# Too Black to Be French

# TOO BLACK TO BE FRENCH

**Isabelle Boni-Claverie**

Translated by
**Joshua David Jordan**

Foreword by
**Kaiama L. Glover**

FORDHAM UNIVERSITY PRESS
NEW YORK 2025

Ouvrage publié avec le concours du Ministère français chargé de la Culture–Centre National du Livre.

This work has been published with the assistance of the French Ministry of Culture–National Center for the Book.

This book was originally published in French as Isabelle Boni-Claverie, Trop Noire pour être française, Copyright © Éditions Tallandier, 2017.

This work received the French Voices Award for excellence in publication and translation. French Voices is a program created and funded by the French Embassy in the United States and FACE Foundation (French American Cultural Exchange). French Voices Logo designed by Serge Bloch.



Fordham University Press also publishes its books in a variety of electronic formats. Some content that appears in print may not be available in electronic books.

Visit us online at www.fordhampress.com.

Library of Congress Cataloging-in-Publication Data available online at https://catalog.loc.gov.

Printed in the United States of America

27 26 25    5 4 3 2 1

First edition

# Contents

# **Foreword by** by Kaiama L. Glover

Race is a social construct, not a biological reality. This has officially been conventional wisdom since about the mid-twentieth century, when UNESCO issued its 1950 Statement on Race, which emphasized the diversity and unity of the human species and declared that racial categories are arbitrary and do not reflect meaningful biological differences. The statement was a response to the horrors of World War II, particularly the Nazi ideology of racial superiority that had led to the racist atrocities with which we are now all too familiar. Mid-century advances in science further contributed to the understanding that human genetic variation does not neatly align with racial categories—that there is more genetic diversity within so-called racial groups than between or among them.

Outside of the natural sciences, scholarly efforts to discredit the notion of biological racial distinction and its consequent racist hierarchies predate the UN's global political proclamation by nearly fifty years. As early as the turn of the twentieth century, sociologist W.E.B. Du Bois in *The Souls of Black Folk* (1903) and anthropologist Franz Boas in *The Mind of Primitive Man* (1911) challenged racial categorizations and argued that race was a product of social and historical contexts rather than a fixed biological trait. The idea of race as a construct has, unquestionably, been around for some time now, and this truth has gained increasingly broad acceptance and understanding in the past few decades.

The Anglophone reader who picks up Isabelle Boni-Claverie's *Too Black to Be French*, impeccably rendered in English by award-winning translator Joshua David Jordan, is likely to have accepted these modern conventions around race and racialization. What a surprise, then, perhaps, for said reader on discovering that the book's very first words point to blood and skin, to hair texture and nose shape, to paternity and biology. Or perhaps there's no surprise there at all. After all, this tension—race is a phantasm, race is real—remains at the very heart of so many of our contemporary debates, on both sides of the Atlantic. For Boni-Claverie—born in Ivory Coast of the fleeting union of a "mixed race" Ivorian-French father and a "Black" Ivorian mother, then adopted by a "mixed race" Ivorian-French paternal aunt and the latter's aristocratic(ish) white French husband and raised in Paris and Abidjan—this tension is threaded into the very fabric of her existence, although it took her quite some time to fully recognize it.

*Too Black to Be French* is the product of Boni-Claverie's awakening to the workings of race in her life and, by reasonable extension, to its workings in the two countries she calls home. The story she tells is in many ways extraordinary: born into an upper-class milieu with roots in Africa and provincial France, she is loved, supported, and claimed by kin in both communities. Her Blackness is singularly complicated: it is transnational, multi-parented, and in many ways class-defiant. Her aunt/mother is a direct and proximate descendant, through the author's Black Ivorian grandfather, of both African royalty and of the French pre- and post-independence political elite. Her family's prestige in sub-Saharan Africa enabled her grandfather to gain access to Europe and ultimately to be influential in both contexts, and this distinguished, long-standing social position meant that some of the most significant elements of France's national and imperial history loomed large in the intimacies of Boni-Claverie's unique childhood.

Boni-Claverie's adoptive parents traveled in elite international circles. As a girl in France, she rode horses and hunted foxes. Surrounded by the whiteness of her Catholic school classmates, the haut bourgeois denizens of her elegant neighborhood, and the swanky guests at her parents' highbrow parties and dinners, Boni-Claverie was an incongruous brown spot in the most rarefied spaces of the republic—spaces of privilege that would be uncommon for any French citizen, much less for a French citizen of color, to occupy. Her left-leaning journalist mother and reactionary conservative father battled over Algeria, though surprisingly little else, considering. They lived a glamorous and cosmopolitan life and, in Boni-Claverie's telling, took real delight in their exclusive position in the world. Danièle and Georges were committed to giving their daughter a life befitting a family of their stature, and if they ever detected an unasked question in a glance that lingered perhaps slightly too long on their many-hued threesome, any discomfiture was muted by the protections of their social class. People in Boni-Claverie's world were generally polite; and when they weren't, her parents refused or feigned not to notice.

Boni-Claverie traces her past with remarkable detail, and race makes only furtive appearances here and there during the early years of her life. This is because she is largely protected by her family's affluence, cloistered by circumstances that elided certain racialized norms, in stark contrast to the world outside the bubble of her privilege. "I was the fulfillment of the republican ideal," Boni-Claverie writes, "and that included its ambiguities." Those ambiguities are the very premises of her book, itself a testament to the insistent presence of racial realities that ultimately could not be ignored, privilege notwithstanding. It is as if Boni-Claverie is viewing her childhood through the photographic archive that presents her and her family's history in all its prominence and good fortune while at the same time looking—and inviting her reader to look—through the querying lens of the adult Black woman she became, still puzzling through those moments in her life when race seemed to be there yet somehow not there, too. Moments when race was present, surely, but unspoken. Unspoken until, of course, the striking instance of Fanonian interpellation—that first time when, at school, six-year-old Isabelle is confronted with a perception of her Black French body that feels flattening, disjunctive, and violently untrue. And so the gaslighting begins . . .

Such moments of disjunction can be as humorous as they are unsettling. The image of the little Black girl and her redheaded white Swiss nanny strolling through the genteel Parc Monceau, for example, presents a funny flipping of the racial script, as does the cast of multinational European characters that make up young Isabelle's personal entourage—her Spanish-Basque nanny and Italian chauffeur; a Portuguese sometimes-driver on loan from the Ivory Coast embassy; the Armenian secretary who helps out with her care every now and again. Little wonder things were never just b/Black and white for Boni-Claverie. Little wonder, too, that she remains for so long struck—and, arguably, empowered—by the kind of "color-blindness" we're more used to understanding as the prerogative of France's white citizens.

Slowly but surely, though, Boni-Claverie begins to "get it." She becomes increasingly attuned to the racial thinking that lay behind incidents in her childhood and young adulthood—incidents that she only much later realizes were microaggressions, so many more and less subtle quotidian acts of derogatory racialization that chipped away at the armor of her gilded life. And these challenges to her belonging were not limited, it must be said, to Boni-Claverie's early experiences as a young Black girl in France. On the contrary, race becomes a decidedly more unsettling presence in her life in Ivory Coast, when she returns to live there with her adoptive parents at the age of eight. Her explicit rejection by Black African classmates in Abidjan is, as it turns out, one of the book's many fascinating twists. "In Abidjan," she tells us, "I discovered that every child was a budding geneticist." Her classmates find her Blackness to be suspect, at once culturally insufficient and inconsistent with her parents' much fairer skin; they ridicule, exclude, and even abuse her. In Ivory Coast, questions about her identity—her legitimacy—turn out to be as much a matter of culture as of color. Though African by birth and by blood, her mind and heart are deemed European, colonial. Thus, whereas any sense of non-belonging she felt in France had been because of her brown skin; in Ivory Coast she did not belong despite it.

Boni-Claverie recounts what one might imagine to have been childhood trauma with a matter-of-factness that refuses our pity. It was what it was, and it is what it is. Yet, while she is wholly uninterested in pathos, she is nonetheless curious about how certain realities came to be. So as she considers the painful racialist misperceptions of her young self in the land of her birth, Boni-Claverie reflects on the broader question of how the changing landscape of the putatively postcolonial relationship between France and Ivory Coast deeply distorted relations among Ivoirians themselves, fracturing those relations along lines of phenotype and class that amalgamated regional traditions with foreign notions of human value. As a child, she felt these tensions acutely; she came to understand them as an adult.

This blend of the experiential and the intellectual is what makes *Too Black to Be French* at once a deeply intimate memoir and a richly documented work of history and social theory. Unique in its geo-cultural expansiveness, it is among the rare first-person francophone narratives to illuminate the experience of Black subjecthood as a sustained dialogue between the metropole and a former colony. Truly, Boni-Claverie's family story is as much a French provincial chronicle as it is Ivorian history. France and Ivory Coast are shown to be inextricably entangled through the three-generations-long account of one "mixed-race" woman who sees in the small story of her own origins the big picture of the French colonial and postcolonial past. Boni-Claverie's access to elite spaces, although exceptional, usefully undermines presumptions regarding the intersectional functioning of race, class, and color in the wake of sub-Saharan African independence—both in francophone Africa and in France. Her insightful and capacious vision engenders an extraordinary tale, one that demands a rethinking of the social realities that typically define nonwhite subjecthood in France. It reveals the inaccuracies and limitations of the tacit forms of essentialism that in so many ways determine the racialized contours of the French public sphere.

Boni-Claverie's personal trajectory opens the door for a transnational and transcontinental inquiry that is robustly grounded in the French Republic's national and imperial history. It is a history of the present that points to the unequivocally transnational, multicultural, and multiracial foundations of the contemporary French state. Her story is a story of France—not just the republic as it now stands, but its prior political iterations, its false starts, and its persistent contradictions. To the extent that the French Republic continues to see itself as an enlightened social democracy while refusing to recognize the unique problems facing its racialized citizens, a work such as this one issues an important corrective. At its core, *Too Black to Be French* is a call for recognition. In one of the book's sharpest passages, Boni-Claverie makes this explicitly clear: "France's former colonies aren't calling for France to repent," she tells us. "They, like French minorities, whose ancestors endured colonization and slavery, are calling for it to recognize what took place. In other words, [. . .] three forms of recognition are demanded: recognition of the facts, recognition of French responsibility, and recognition of the harm done." Distinct from repentance or any other emotionally charged performance, like love or even remorse, recognition is a matter of truthful perception. "I couldn't care less if someone loved Africa or African people," she insists. "I wanted nothing to do with a love that negated me as a person."

*Too Black to Be French* belongs to an expanding corpus of first-person narratives by Black French women that address the workings of race in a nation that explicitly refuses to admit race as a category of social and political being, among which, Maboula Soumahoro's memoir *Le Triangle et L'Hexagone: Réflexions sur une identité noire* (Éditions la Découverte, 2020), published in English as *Black is the Journey, Africana the Name* (Polity Press, 2021); Audrey Celestine's family history *Une famille française* (Textuel, 2018), (forthcoming in English as A French Family), and Mame-Fatou Niang's documentary film *Mariannes noires* (2016) (Black Mariannes). Every one of these works calls in no uncertain terms for national recognition from the singular space of an individual's gendered and racialized experience. Indeed, at this particular moment in time, when France's minority populations—peoples of color, descendants of empire—are demanding with increasing force that France grapple meaningfully with the nation's past and recalibrate its present conditions of citizenship and belonging, the notion that a citizen of the republic can be "too Black to be French" is a profoundly necessary provocation.

# Acknowledgments

I would like to express my particular gratitude to Frédéric Viguier, without whom this book would never have existed in English, and to Emmanuelle Ertel and the Cultural Services of the French Embassy in New York.

I would also like to extend my many thanks to Joshua David Jordan for his translation and unwavering commitment to this project, which owes so much to his work.

Finally, a heartfelt thank you to Thomas Lay for his kind support throughout the process.

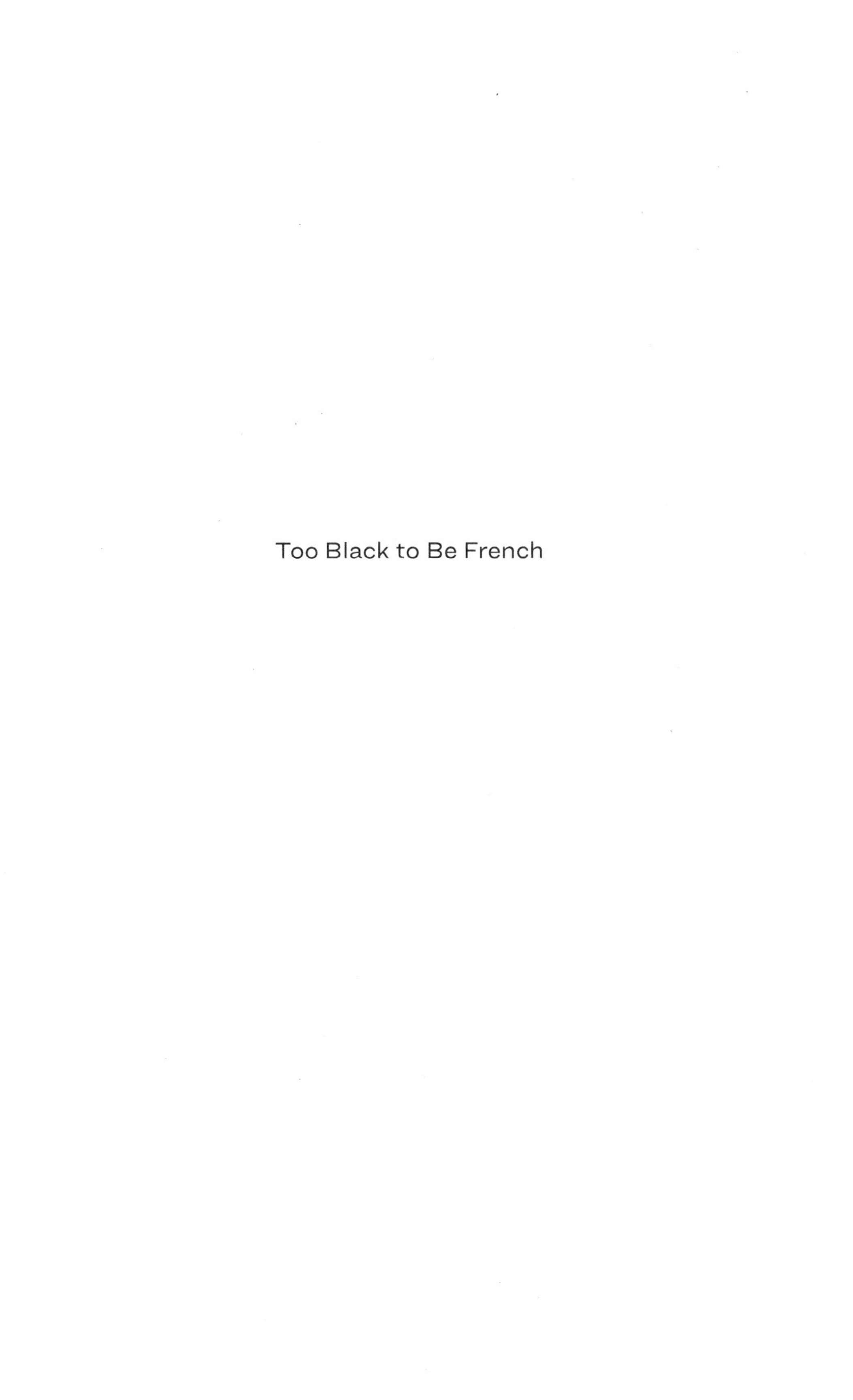

Too Black to Be French

# 1 If Only You'd Been Lighter

My skin color has always been an issue.

My biological father was mixed race. His father was Ivorian, his mother French. He was light skinned, with wavy hair and a thin nose. My biological mother was Ivorian and Black. Her phenotype was thoroughly African. Under pressure from their families, they separated shortly after my birth. They weren't married.

When I was born, my mother feared that my dark complexion might discredit me in the eyes of my father's family. But there was never a doubt about his paternity. As a baby, I was the spitting image of my father.

My mother was promptly shunted aside. My paternal grandparents thought she was too young and her background too modest for her to take care of me. This was the early seventies, in Ivory Coast. My grandfather was president of the Supreme Court. His position, combined with his noble birth, made ours, as people said, a "great family." I bore the surname, which still carried weight at the time. Since my mother hoped to continue her studies, she was packed off to a boarding school in the country's interior while others pondered my fate. My father left for his first diplomatic posting at the Ivory Coast embassy in Washington, D.C. This was not an era rife with single fathers, and burdening himself with a baby never crossed his mind. My grandparents were old. They briefly considered sending me to Gaillac, a small town in France, to live with my grandmother's French family. But then a solution came from one of my father's younger sisters, Danièle, who lived in Lausanne with her husband and offered to take me in.

I was four months old when I left Ivory Coast for Switzerland in my grandmother's arms. She handed me over to my aunt, to a new country, a new life. The memory of my birth mother quickly faded. I was an adult before I saw her again.

Although my mother was conscious of being pushed aside because her modest background was incompatible in my grandparents' eyes with the plans they had for their son—the oldest child, the only boy, the heir to the family name—she nonetheless remained convinced that she had also been rejected because she was Black. She was sure that my white grandmother had done all she could to dissuade her mixed-race son from marrying a Black woman. As proof, she cited my biological father's subsequent marriage to a woman of mixed race. She didn't know that his wife, just like her—indeed, more than her, since his wife would have to endure constant humiliations throughout their marriage—was never actually accepted by my father's parents and sisters. The reason? The same: her family's social status, which they considered unsuitable.

I was eighteen months old when my aunt Danièle divorced and brought me to Toulouse, where my grandparents owned an apartment. Soon after, she met Georges, her second husband, a dandy from a good family, the son of one of the city's most prominent legal families. Georges had the self-confidence of someone who knew himself well-born; he had the casual handsomeness of a leading man, a keen intellect, and the smooth-talker's gift of gab. He drove a Porsche, lived in a penthouse, had a table reserved every evening at a five-star hotel, and maintained his flawless style by dressing exclusively in tailor-made attire. On the weekends during the season, he went foxhunting near Pau.

Unlike Danièle's first husband, who was Ivorian, Georges was French. We soon left the south of France for Paris. I was three years old when they married. That was when my aunt decided that she and Georges would be my only parents. She refused to return me to my father, who was by then calling for me to join him, made my mother believe that she might still be able to see me during vacations, and gradually erased my relationship with both of them. To a certain extent, it was a clever move: she and Georges would never have any children of their own, so I became their daughter. Their only child, but imperfect. For there was always the question of my Black skin, which stubbornly contradicted the tale that, whenever I asked, as they later maintained, they tried to keep up for my benefit: namely, that I was their biological daughter, born of Danièle's womb, the sole daughter of a mixed-race woman and a white man. Now, a common bloodline between us might have been plausible enough; after all, she was half Black herself and I looked somewhat like her. People might have assumed that she had had me with a man—a Black man, of course—whose identity she never revealed. And people certainly pretended it was normal for me to call my white stepfather Papa. But in the end no one except me was ever really fooled.

To complicate things still further, Jean-Pierre, my birth father, would occasionally find time between his diplomatic assignments to come visit us. He, too, was a dandy in his way. Mesmerized, I would watch his ivory cigarette-holder gracefully twirling between his long fingers and carefully manicured nails. On his pinky, he wore a signet ring and, on his wrist, a gold bracelet, which on anyone else would have seemed in bad taste but which on him provided an added note of sophistication. Sometimes, by chance, we would find ourselves alone in a hallway or just the two of us in a room. Hurriedly, in a voice at once firm and forlorn, he'd tell me: Don't forget I'm your father.

Bewildered, I never said a word.

Even today, although to make things easier on others I say that Danièle and Georges are my adoptive parents, I continue to think of them as my mother and father. So, that's how I will refer to them here. My mother. My father. My parents. There will also be times, as often happens to me in everyday life, when I call them by their first names. When I speak of the two people who brought me into this world, I will specifically refer to my biological father or birth mother.

I'm clarifying everything now because in general no one understands a thing about my family. I myself only slowly came to terms with the idea that I had four parents, which is another way of saying that I have never had a single parent whose child I am entirely.

Sometimes, as I grew up, my parents would express a certain remorse about the past.

With carefully studied pathos, Danièle would tell me that, when I was born, my biological mother had rubbed my body with whitening cream in an effort to make me look more mixed. When I took you in, she would say, your skin was burnt from head to toe. Upon further inquiry, it turns out that the reason for the cream was a slight rash on my backside.

Other times, Georges would look at me sadly and say: "If only you'd been lighter, no one would have asked any questions, everyone would have thought you were my daughter." A vague feeling of guilt overtook me. Black. Too Black. I had been stuck with the wrong genes. A twist of fate had engraved in me, on me, like a mark of defiance, the trace of this African woman, whose presence, although responsible for my birth, they never stopped trying to erase.

# 2 A Black Princess and White Nannies

In Paris, my parents and I lived in a very large apartment in the seventeenth arrondissement, near the chic Plaine-Monceau neighborhood. Georges, who at the time worked as a licensed legal advisor, a profession that no longer exists, had set up his practice at home. From my bedroom, I would follow the hallway of my dressing room, slip into the pitch-black storage closet, then, without a peep, silently enter his secretary's office. The secretary, Jacqueline, a Sephardic Jew with olive skin, eyes lined with thick strokes of kohl, and beautiful curly brown hair, would welcome me in with a smile. I would sit there watching her type. Her beauty, the sensuality she exuded, fascinated me, as did the liberty she took in calling my father by his first name and her use of the familiar French pronoun "tu" with him, whereas I myself still found him somewhat intimidating.

Like every rich child whose parents work, I spent the bulk of my time with the house staff. They usually came in pairs: a kind of jack-of-all-trades, whom we grandiloquently called a butler, and a full-time nanny who took care of me. They each lived in a servant's room with shared showers and toilets on the building's top floor, accessible only from the service stairs. The few times I ventured there, I thought I had landed in another world, one that I found oppressive. I naively asked why there was no proper bathroom. Even today, service entrances, shared or Turkish toilets—these overt markers of class difference that the well-off demand—make me uncomfortable.

My first nannies came from Ivory Coast. They were young and pretty, frivolous perhaps, or simply shrewd. Once they became acclimated to Parisian life, they took to their heels. Exasperated, my mother hired a Swiss—in other words, white—nanny, who had previously looked after the daughter of Thérèse Houphouët-Boigny, the wife of the Ivorian president. She was brusque and affected, and I took an immediate dislike to her. She thought she could break me through exemplary discipline. Without my parents around, we engaged in an insidious power struggle. One afternoon, she forced me to eat an avocado, a fruit I abhorred at the time. After an hour resisting, I finally gave in and she made sure not a speck of it remained on my plate. At which point, I vomited everything onto her dress. To maintain her credibility, she didn't denounce me to my parents. As for my mother, she found that I had become more obedient and that my manners had improved.

When warm weather arrived, my redheaded nanny, whose milky skin was sensitive to sunlight, would take us on walks, flourishing her umbrella like a parasol. I wonder what impression the two of us made on the other parkgoers.

One day, when I was being particularly unctuous toward my mother, she caught me sticking my tongue out at the nanny behind her back. The verdict was swiftly rendered; the nanny was let go. Anyway, she watched too much TV. The butler was dismissed along with her. He was an alcoholic, and one night in his servant's room had gotten into a fight that turned bloody. Another man, Yeo, replaced him. And Yeo I liked. After school, as he ironed, I would sit next to him eating my little tartlet cookies—always the edges first, the jam last—and telling him about my day. He taught me how to tell time and plenty of other things. Then, like the others, he left too—to work in hospitality, I believe.

My mother had had enough of these two-person teams. They were replaced by a sturdy Spanish-Basque woman, Pilar, whom I loved. In the evenings, when my parents went out, we would secretly go to the caretaker's lodge. Spanish like Pilar, the caretaker would give me a raspberry lollipop whose wrapper always stuck. Sometimes a bowl of hot chocolate. They spoke in their language, which at the time I didn't understand, while I watched TV. The atmosphere was pleasant and warm. I felt good.

When I came home in the afternoons, Pilar would make *chocolate a la taza* with bars of dark chocolate and flour that Georges's sister sent from Spain. Once melted in a pot with milk, the chocolate was supposed to be thick enough to hold a *churro* standing up. She would load a tray and tap on the door to my father's office. With some formality, he would invite me to take a seat on the sofa. We unfolded our white napkins. I was proud of our tête-à-têtes, which made me feel like a grown-up.

Georges was an experienced horseback rider. I learned to ride a horse before I learned to ride a bike. On Wednesdays, my cousin and I rode ponies on the outskirts of the city. My mother's driver took us—a talkative Italian with salt-and-pepper curls, who brought back leather bags from his vacations in Italy to resell in Paris. He once gave me a wooden Pinocchio with an extendable rubber nose. When he wasn't available, the Ivory Coast embassy's Portuguese driver took care of us. My mother, a correspondent for Ivorian radio and television in France, had managed to procure a diplomatic passport through one of her expert sleights of hand (although it conflicted with her job as a journalist). She thus enjoyed, and we with her, the same advantages as Ivorian diplomats.

With summer began the game of au pair musical chairs: the young European women who wanted to learn French and accompanied us on our vacations. Sometimes, the sweet blonde shampooer from my mother's hair salon played babysitter. We would have dinner with her grandmother, a little Old Mother Hubbard–looking woman, nestled in a tiny two-room apartment. Her grandmother brought out a very old suitcase from which she presented me with children's clothes from a distant age. I remember a pink-and-white checkered bloomer that was a pure delight. Danièle grimaced. She didn't like women other than herself giving me presents.

My mother's secretary, from Armenia, I believe, and on maternity leave, looked after me at her home from time to time as a favor. While she changed her baby in the mezzanine bedroom, I thumbed through the comic books in the living room. She had a huge collection of the cartoonist Jean-Marc Reiser. I slyly lingered over his drawings of nude women and men. We took her baby to the nearby park. She bought me candy necklaces. One day, she asked my mother for permission to bring me to a birthday party her family was throwing. I remember running every which way with a mob of other children and hearing adults speaking a foreign language.

Thirty years later, still living in the same part of Paris, I was out for a walk one day with my newborn children in their double stroller. It was winter. They were so wrapped up you could barely see their faces. I was running an errand at the shopping center where African nannies often met. Ignoring their white employers' children for a bit, they chatted among themselves. Suddenly, they noticed me, then eyed me curiously, as if to say, "Look, a new one." One of them greeted me with a nod, but the other women's faces hardened as I passed. They took me for stuck up, the kind of woman who doesn't bother introducing herself to her peers. Another woman, still unsure, examined my purse to try to pin down my social status. At the shopping center, numerous customers, intrigued by my imposing twin stroller, also stared at me uncertainly. Was I the mother or nanny of these swaddled, faceless children who could very well be white?

The questions I ask myself are different. What image of Black women will these upscale-neighborhood children have once they become adults? Will they develop the curt and condescending emotional attachment that Scarlett O'Hara showed for Mammy, the sweet fat Black servant—and slave—in *Gone with the Wind*? Some affection, to be sure, but everyone in their proper place. On one side, the rich Northern bosses; on the other, the proletariat, the precarious wage-earners, of the South.[1] Or will they feel the nagging guilt of a Kathryn Stockett, the best-selling author of *The Help*?[2]

When these little boys become men, will they have tender memories of being cuddled on their Black nannies' laps? Will they be erotically attracted to Black women, though not quite enough to actually marry them? Or will they keep to a strict class and racial divide?

In 2015, I directed a documentary film on the place of Blacks in France, also entitled *Too Black to Be French*, albeit with a question mark at the end, because it was still a question I was asking myself at the time. I've found an answer since then.

In the documentary, I presented some of my family history. After it was aired on television, I was invited to numerous screenings. At the conclusion of one of them, held in one of Paris's best private schools, a young woman (white, from a wealthy family) came up to me. She told me she had really liked the film and the discussion afterward. With great emotion, on the verge of tears, she thanked me: You, at least, are comfortable with who you are. She added that she had had a Black nanny who hadn't at all come to terms with her skin color. The young student's sincerity was touching. However, I found it curious that she would associate me with her nanny, that the one Black person whom she had gotten to know enough in life to serve as a point of reference would be this woman. When I asked the two hundred students present if they had Black friends, the overwhelming majority had raised their hands. Had she, too?

Kathryn Stockett says in her afterword:

> I'm pretty sure I can say that no one in my family ever asked Demetrie what it felt like to be black in Mississippi, working for our white family. It never occurred to us to ask. It was everyday life. It wasn't something people felt compelled to examine. I have wished, for many years, that I'd been old enough and thoughtful enough to ask Demetrie that question. She died when I was sixteen. I've spent years imagining what her answer would be. And that is why I wrote this book.[3]

I never asked—and, in all honesty, I couldn't care less—what it was like for my parents' white employees to work for a mixed-race woman and a Black girl, the opposite of the usual socioracial hierarchy. With their merry-go-round of personnel of every background and nationality, Georges and Danièle taught me to dissociate race and class, to refrain from social judgments of others based on their ethnicity. Thanks to them, I didn't attach any type of social inferiority to the fact of being Black.

Yet there was the historical reality of immigration and, before it, of slavery, Blacks ever and always the workforce of whites. There was what I saw—no Blacks in my neighborhood besides the street sweepers in the morning on my way to school. Then there was my parents' value system, the only one that actually mattered to me back then. Within this system, Blacks enjoyed the same social status as whites.

# 3 You Will Play Balthazar, My Dear

I was six years old, attending a Catholic school run by Ursuline nuns. No one seemed to give a second thought to my skin color—at least none of the other children did. Impervious to my pigmentation, they nicknamed me China Girl because of the especially tight, eye-stretching buns my mother made me wear to tidy up my kinky hair.

I had many friends at school. And at recess our games were raucous. But whatever foolishness we got up to, the nuns never punished us, figuring they could sort most anything out by talking it through. This was the late seventies. The decade's libertarian spirit, it seems, had reached even as far as my Catholic school. I remember working little and enjoying myself a lot during the many outings and activities that punctuated our days.

As was the case every year as Christmas approached, one class was chosen to perform the nativity scene. It was our turn. I immediately pictured myself playing the Virgin Mary, kneeling center stage, a long blue veil covering my hair, as I cradled the pink celluloid doll that represented the Baby Jesus. In short, the star of the show. Until, that is, our teacher, a stern middle-aged woman, announced that Julie, the daughter of the school's custodian, would be taking the role. "As for you, Isabelle," she said, "you will play Balthazar, the Wise Man from Africa."

I was dumbstruck, I wanted to cry. How could my teacher inflict this kind of humiliation on me? How could she force me to play a boy's role when she knew very well I was a girl? Why was I the only one beset with such bad luck? For my teacher, the rationale was simple: there was no other Black student in the class. Nor probably in the entire school at the time.

Black. No one had ever said that to me before. Until then, although I was too dark to bear out the tales my parents told about me, I wasn't Black. I was dark brown.

Black.

What was this mysterious term that trumped everything else and even defined who I was? Why was it the opposite of being white? I had a white grandmother. She was my flesh and blood and I was hers. I had cousins, uncles, and aunts with skin of every shade from white to black. I was raised by a white man who, although not my father, considered me his daughter, as did his entire family, which had accepted me without question. One of Georges's sisters often looked after me. She never batted an eye when she introduced me as her niece, never tried to explain how she herself could measure just under five feet, weigh a mere ninety pounds, have straight hair and white skin whereas I was tall and dark with a head of kinky curls. Let others puzzle out our family ties whichever way they please; we know that it's the bonds of love that matter most.

I wasn't Black. I was dark brown. I didn't want to play Balthazar in the nativity scene. I wanted to remain that same multifaceted, composite Isabelle and—something else that was important for me at an age when I was just getting a sense of my gender identity—I wanted to remain a girl.

Once home, I counted on my mother to save me from my predicament. But she thought it was an excellent idea and promised me, as consolation, a handsome costume befitting a king.

The day of the nativity scene, I again had the urge to cry. My costume amounted to a red turtleneck, which in winter I already wore nearly every week, and velour pants. No mistaking it, I would look like a boy. My mother draped me in several yards of shapeless red satin, whether to evoke the pagnes of Akan chiefs or a Roman toga, it was hard to say. Satisfied with her work, she placed a crown on my head. And what a crown it was! The kind that bakeries gave away for free at Epiphany, the ones in gold paper, with glued-on colored dots passed off as gemstones. I held a dirty-brown box supposedly representing the chest of myrrh Balthazar gave the Baby Jesus. Suffice it to say, by the time I stepped forward to deliver my gift to Mary and Joseph, every bit of Christian charity had long since abandoned me. If daggers could have shot from my eyes, I would have murdered Julie-who-got-to-play-Mary, my teacher, and every one of the organizers of the nativity farce.

There was no one among my family or friends to tell me that it wasn't normal to be assigned a Black role, that I shouldn't be essentialized or be made the representative of all the people—around a billion, mind you—who shared the same pigmentation as mine.

Yet my parents were extremely interested in politics. Danièle was a political journalist. There was no French politician at the time whom she hadn't interviewed or met. Her favorite, she often said, was one of France's leading Socialist Party figures, Michel Rocard. Every day, she listened to and watched the different TV news programs, read the press, and devoured the weekly political magazines. Whole bookcases of our home library were dedicated to the subject. She was especially passionate about intellectuals like Solzhenitsyn and Oriana Fallaci, who, in 1979, published *A Man*, a novel in which the author recounted the life of a Greek resistance member during the junta with whom she was passionately in love. My mother unequivocally positioned herself on the side of freedom and against oppression.

Georges, too, was passionate about history and politics, as soon as they had to do with France or, possibly, Spain. A hypermnesic, he showed impressive erudition in support of ideas that at home we politely referred to as reactionary. Although he never mentioned Hitler except to revel in his defeat, he had a marked affinity for every far-right dictator on the planet. He recited from memory the speeches of a well-known right-wing politician, professed the need for strongman regimes, especially in developing countries, and execrated the French Revolution, May '68, and General de Gaulle. He held that Pétain had saved France from disaster and dreamed nostalgically of a return to the monarchy. Even though he knew such a dream was impossible, he nonetheless clung to it thanks to his diligent reading of the royalist gossip magazine *Point de vue. Images du monde*.

To round off his education and to give him a certain cosmopolitan veneer, his parents had sent the still-teenage Georges to study in Barcelona at the height of the Francoist dictatorship. Since then, he had retained a particular soft spot for Franco, whom he affectionately called *el caudillo*. Never a man lacking in contradictions, Georges would sometimes recite entire poems by García Lorca to me in Spanish.

On the Boni side of the family, we maintained an emotional attachment to the French politician and president François Mitterrand. When my grandfather arrived in France at the age of fifteen, he was put into the same middle-school class as Robert Mitterrand, François's older brother. They spent their entire secondary schooling together. And my grandfather, it seems, was often invited to the Mitterrand family house in southwestern France during school vacations.[1]

Once—a scene etched in my memory despite my young age—just as we were leaving the Pau airport on a visit to Georges's family, François came rushing in. Stepping aside to let us pass, he recognized Danièle and, on the spur of the moment, suggested we all grab a drink at the bar. My mother was on the verge of accepting when Georges, so irritated that a grimace was the most he could muster for a smile, declared that we were in a hurry, that people were waiting for us, that unfortunately we just didn't have the time. Danièle put on a brave face. Then, once François left, she unloaded on Georges. A journalist to her bones, she accused him of having cost her a prized off-the-record conversation. For my father, sharing a drink with a leftist politician was simply inconceivable.

As a rule, however, he put on a good show. He had a flair for professing his opinions tongue in cheek, as if he didn't wholly believe the ideas he expressed, or as if they were merely a form of politically incorrect affectation. Danièle, smiling ironically, settled for calling him a chauvinist and reactionary. Like her, I preferred to make light of my father's idiosyncrasies.

Yet shortly before his death, as one of our last conversations turned to Augusto Pinochet, one of the military dictators he was so fond of, Georges vehemently protested the Chilean general's imprisonment. Given the obvious sincerity of his indignation, I finally understood that he was, that he had always been, on the most extreme fringe of the political right.

There was, however, one topic about which Georges never made light: the Algerian War. Called up when he was twenty years old, he was initially assigned to France's First Parachute Regiment, before joining the Fifth Algerian Spahi Regiment, a calvary unit composed of Algerian soldiers led by their French counterparts.

There must have been something romantic about this kind of combat for the young Georges, who had been fed stories of chivalry from childhood. The Algerian War, which he spent three years fighting, would haunt him to the end of his days. He would tell me how, as a young lieutenant, he would ride to the front on his tall bay horse in white gloves and immaculately shined boots. In the mess hall, he would eat the pistachio-flavored pudding that, along with the storied white gloves, his mother sent him by the crate. In a village decimated by the National Liberation Front (FLN), he took a young Algerian woman under his wing and fell madly in love with her. She became his mistress. I wonder if she really had a choice.

My parents chose the war as their ideological battleground. Not a day passed without an argument over Algeria, which, according to Georges, should have remained French.

For her part, Danièle defended the right of all peoples to self-determination and to choose their fate freely. She excoriated Georges for his colonial predilections, while Georges defended himself by arguing that those seeking true *fraternité* were on the side of French Algeria, that if de Gaulle had kept his word, nine million Muslims would have had the same right to vote as the one million Frenchmen living there. According to him, the true racist was de Gaulle, who, one year after his famous Mostaganem speech[2]—"From today onward, I proclaim here and now and give you my word, there are only full-fledged Frenchmen, compatriots, fellow citizens, brothers who will henceforth walk through life hand-in-hand"—privately told Alain Peyrefitte,

> It is all fine and good that there are yellow Frenchmen, Black Frenchmen, and brown Frenchmen. They demonstrate that France is open to all races and that her calling is universal. But on one condition: that they remain a small minority. Otherwise,

> France will no longer be France. We are still first and foremost a European people of the white race, Greek and Latin culture, and Christian faith [. . .]. If we were to integrate, if all the Arabs and Berbers from Algeria were considered French, how could we stop them from settling in mainland France, where the living standard is so much higher? My own village would no longer be Colombey-les-Deux-Églises, it would be Colombey-les-Deux-Mosquées![3]

These remarks, which most of today's French right and even some on the left wouldn't disagree with, were reproduced on posters by the far-right National Front party in 2009, then repeated, more recently, by Nadine Morano, a deputy from the center-right party Les Républicains.[4]

Without fail, the discussion veered from Algeria to sub-Saharan Africa. Annoyed, Danièle protested, "So, what you're saying is we shouldn't have given French African countries their independence?"

"Their independence came too early," Georges countered, "when those countries, not even nations yet, had no experts to run them and no army worthy of the name to ensure their sovereignty."

"Nonsense!" Danièle retorted categorically. "Just come out and say we aren't capable of governing ourselves." At which point, Georges, who didn't want to pass for the kind of person he in fact was, preferred to keep quiet. Or he simply recalled that de Gaulle didn't give Africans their independence out of the goodness of his heart but to rid himself of colonies that had become an albatross. He wasn't wrong on that score. Again, according to Peyrefitte, the General supposedly admitted,

> You know, it was an opportunity for us to seize upon, to unload a burden that had grown much too heavy for us to bear, the more desperate for equality those people became. We escaped the worst! [. . .] Luckily, most of our Africans were happy to take the peaceful route of self-government before independence.[5]

Let's note in passing the paternalistic "our Africans."

Georges harbored no anger about all this. Françafrique, France's privileged postcolonial sphere of influence, was there to ease his mind. And even if Georges found Danièle's arguments a bit thin, he always let her have the last word. Curiously, though, even if the issue of race provided the ever-present subtext of their disagreements, they never once brought it up.

# 4 Does Class Erase Race?

"Race" has become a dirty word in France. It has been removed from legislative texts, and people no longer dare to use it except, perhaps, to point out that there is only a single human race. When I use the word, I'm not referring to the supposed existence of several species of human being with different biological, intellectual, or moral capacities—that old conception of race.

People have always strived to distinguish themselves from others based on their physical traits and cultural practices, each group generally believing itself superior to its neighbor. The Peruvian sociologist Aníbal Quijano traces the origins of racial classification to the fifteenth century, when Spanish and Portuguese colonizers, confronted with the physical differences of Latin American indigenous peoples, began to think of themselves as "white" and to associate this physical feature with a kind of essential superiority.[1] As we know, the biological notion of race was deployed as part of the systematic enslavement of Africans during the subsequent four centuries. Such a criminal undertaking needed justification.

It was at the end of the Second World War, when the horrors of the Holocaust became known, that UNESCO developed a program on "The Race Question" over the course of three decades. It published several official declarations aimed at invalidating the principle of inequality between human "races" and at combating the prejudice that made "race mixture" a cause of human degeneracy.

The first declaration on race adopted on December 14, 1949, states:

> From the biological standpoint, the species *Homo sapiens* is made up of a number of populations, each one of which differs

> from the others in the frequency of one or more genes. Such genes [. . .] are always few when compared to the whole genetic constitution of man and to the vast number of genes common to all human beings [. . .].[2]

In 2000, human genome sequencing led to a similar conclusion: the DNA of the planet's more than seven billion people is 99.99% identical. Without question, there is only one human race.

That's certainly reassuring; it pulls the rug out from under people who continue to defend a biological basis for racism. Yet it doesn't eradicate other forms of racism, specifically cultural racism. Proving that there is only one human race doesn't erase five centuries of world domination or the political thinking that has gone with it. Nor does it erase the extraordinary intellectual and cultural production that accompanied first the enslavement of African people then the colonization of Africa in order to convince public opinion of the soundness of these enterprises. Nor does it erase the indelible scars that resulted, the ethnocentrism, the prejudice. The conviction that whites are the standard of world humanity against which anything non-white is deviant and inherently inferior. And all of it with a clear conscience.

Race in its social, political, and cultural sense continues to be ubiquitous. It very effectively maintains a distribution of power that favors a minority we call white, and that was for a long time European then, more broadly, Western.

My parents couldn't have been ignorant of all this. Why did they dodge the issue? To preserve their mixed-race couple? My father: to avoid revealing the extremes of his right-wing opinions? My mother: because she simply hadn't thought about it enough? Indeed, despite her emancipatory politics, her views proved to be extremely fluid in everyday life.

She complained to my school's principal about a documentary shown in class that gave an outdated picture of Africa. "Africa, Africans, live in the twentieth century just like you!" But she approved when my teacher assigned me the role of the token Black in the nativity scene. Prior to that, she had refused the school's request that I redo my final year of kindergarten because I would be underage entering first grade. She agreed, however, to have me take IQ tests to assess my intellectual maturity. Talking things over with the psychologist who met with us, she declared with astonishing bad faith, “Don’t forget that Isabelle is African. She doesn’t have the same cultural references as the children you usually see. So don’t go showing her pictures of snowmen hoping she’ll get the right answer.”

Yet at that point I had lived in Switzerland from the age of four to eighteen months and in France after that. In winter, I went sledding with my grandmother in the Pyrenees. The sole African country I knew was Ivory Coast, which I only visited occasionally during summer vacations. Did Black skin have special properties that made one clueless about snow and cold climates?

My mother must have really been afraid I wouldn’t pass the tests for her to resort to such crude essentialism. The more surprising thing is that the psychologist took what she said into account.

In 1976, Danièle met President Giscard d’Estaing at the Élysée Palace. She was, it appears, the first woman journalist of African origin to interview a French head of state. The event was sufficiently newsworthy—and the Ivory Coast embassy’s press office was sufficiently persuasive—that it earned her a two-page spread in the now defunct magazine *Jours de France* (resurrected a few years ago by the newspaper *Le Figaro*), a kind of alternative *Paris Match* aimed at women readers.

Edgar Schneider, a society journalist popular at the time, wrote the following: “Danièle Boni-Claverie comes to us from Ivory Coast. Suffice it to say that her appeal is in no need of a suntan. She will always be a day at the beach ahead of all the other Parisiennes, with the added advantage that her color is in no danger of fading when summer comes to an end.” Further on, he noted:

> Danièle, a seasoned journalist, wasn’t chosen solely for her charm, I hasten to add. First of all—as I convincingly learned at a recent lunch—she speaks effortless French, all the more so because, although Ivorian on her father’s side, she is from

> the Southwest on her mother's, and her husband hails from the Béarn. Moreover, she owes her professional skills to the National Center for Journalism in the Rue du Louvre, after a childhood split between France and Africa depending on her father's judicial postings.[3]

The commentary, which oscillated between racism and paternalism, was like water off a duck's back to Danièle. She kept dozens of copies of that issue of *Jours de France* in her desk to offer proudly to people she knew. She was hurt, however, by the rumor that she had had an affair with Giscard, whose taste for Black and mixed-race women was well known. She found it exceedingly sexist. Nowadays, sociologists would speak of intersectionality and underscore the accumulation of discriminatory factors linked to her status both as a woman and as a Black woman. At the time, the term wasn't used. And my mother fought solely on the side of feminism.

In any event, what mattered most to my parents wasn't race but class. That undoubtedly explains how Georges, without undermining his own value system, could marry a woman of mixed race, the daughter of one of those colonized peoples whom he would have so liked to keep within the French fold.

Danièle was upper-middle class and her father, Alphonse, an important political figure in Ivory Coast. The fact that he had studied in France guaranteed, in Georges's eyes, the seriousness of his education. And to top it all off, Alphonse was of noble lineage; money and power had circulated in his family for generations. He didn't belong to that recent class of African "nouveaux riches" who had sprung up after decolonization, whom Georges loathed, and whose excesses, like their lack of taste, he derided. But what kind of taste are we talking about? What kind of propriety or good manners? Who decides? According to what cultural criteria?

Georges's friends assured me that they never gave a second thought to Danièle's skin color. Her mixed race, her half-African background, was, they told me, a non-issue. She was beautiful, intelligent, and cultured. That was enough. Some of them, like Georges, held political beliefs that ran counter to their personal affections.

Like Georges, they saw no reason to justify themselves. How did they square their contradictions? These weren't things one talked about.

With other people, I've observed first-hand that the argument generally used to justify this kind of disconnect is "You aren't like the others." Not like other Blacks, not like Arabs, not like "suburban youth," which in French elicits similarly negative connotations as "inner-city youth" does in English. It's all too easy for people to believe that they don't have a racist bone in their bodies and that it's other people who are inadequate.

At the school my children attend, a parent spoke to me about one of the other mothers, a practicing Muslim, who wore a jilbāb, a long robe and a veil that covered her entire body except for her face. "I like her a lot," she took the precaution of telling me first, "but, you know, her son doesn't come to any birthdays." Meaning: they want to be separate, they refuse to be like us, with us.

I met the boy once at one of those vaunted after-school get-togethers. He probably would have gone to plenty of birthdays if people had simply thought to invite him.

For my father's circle, was Danièle—civilized, assimilated, assimilable, and acceptable Danièle—an "African unlike the others"? The compliment, since my mother was meant to understand it as a compliment, came from the media mogul and Mitterrand confidant André Rousselet at a dinner I once attended. We were worlds away from Georges's crowd. Yet this prominent man of the left had no sense of how paternalistic and, ultimately, scornful his words were. My mother simply smiled.

She herself wasn't without contradictions. Why would she marry a man whose beliefs were so diametrically opposed to hers? She was in love, she told me, whereas for Georges it was a marriage of convenience. Except that Georges's friends talked about love at first sight. Where does the truth of a couple lie?

Among our family photos, a stray black-and-white picture shows Danièle, not much older than eighteen, next to Prince Claus, the now deceased husband of Queen Beatrix of the Netherlands. They are talking, seated side by side on a beach in Ivory Coast, probably in Assinie or Grand-Bassam, not far from Abidjan.

Claus, tall and blond, with delicate, even features, wearing only a pair of dark swimming trunks, is remarkably handsome, the embodiment of Northern European perfection. Next to him, in a gingham bikini, knees tucked under her chin, pouty, a long cigarette between her fingertips, Danièle looks like a Black Bardot. The two of them are superb. The photo reveals a genuine affection but also a distance between them, the distance that separates two people who have forbidden themselves greater intimacy. Giving free rein to my imagination, I have often wondered if they ever had a little fling. Claus von Amsberg was then second counsel at the German embassy in Ivory Coast. He had become friends with Jean-Pierre, my biological father, Danièle's older brother, who was also headed for a diplomatic career.

Whether based on a real or distorted memory, Danièle recalled an evening in Abidjan. She had gone to Claus's villa unannounced. As usual in the tropics, night had fallen all at once. She was about to knock on his door when, through the partially opened living-room shutters, she saw him in the half-light giving the Nazi salute. Deeply disturbed, she left, not knowing what to think of something she wasn't supposed to see. Claus, who had grown up in the German colony of Tanganyika, present-day Tanzania, had been enrolled, like all young Germans, in the Hitler Youth. Back in Germany after secondary school, he had served two years in the Wehrmacht. Was he reviving or purging a difficult past? Whichever it was, the incident didn't harm their friendship.

In 1966, Jean-Pierre and Danièle attended Claus and Beatrix's wedding. Danièle wore a long, light-colored satin dress with matching gloves, her hair in a bun. She was ravishing. Juan Carlos of Spain made a pass at her, she remembered, in a very cavalier way. Constantine II of Greece, not yet deposed, offered her land on a desert island if she accepted to be his mistress. She found the offer ridiculous. She did, however, get along very well with Beatrix, the future queen of the Netherlands.

Some years later—I must have been two and a half or slightly older—Danièle and I spent our summer vacation with the royal couple. I obviously have no memories of our time in the Netherlands, but the wealth of photos from our trip were part of my childhood. In one picture, I'm on a yacht, knee-high to a grasshopper, plump, chubby-cheeked, with short braids, surrounded by three blond heads, three crown princes, crowding around me. One of the boys is putting a raincoat on my shoulders to protect me from the sea spray. The other is kissing my cheek. Another watches my mother dry me off with a towel. In other photos, in the park around the palace, I glide down a slide under the watchful eyes of the future queen. I'm wearing atrocious orange terry-cloth shorts, the fashion in the seventies, with a light-weight white sweater and matching knee-high socks. A tent is set up on the lawn. Inside, with the conscientiousness of a very young child, I play with a piece of clay as if my life depended on it. Around me, the three little princes, including the current king, gaze at me tenderly. I don't look up, not even to smile, instinctively aware of my girlish privilege. On my face, however, you can see that I'm ever so pleased.

I have occasionally wondered why these three boys, each of them a year apart, probably between five and seven years old at the time, were so fascinated by me. Was this the first time they had spent time with a Black girl? Perhaps their father had raised them on stories of the Africa he had known and loved growing up, an Africa to which he remained connected later in life through his cultural foundation and its support of numerous African filmmakers. Or perhaps they were quite simply won over by my personality, although I would be hard-pressed to describe what it might have consisted of at that age.

I never saw them again in person, but the Dutch family's friendship with mine never wavered. In 1998, Danièle and Georges were invited to Queen Beatrix's sixtieth birthday. Spotting her from afar in the banquet hall filled with European aristocrats, Claus, overjoyed to see my mother again, thunderously shouted her name. As for Georges, he was living a dream. Every crowned head of Europe, whose lives he followed assiduously in *Point de vue* and on TV shows devoted to high society, had suddenly come to life only a few inches from him.

When I try to imagine this moment, I picture the scene in the video by 50 Cent when the door of a mansion opens to a room filled with gorgeous women, one of them purring, "Welcome to the candy shop."[4] A giant candy shop. That's exactly the feeling Georges must have had. He managed to tell Prince Charles about the team of English foxhounds he was master of in Pau. He clearly nourished the hope of inviting the prince to come there to hunt. Less than a year later, however, Georges was dying. As at every funeral in my family—and there have been many—a wreath of orange and white flowers, the colors of the House of Orange, stood at the center of the church, in memory of a friendship born forty years before in the stifling heat of a young, newly independent African country.

Because of his propensity for the aristocratic, quite a few of my father's close friends had a particule—an aristocratic "de"—in their names. In Paris, two of Danièle's best friends were from old German nobility. They didn't know one another, but both had fled Germany when the Russians arrived, leaving behind most of their belongings and no doubt a large part of themselves. I often spent the night at one or the other's house.

The first friend lived in Saint-Nom-la-Bretèche, west of Paris, with a French architect, in a house I loved, where we picked apples and cherries to make jam. Her husband, who was also named Georges, had adopted a daughter during his first marriage—a girl known for being temperamental but who, it seems, was calmed by my presence. I remember that we spent a lot of time playing together.

The other friend was a journalist like Danièle. Married to an Alsatian aristocrat, she lived, in classical style, in an old family apartment a few steps from the Champ-de-Mars in the seventh arrondissement, a neighborhood traditional France is very fond of. I appreciated her impulsiveness, her oldest daughter's sense of humor and freedom, the kindness of her two younger sons, and the way she had of treating me like one of the family when I stayed with her. I sometimes had to adapt to her extraordinarily exotic ways: for example, children drank milk at meals, as they do in Germany. For everything else, I made out pretty well. My mother had sufficiently coached me growing up, and a thousand clues were there to remind me that, in this milieu, which wasn't completely mine—where they kept an exact count of noble lineage, where mothers enrolled their daughters in rock 'n' roll dance lessons to prepare them for the array of balls to come—the most important thing was impeccable manners. My ethnic origins were never brought up. Only the quality of my conduct mattered, for in this setting, more than elsewhere, class trumped everything else.

It was only when I went to live in Ivory Coast that the issue of race hit me square in the face.

# 5 A "Little French Girl" in Ivory Coast

In the early eighties, we left Paris for Abidjan. Danièle felt she had hit a glass ceiling in France. She was no longer satisfied chairing the Foreign Press Association or interviewing politicians—she wanted to become one herself. At the end of the year, Ivory Coast was holding elections, as it did every five years. Even if people already knew that, barring any opposition, Félix Houphouët-Boigny would be reelected president, things were still up for grabs in the legislative and municipal elections. Danièle chose to run for parliament in the district my grandfather was from.

Leaving behind the cocoon of our large Parisian apartment on the Place Malesherbes was heart-wrenching. It also meant leaving Pilar, our Spanish maid and my nanny, whose sturdy presence had always reassured me.

Arriving in Ivory Coast was a shock. Was it because I knew I'd be living there permanently? My perception of the place was no longer the same as when I'd visited on vacation. The heat and humidity; the thick blanket of clouds that made the skies perpetually gray; the gloomy green of the forests along the road we took on weekend trips to my grandfather's hometown; the stench of open-air garbage in the streets of Abidjan—I found it all oppressive. I couldn't stand having to call people I didn't know "uncle" and "auntie," on the dubious grounds that "it's like that here." At my new school, whose rules seemed straight out of the fifties, we had to stand when the teacher entered and curtsey for the principal. At my Catholic school in Paris, we were never punished. In Ivory Coast, at a secular private school, the discipline was strict and the standards exacting. I'd barely arrived when the teacher declared in front of the class that my handwriting looked like chicken scratch. Mortified, I asked my grandmother's driver to take me to a stationery store. I bought several notebooks and when I got home that afternoon, I sat alone in my room writing line after line of cursive. Even today, people compliment me on my handwriting.

As in every formerly colonized country where a rigorous social hierarchy had been established according to color—a hierarchy separating whites from Blacks, giving rights and privileges to the former that the latter lacked, and attaching a special status to people of mixed race—Ivorians had become particularly attentive to gradations of color.

In Paris, my classmates hadn't bothered me about my bloodlines. Georges was my father, Danièle my mother, and no one compared my pigmentation to theirs. In Abidjan, on the other hand, I discovered that every child was a budding geneticist.

On the playground, the Ivorian children chanted, "Bastard! Bastard!" They accused me of having no father. I tried to rebut them by bringing up Georges, but they shot back scornfully that I was too dark to be the daughter of a white man and a mixed-race woman. Some of them, who may have heard about Danièle's first marriage from their parents, simply invented a Black father for me. They felt sure she was my birth mother, so focused their attacks on my supposed lack of a paternal line. A bastard. An orphan. Fatherless. Every one of their words cut me to the quick. To avoid crying in front of them, I defended myself with my fists. Which was a bad choice. Even born with a silver spoon in their mouths, the Ivory Coast kids had extensive practice in hand-to-hand combat and got the better of me every time.

Some of the children I played with made fun of me for my Parisian accent, for not understanding Abidjan slang, or for going horseback riding in my free time like a "little white girl." I felt out of place. It took me a while to understand that what their criticisms revealed was less a rejection of me personally than a complex best described as "colonial." The Ivorian children were persuaded that, with my very French manners, I was making a show of my superiority, although I was only being myself. Their suspicions were reinforced by my parents' social status. At school, I was the "daughter of": a snob looking down her nose at them, flaunting her mastery of cultural codes imported from France, someone they protected themselves from through ridicule. Which meant that they implicitly placed special value on being or seeming to be French; that they would undoubtedly have liked to have the same mastery of the former colonizer's culture; that, despite appearances, they devalued their own Ivorian identity; and that they definitely couldn't say so, let alone admit it to themselves, because such things simply weren't said in a country that officially claimed to be proud of its independence, even if it remained a bastion of Françafrique.

For such young children to have already internalized all this, their parents, and more broadly the society in which they lived, already had to be thinking along these lines. The colonizer had done his work well, instilling in the psyches of the colonized the self-evidence of his superiority.

I thus discovered in Ivory Coast a bipolar country where people proclaimed their pride in being Ivorian but where it was more reassuring to be ruled by Europeans, where the closest advisors to the head of state were French, and where there persisted a kind of naïve admiration for every form of Western modernity. Didn't people frequently say "the white man's really something" as soon as some new technology arrived (needless to say) from the North? Didn't Ivorians call each other "bushmen" and "savages"? Between the lines lay the idea that civilization was something that came from the city, that it meant mastering a Western way of life. At the same time, Ivorians wanted to show pride in their traditions, which were highlighted on TV. Yet people had become so accustomed of thinking of themselves according to exogenous criteria that in restaurants an "exotic" fruit salad consisted of pineapple, mango, and papaya, in other words, of fruits grown locally.

When I went to live in Ivory Coast, the country had been independent for only twenty years, and you could feel it. The country had been a French colony for nearly seventy years. That isn't so long in historical time, but the colonizer's work of dispossessing the population had been remarkably effective, all the more so because it was accomplished in a place that had never comprised a unified political entity before the French arrival. There had been kingdoms, clans, and chiefdoms, but Ivory Coast itself was a colonial invention. It remained so until well after its independence. It was only in 2004, with the so-called "war against France," that the French yoke was symbolically broken.

Until then, as difficult as it was to admit, the idea of French superiority over Ivorians, of Europeans over Africans, of whites over Blacks, continued to be deeply entrenched in people's minds. It oozed and it festered like an untreated wound. Not surprisingly, things finally erupted in violence.

Ivorians' relationship with people of mixed race—the white man's children, to borrow the title of Sarah Bouyain's documentary film[1]—is symptomatic of the colonial complex.

Popular opinion holds that they form a separate caste, that they don't mix with other groups, that they live and marry among themselves. What gets forgotten is that during colonization these children of what were rarely consensual relationships between colonizers and African women were herded off to an orphanage specifically for them in Bingerville, the country's former capital. Forcibly separated from their mothers and abandoned by fathers who, with or without recognizing them legally, had in some cases already gone back to France, these mixed-race children had no one to turn to. Wasn't it only natural for them to forge especially strong bonds with each other? On the other hand, all of them, boys and girls alike, were sent to school and provided an education that at the time only a handful of Ivorians received. It allowed them to secure well-paying jobs and, for many of them, to enter the newly independent country's upper classes.

In Sarah Bouyain's documentary, a mixed-race woman born during colonization recounts feeling rejected by whites but at the same time sensing a kind of discomfort from Africans, who didn't feel they could have a straightforward, genuine relationship with children who, like her, had unwittingly inherited the white man's prestige.

One of my distant cousins, the daughter of a white priest who had long since broken his vow of celibacy, told me that the day she set up a stall in the local market, the other women vendors made fun of her. They simply couldn't understand how a mixed-race woman could do work as humble as theirs, and they assumed from the get-go that she would fail because she wasn't where she belonged. As if the genetic link to the white man could protect her from poverty, as if being white weren't merely a skin color but wealth itself and a symbol of power.

At the height of her fame, the singer Nayanka Bell, a sublime mixed-race French-Ivorian woman, had the misfortune of saying in an interview, "The future belongs to people of mixed race." A major scandal ensued. Public opinion united against her, tongues sharper than machetes. What was she trying to say, that Black Ivorians weren't good enough for her?

Overnight, her career came to a screeching halt, even though she had simply wanted to convey, albeit somewhat clumsily, an inclusive message about the interdependence of peoples and cultures.

Yet among the same people who vilified her, I have zero doubt that most of them dreamed either of looking like her or having her as a mistress, because on a scale of sex appeal, people of mixed race won out. When I was living in Ivory Coast and for a long time afterward, the absolute fantasy was a West Indian Creole woman or an American like Beyoncé. Caramel complexion, long curly hair, and if, to top it all off, light-colored eyes—you had definitely hit the jackpot. At a time when Denzel Washington and Wesley Snipes were equally famous, women dreamed of Denzel and his light-brown skin, not of Snipes, who was too Black, too *nègre*.[2] That model already existed at home.

When colored contact lenses came out, Abidjan suddenly teemed with glassy blue- and hazelnut-eyed aliens. Women were constantly sewing hair onto their head—fake hair as straight as chopsticks or real hair cut from the heads of destitute Indians. The most diehard slathered themselves with lightening cream. Whatever it took, it seems, to acquire the physical attributes of whites. But when Nayanka Bell had the temerity to say that the future belonged to people of mixed race, she was pilloried by the Ivorian public.

When I arrived in Ivory Coast, I was surprised to discover these contradictions. Even if I wouldn't have been able to put it so clearly at that age, one fact had obviously shaped who I was: my grandfather's unique history had freed our family from the inferiority complex the colonizer had instilled.

Alphonse had accomplished the work of our emancipation for us, by overcoming or even reversing those factors that in his time proved so determinative. For example, the issue of mixed race. We had the good fortune that our skin color wasn't the result of colonial domination. Although we had been mixed race for three generations, it wasn't because a colonizer had set his sights on a native woman, knocked her up, as they say, then, with or without recognizing his paternity, dispatched the child to the mixed-race orphanage (renamed the "Home for the Mixed-Race" in 1939) and, in the best of cases, sent for him once he returned to France, became a good father, raised him well, but without ever—never ever—marrying the mother, whom he left to her native Africa.

We were mixed race because my grandfather was the first Ivorian to marry a Frenchwoman, breaking one of the fundamental taboos of slave and colonial societies: never touch a white woman.

# 6 My Grandfather, Alphonse Boni

Alphonse Boni was born on March 1, 1909. That's at least what most of the official documents say. Other forms have January 1909, whereas the career record for his time as a French magistrate[1] mentions December 22, 1909.

In fact, no one knows exactly when my grandfather was born. We assume he took his first breath sometime in 1909. To comply with the norms of the French civil service, the colonial administration assigned him a day and month, both as arbitrary as they were uncertain. It did the same for his name.

My grandfather's real given name was Boni and his surname Ehouman. In Ivory Coast, it was customary, at least within his ethnic group, to introduce oneself with one's surname first: Ehouman Boni. One further nuance: in certain circumstances, the son would take his father's given name as his surname. My great-grandfather was called Tano Ehouman, my grandfather Ehouman Boni. And, in fact, my biological father should have been the first with Boni as a surname: Boni Ehouman Jean-Pierre. But my grandfather's patronym was transcribed according to French custom and Boni became his surname. When he wanted to continue his primary schooling, he was required to get baptized, at which point he chose a Christian name, and his actual surname was simply omitted. That explains why on paper, and no doubt elsewhere, his identity ended up entirely reworked. It was at that point that he decided to not merely accept things as they were and that he and his family made the somewhat extraordinary decision that would radically change the course of his life.

I suspect that the sense of freedom they displayed at that moment, the way they said "enough!" to the colonizer in an effort to regain their dignity, the scornful pride that that extraordinary decision implied—all this was possible because the family had long drawn strength from a rich and ancient history.

Although my grandfather grew up in Tiassalé, a small, flourishing town in southeast Ivory Coast, his family originally came from farther away. Through his parents, Alphonse was both Agni and Baoulé, two ethnicities belonging to the powerful Akan group, whose first kingdoms historians date to the late thirteenth century.[2] The Agni and Baoulé migrated from present-day Ghana, but I couldn't say where exactly the Agni branch of my grandfather's family is from. There is no doubt, however, that his Baoulé relatives descended from the influential Ashanti empire, founded by Osei Tutu in 1701. They arrived in Ivory Coast in the first half of the eighteenth century, following in the footsteps of Queen Pokou, a West African figure of both history and myth.

Abla Pokou, King Osei Tutu's niece, was the sister of his successor, Opoku Ware, and of the latter's designated successor, Dakon. She was at the center of power, since succession passed through the female line among the Akan, although the men governed. The queen mother, who, in fact, may also have been the king's sister, played an equally important role in the kingdom's affairs, as she was the only one allowed to contradict the *Asantehene*, the sovereign.

Before Abla Pokou's brother Dakon could take power, he was killed by a pretender to the throne. Realizing she would soon suffer the same fate, Abla gathered her people, her brother's supporters, and their allies and fled northwest with several thousand followers. She was a woman of around forty whom people had long believed to be infertile, until late in life she gave birth to a son. With her enemies in pursuit, she arrived at the Comoé River, whose swelling waters blocked her passage. This is where the myth comes in.

Through Pokou's soothsayer, the river gods told her that in order for her and her fellow exiles to pass, they had to provide a gift of their most prized possessions. The women immediately took off their jewelry and collected the Ashanti gold, the very gold that had ensured the power of the empire. But that wasn't enough. Material belongings could be replaced, but not a human life. What the gods wanted was the sacrifice of something pure, a being yet untainted by the vicissitudes of life.

According to the transcription of Ivorian oral accounts taken in 1901 by Maurice Delafosse:[3]

> Queen Pokou then turned to them and said, "All of you here must take your newborns and throw them in the river." But they refused. Queen Pokou had an only son; she took a great many pieces of gold jewelry, adorned her son's body with them, and cast him into the river. An enormous silk-cotton tree then rose on the opposite bank and bent forward until its top touched the bank where Pokou and her followers stood. All of them then climbed onto the trunk and advanced across the bridge. The crossing lasted a long time; after sixteen days, they had still not completed their journey. In the end, it took them eighteen days to reach the other side.
>
> Then their Ashanti pursuers arrived at the river. The silk-cotton tree, which stretched like a bridge across the water, suddenly rose, and the Ashanti, who had no canoes, were unable to cross the Comoé.[4]

Once safely on the other side of the river, Abla Pokou, heartbroken, cried out, "Baou-li!" "The child is dead!" Her sacrifice and selflessness marked her out as queen of a new people, who took the name Baoulé in homage to her loss.

Because of her example, it was accepted among the Ivorian Akan that women were entitled to rule. Thus, Pokou's niece, Akwa Boni, who succeeded the queen after her death in 1760, and later Tanoh Adjo, who founded Tiassalé.

According to the story that my grandfather's first cousin told me one night, the founder of our clan was an officer in Abla Pokou's guards. To thank him for his bravery, the queen allowed him to marry a "princess of the chair," that is, a princess of royal blood. Which princess was she? He didn't tell me or I don't remember. Our elders die and with them a part of our collective memory.

On the other hand, I remember very well Alphonse's funeral in 1989. A national day of mourning was declared. We walked behind the coffin to the National Assembly where people paid their respects. The men of the family who carried him said that the coffin trembled, a sign of my grandfather's spiritual power. Or perhaps the coffin wobbled from the bearers' shaky steps.

In Tiassalé, along the river where he grew up, the traditional drums beat, invoking, in their coded language, his secret name, which my great-uncles refused to tell me. My mother had workers clear the vast piece of municipal land in front of the modest little house where my grandfather came to relax on weekends. Several hundred, perhaps a thousand, people gathered under canvas canopies or directly under the beating sun. Félix Houphouët-Boigny, the President of the Republic, attended, along with Ivory Coast's political patriciate, diplomatic corps, and our extended family. But what struck me most was the delegation of bare-chested men facing us at the other end of the lawn, all of them wrapped in awesome red- and black-silk pagnes, the mourning colors of the Akan. The men had traveled from Ghana to remind those present that one of their own, a descendant of the Kumasi Ashanti, had just died and that as such he should be honored. Two and a half centuries after Queen Pokou's flight, the circle was complete.

If I have digressed a bit to recount the funeral of a man whose birth I have only just mentioned, that is because when people—at least, in France—speak of colonialism, they too often forget that it involved conquest. Obviously, Africa had been weakened demographically and politically by four centuries of the slave trade, but it wasn't inhabited by mewling dim-witted hordes aching to surrender themselves to the invading liberators.

Whether acquired through war or the cunning of "protectorate" treaties, the territory the European powers colonized over the nineteenth century was wrested from those to whom it legitimately belonged. The French didn't come to Africa to celebrate friendship between peoples; they came for gain. And of course, as was true with other Europeans, their appetite for conquest met with resistance, and that resistance was suppressed with bloodshed. In West Africa, the most well-known resistance struggles were led by Béhanzine and Samory Touré, but there were plenty of smaller-scale revolts as well.

In 1893, French Captain Jean-Baptiste Marchand, who was on a "mission de pénétration," in other words, on a mission of annexation, along the Bandama River, arrived in Tiassalé. My grandfather's ancestors, proud of their long history, were intent on preserving their independence. They armed their canoes, drew their bows, and loaded their guns to fight off the invader. To be honest, though, their defenses were sorely ineffective. They were defeated without much difficulty and Tiassalé was annexed to the new colony of Ivory Coast, officially created in the same year.

To avoid the humiliation of having their chief captured, my forebears hid him in the forest and disguised a commoner to take his place. As for Marchand, he cut short his "mission" and headed north to fight Samory Touré. After which, he embarked on the African adventure that would make him the "hero of Fashoda" and a celebrity among the French public: the famous expedition designed to establish French outposts along the Congo-Nile axis and eventually eat away at Britain's Egyptian possessions.

I find it quite ironic that the single feat this French military man accomplished in Ivory Coast was to bring my family members to heel.

To return to my grandfather, in 1924, his family made the decision that would change his life forever.

According to Alphonse's cousin, it sprang from an incident involving the patriarch of our clan, my great-great-great-uncle. Accused of murdering another Ivorian, he was brought before a French court, probably in Grand-Bassam. Since he was by no means poor, he procured the services of a French lawyer, who got the case dismissed, even though it's quite possible that he had in fact committed the crime. He was known for being hot-headed, and I have been told that to scare the children of the region, people told them at the time, "If you don't behave, we'll send you to the Big Bitty," the clan patriarch.

The proud chief learned a single lesson from the episode: the humiliation of being subjected to a trial, whereas before the whites arrived, he himself had embodied judicial authority. He assembled the family council and asked them to name a boy among his descendants whom they would send to France to become an attorney, and who would return to Ivory Coast to protect the family. My grandfather was just finishing primary school. He was a good student. So, according to this account, that is how he ended up on a boat bound for France.

My grandmother, Rose-Marie Boni, was well aware of her husband's unique path in life and endeavored to recount his experiences and how they met in a manuscript that she never ultimately completed. In her telling, an entirely different reason explains Alphonse's departure. My great-grandfather, to whom power would traditionally be handed down, had been named chief of the Tiassalé canton by the colonial administration. Alphonse was his third son. He sent him to study in a little village school in Tiassalé. Why him instead of his two older sons? No doubt because after several years living under occupation, Tano Ehouman understood the importance of acquiring the white man's knowledge in the new order then being imposed. When Alphonse's good grades allowed him to continue his education, his father agreed to send him to the regional school in Bouaké, in the center of Ivory Coast. That decision caused him some grief.

"The subdivision chief, in his white starch-hardened jacket, was slumped over his desk," my grandmother writes in her manuscript.[5]

> He was sweating profusely, as much from anger as from the heat. He was waiting for Tano, the young canton chief who had dared to violate his orders. Tano, his large shadow preceding him, entered the office, poised and dignified. Seeing the two of them side by side, one wondered which was the chief, the one slouched in his chair, teary-eyed, with drooping red-blotched cheeks, or the tall, proud young man who preferred not to sit down.
>
> "Where's your son?"

"In Bouaké."

"What's he doing in Bouaké? Why is he mucking about there instead of here in school?"

"My son has been at the regional school since October 1st."

An angry furrow cut across the chief's brow.

"Liar! What impudence! Why don't you mull things over in jail since you don't know how to tell the truth."

Tano left the office without betraying his humiliation. Even the guard, sent to accompany him to the crude shack people called a jail, felt embarrassed as he followed Tano deferentially down the hall. But before the chief had time to ask his colleague in Bouaké to verify Tano's story, the regional school director, already alerted, telegraphed to inform him that he did indeed have the young Boni boy among his pupils. Beside himself, the subdivision chief had no choice but to let Tano go. Tano returned home to the sound of tom-toms, which, in their special language, ridiculed the chief.

Of course, at the time, attending school, even to learn the basics of the French language, was the exception among Ivorian children. In 1924, out of an estimated population of two million, only 4,354 young Ivorians attended school, "among whom there were only 211 girls."[6]

In Bouaké, my grandfather earned his lower primary school certificate, which allowed him to enroll in the only upper primary school in the colony, located in Bingerville. Unlike Senegal, Ivory Coast had no secondary schools, so Bingerville represented the height of what a young Ivorian could aspire to. The upper primary certificate, which in France officially recognized the completion of one's primary schooling, didn't even exist.

In Bingerville, life was immediately different. Students had to wear gray cotton-drill uniforms. They were split into three dormitories, one for pupils of mixed race, one for those from the coast, and the last for those from the country's interior. The thinking was that grouping students by ethnicity would alleviate their homesickness.

Another big difference: although French schools had been secular since 1882, young Ivorians—"French natives," as they were called—arriving in Bingerville had to be baptized before beginning school. Renouncing their religions and first names, they cast off their previous identities at the altar of French schooling in order to embrace a new identity that would allow them to rise in Ivorian society. At least that was the prevailing belief. Particularly so at the one federal school in French West Africa (AOF) and French Equatorial Africa (AEF), the École William Ponty, on the island of Gorée in Dakar.[7] At that elite secondary school, admission to which depended on a competitive entrance exam, the best students of France's Black African colonies studied to become teachers or civil servants. They could also prepare for the entrance exam to medical school, likewise in Dakar, where they would train to become French doctors' medical and pharmaceutical "auxiliaries" as well as midwives and nurses.

None of the professional degrees was recognized outside the colonies. The degrees didn't provide students with a baccalaureate equivalent, which would have allowed them to enroll at a university. Yet to the colonized youth of the day, the degrees offered the guarantee of a better life. Attending William Ponty, having its badge on one's uniform, was extremely prestigious, and its students—the "Pontins"—comprised a kind of colonial elite.

As soon as my grandfather arrived in Bingerville, he began studying for the William Ponty entrance exam. Unfortunately, he didn't make the cut, nor did the rest of his classmates that year.

My grandmother attributed his failure to discrimination:

> The reader should bear in mind that although progress among the elites is gaining momentum today, such was not the case during the period immediately following the First World War. It was considered good form to reserve access to secondary school for the Senegalese. The young elites from other AOF colonies lost out. The scant number of spots weren't always granted to students who merited them for the quality of their work. So many bright young minds, who only asked to be given a chance, were simply swept aside.

Whatever the reason for Alphonse's failure, his disappointment was immense. Beyond his father's plantations, the only future he now foresaw for himself was a career as someone's assistant. Unable to accept such limited prospects, he left Bingerville without completing his second and final year of upper primary school and asked his father to send him to France. The family council met and approved the decision; my great-great-great-uncle was especially supportive. Was it his chance to get a kind of symbolic revenge for the trial the colonial authorities had put him through? Did he now understand that the new elite would no longer be made up of traditional chiefs but of the young men and women who attended French schools?

Whatever the case, at the time, it was extremely rare for Africans to study in France. By way of comparison, it was only in 1946, twenty-two years after Alphonse left, that then-French deputy Houphouët-Boigny succeeded in sending 146 Ivorian children to pursue their education in France. And Ivory Coast still had no secondary school.

On the other hand, Senegal, whose ties with France were older, had two public high schools, one in Saint Louis, the other in Dakar, where Léopold Sédar Senghor completed his baccalaureate. But attending university was a whole different story. So, when Senghor wanted to study humanities in Paris in 1928, his teachers had to move heaven and earth to convince the AOF Governor General to grant him a scholarship. And even then it was only a "half-scholarship" of 250 francs.[8]

My family managed to avoid the same difficulty with Alphonse's secondary education because they paid everything out of their own pocket. The surprising boldness of their decision as well as the financial cost show that the entire clan had become invested in my grandfather's education and that his success was part of their strategy to conserve their influence.

Alphonse had no inkling about schools in France. According to my grandmother, he sought the help of Bingerville's regional school director, who knew the father superior of a Jesuit middle school in Angoulême, the Collège Saint-Paul, which had hosted an African student in the past. Skeptical of Alphonse's chances, the director provided a lukewarm recommendation of my grandfather.

According to Rose-Marie's manuscript:

> "Six years of study for the baccalaureate," the director said to himself. "He'll give up well before then. Blacks don't persevere and they're incapable of planting roots. In three or four years, he'll come back to us without a diploma and full of self-importance. I'll still write the recommendation, if only to keep my word."

My grandfather's family, it seems, gave him the sizeable sum of 15,000 francs to cover his trip and pay for tuition. Then they sent him to Grand-Bassam, where the boats left for France.

> With his uncle's help, Alphonse had tackled all the administrative hurdles, but when he went up to the ticket counter alone, the agent laughed in his face.
>
> "Sir, I want a third-class ticket to France."
>
> "What are you going to go do in France?"
>
> "Go to middle school, sir. I have money for the ticket."
>
> A colonizer overhearing the exchange chimed in, paternally, "Come with me. I'll take you on as my cabin boy."
>
> "Me? Your boy, sir? Never!" Alphonse replied, furiously. "I have the money for my ticket. I want my ticket."
>
> "What is this big-headed child going on about?" the ticket agent wondered. "That's the first time in my career I've seen a little *nègre* wanting to leave for school. As if he needed an education. As if we aren't already here."

Alphonse finally got his third-class ticket. On December 10, 1924, he made the trip to Bordeaux. He was fifteen years old, with a pair of new shoes and three suits in his suitcase. He was leaving for the unknown, never suspecting that it would be many years before he would see his country again. Like some messiah, he arrived in Angoulême on December 24, in the middle of winter. The boarding school was closed for school vacation and Alphonse was the only student there. The priests thought the transition period would help him get acclimated—in the literal sense of the word. This was the first time Alphonse experienced a French winter. He nearly froze to death in his thin suits.

When school resumed in January, he was introduced to his new classmates. While they were impatient to meet the new African arrival, my grandfather had a hard time concealing his surprise: he had never seen so many white people. The French colonizers at the time, my grandmother writes, usually sent their school-age children to France, so there were very few French children in Ivory Coast and just as few Africans in France. According to the Colonial Ministry's 1926 census, there were 2,524 Africans and Malagasy in French territory. According to researchers, it would be more accurate to put the number at between five and seven thousand.[9] Out of a population of more than forty-one million, the figure remains miniscule.

My grandfather liked to tell the story of how, when he entered the dining hall at lunchtime, all the schoolboys pounded their silverware on the table to welcome him. He had wonderful memories of his years among the Jesuits, with whom he said he found a second family. During school vacations, he was sent home with fellow students so that he wouldn't have to spend the time alone. And when the coffee or cocoa harvests back in Ivory Coast weren't good, the priests never raised an eyebrow if the tuition money came late.

Despite everything, when I look at the class picture I included in my documentary film *Too Black to Be French?*—a photo sent to me by the niece of one of my grandfather's closest friends at school—the solitude he exudes hits me each time. Everything sets him apart from the other students. His skin color in the middle of an entirely white class. His height and build, revealing him to be older than the other boys. And even the black and white of the photograph, the austere uniforms of these teenagers who, transporting us back to the 1920s, remind us of how exceptional it was for a little African boy to be going to school in France, and of how alone Alphonse, however well looked after he may have been, must have felt during all those years spent far away from his family, his country, and his native language.

# 7 Slavery and the Holocaust: Why I Am a Humanist

When I arrived in Ivory Coast, I too was an exile, but an exile in my own country. Pestered by my young Ivorian classmates, I turned to those who accepted me as I was and with whom I shared the same cultural codes. My first friends were French or mixed-race.

I went horseback riding three or four times a week; Georges made a point of it. There were several riding clubs in Abidjan. Their members were almost exclusively French and lived like caricatures of expatriates in Africa. Narcissists, they enjoyed a social status they never would have had in France and always stuck to their own kind, knowing no more of Ivory Coast than Abidjan, the Assinie beaches, and Yamoussoukro, the museum-city of the country's president. To the African stable hands, they spoke pidgin or in what purported to be an Ivorian accent. This was a crowd I avoided.

My father had an extremely manly, not to say martial, view of horseback riding. He believed that only by working with bad horses did one learn to ride well. I was forbidden to cry if I fell and required to remount immediately to keep the fear away. I've lost count of all my falls and fractures.

When I was thirteen, Dominique Bentejac, one of Georges's very good friends, a runner-up in the World Eventing Championship, had me ride my father's horse, which was known for being difficult to handle, its fiery temperament, and not least its power. The whole club came out to see how I would manage. Fully determined not to fall, I went with my instincts and put my trust in the horse. No power struggle; I didn't try to impose my will. I followed along, light as a feather. We flew over the bars of the obstacle course that

Dominique had set up, and afterward Georges was so proud of me that he gave me his horse. Done were the days of ill-natured nags. After eight years of weekly practice, I had at last earned my rider's stripes. Although horseback riding didn't bring me any closer to Ivorians, it taught me courage and perseverance.

All the same, as an adolescent, I began to have doubts about the company I kept. One evening, I went with two of my best friends—sisters who lived across the street—and a big group of girlfriends to a "white party" at a local nightclub. We stopped for a burger first. At the table next to us, Alpha Blondy sat eating alone. The country's first "rude boy," my absolute idol ever since, as an eleven-year-old concertgoer in my good-little-girl dress, I had seen him sing "Brigadier Sabari" at the Hôtel Ivoire. His photos covered my school notebooks. I thought he was beautiful. I thought he had talent. I *luuuved* him. He good-naturedly indulged us for a round of pictures and autographs. Afterward, he invited us for a glass of champagne with the French singer Bernard Lavilliers.

A few weeks later, I looked through the pictures. We were ravishing, all dressed in white. Yet something was off. How was it that, in this group of young women in the full flower of our youth, I was the only Black girl? We were in Ivory Coast, after all, but these little French girls had no African friends except me. My sense of not really belonging only intensified when my two neighbors, the sisters, explained to me, as naturally as could be, that they could never date a Black man. Their disgust was almost physical, even though they were born in Ivory Coast and, unlike me, had lived there their entire lives. All they knew of France was summers on the Riviera. Their minds were nevertheless made up. No romance with an African. What, then, was Ivory Coast to them? Scenery? A giant amusement park? Can one claim to love a country but not its inhabitants? What color was I in their eyes for them to feel free to tell me this? Something in me faltered.

In addition to being neighbors, these two friends and I attended the same private middle school, undoubtedly the best school in the country in terms of academics. It brought in young people of every nationality; Ivorians, of course, including some on scholarship; many Africans from across the continent, Abidjan being the headquarters of several regional and international organizations; children of expats and diplomats, and of people from Lebanon who had fled the war or moved for business. It all made for a wonderful melting pot in school pictures. On the playground, though, things were different. I had never paid attention before, but the whites and Lebanese students were always together. The Africans kept to themselves. The mixed-race kids navigated between the two. As always, I belonged to no group. Once again, I was a victim of harassment.

This time around, several Ivorian girls targeted me. They waited until classes got out and converged on me with a flurry of slaps and punches. I suppose they were jealous. Abidjan was then an oversized village of two million people. A few middle schools and high schools, public and private, formed the upper crust, and rumors traveled at lightning speed between them. Despite myself, I was one of my cohort's fashionable girls—today, we'd say an It girl. I made the most of my vacations in France to soak up the latest trends. When Vanessa Paradis hit it big with "Joe le Taxi," sporting ripped jeans in her video, I asked my father to buy me a new pair. I took a scissors and meticulously slashed them, then added bits of embroidery and fabric for some personal flair. Clad in his gray three-piece suit and astutely matched tie and handkerchief, Georges wouldn't let me on the plane with him. When I refused to change outfits, he called Danièle, who advised him not to raise a fuss. When people saw me in my ripped jeans in the streets of Abidjan, they asked me anxiously if I'd fallen, if I'd hurt myself, if I needed help.

But I was terrorized back at school. For a time, our driver even walked with me to the gate, which did little to change things. The girls still waited for me at the sound of the bell. And then, in the middle of the school year, out of the blue, Nathalie arrived. Nathalie had dreads and long hooked nails, like bird claws, she painted red. She was no fan of injustice. She made it loud and clear that whoever picked a fight with me, the youngest of the class, was a coward and that from then on, whoever did would have to deal with her. It seems that no one wanted a taste of her nails, because my tormenters, as if by magic, left me in peace.

Nathalie was my first African friend. We hung out with members of the Solar System, Alpha Blondy's band. I snuck out with her to see Burning Spear in one of Abidjan's working-class neighborhoods, where my parents would never have allowed me to go. I went with her to my first *maquis*,[1] where people from the neighborhood went to drink beer.

At around the same time, an Ivorian girl in my class told me that her cousin, one of the year's It boys who was slightly older than me and attended a different school, had noticed me and wanted to meet. An interschool outing was planned for Boulay Island, a leisure spot off the coast of Abidjan. We agreed that she would introduce me to him there. Her cousin was very cute and looked friendly. Despite the huge cold sore that my anxiety had planted on my face, he still seemed interested in me. My classmate rubbed her hands together slyly: on the agenda for the day, first lunch, then dancing. That was her plan to bring the two of us together.

First one song came on, then a second, then a third. Helplessly, I didn't budge from my seat. The DJ played only makossa pop and Zaïko Langa Langa, and I was too embarrassed to tell anyone that I didn't know how to dance to African music. I remained frozen in place. Until, at long last, I realized just how absurd the scene was. At which point, I strode out onto the dance floor and asked my friends to teach me to dance like them. To my immense surprise, instead of making fun of me, they were all too happy to show me and cheered with joy as I made my first successful hip rolls.

A few weeks later, I went out with the long-awaited cousin.

From then on, as if the tide had suddenly turned, all the criticisms stopped. The other girls quit shaming me for being too French or not Ivorian enough. I was considered a native while also accepted for my differences. Deep down, however, nothing had really changed.

At home in Ivory Coast, we lived the same way as we had in Paris, in other words, à la française. Georges didn't like Ivorian cuisine, so we ate French. Danièle listened to opera. And Georges? We generally stopped him from buying records, otherwise it would have been hunting horns and military marches all day long. The two albums of African music we had were by Miriam Makeba and

Manu Dibango—and the latter only because Manu Dibango himself had given it to my mother as a gift.

A compulsive reader, I regularly went (you can't invent this kind of thing) to the Librairie de France, the largest bookstore in Abidjan, to stock up on novels from the green- or pink-spined series for children and young adults: Fantômette, Noddy, the Club des Cinq (aka the Famous Five), Alec Ramsay, and the Black Stallion. All my heroes were white. When I was ten years old, I started raiding my parents' massive library. It didn't contain a single African author.

At the video store, not one African movie figured among the blithely pirated titles.

On the other hand, there was television. My exposure to Ivorian culture came through ultra-popular TV shows—the comics Toto and Dago, the satirist Léonard Groguhet and his pioneering series "Comment ça va?"—and advertisements, some of which are genuine classics today. For example, the mosquito-swatting choreography in ads for the bug spray Super Timor. Or the happy customer of Pharmapur soap, who, ever since he started using it, has people telling him, "Lambert, you really are getting handsome," a phrase, like so many others from popular ads, we repeated like personal taglines.

Movies, literature, painting—all the culture I so avidly consumed at the time was created by Westerners. I'm not saying white, because Danièle made sure to introduce me to the history of slavery and its consequences from very early on. She had me read Richard Wright's *Black Boy*, although she neglected to tell me it was an autobiography. For me, Wright was American, like Romain Gary, whose novel *White Dog* she bought me, a book that had blown her away when she was young, and like Vernon Sullivan, whose book *I Spit on Your Graves* I simply devoured. In other words, except for Wright, the authors I read had no color.

I didn't know that Sullivan was Boris Vian's pseudonym and that he and Romain Gary were French. I was fascinated listening to my mother talk to me about segregation in the United States, about these almost-white Blacks who had crossed the color line but got caught because of the pigment of the half-moons of their fingernails. Later, of course, I saw Douglas Sirk's *Imitation of Life*, a marvelous melodrama about racism. Danièle made me relive Martin Luther King, Jr.'s visionary speech "I Have a Dream" and chanted James Brown's "I'm Black and I'm Proud" for me. She told me about the Ku Klux Klan massacres as if she had been there herself. She was an excellent storyteller, and I was petrified. Just as I was petrified watching *Roots* on TV and seeing Kunta Kinte chained up on the slave ship.

After hearing Danièle's glowing enthusiasm for *The Covenant*, the James Michener novel about South Africa, I too polished off the saga's 800 pages. I was at most nine years old that summer and knew from then on what apartheid was. Although I grasped that the violence perpetrated against Blacks stemmed solely from their being Black, I never made the connection between their history and my own. It was history, a state of the world that had once existed but existed no longer or that, in the case of South Africa, was fated to disappear. I couldn't see how that history directly affected my present circumstances and who I was, and Danièle didn't provide me with the tools necessary to discern the relationship. I didn't even make the connection between slavery and colonialism. Slavery, racism, and segregation were atrocities that taught me about the human capacity for evil. I felt exactly the same emotion and indignation when I saw pictures from and read stories about the Holocaust, a subject Danièle steeped me in with the same intensity. She was part of the generation born during the Second World War that turned twenty in the 1960s, when after years of silence and denial, people began to speak openly about the extermination of the Jews. She told me about the final sequence of Gillo Pontecorvo's film *Kapo*, emphasizing the melodrama underpinning a story about a female concentration camp kapo, who, as she is about to die, recites the Kaddish, thus revealing her Jewish identity to the German guards. With the same fervor as we had followed *Roots*, we watched every episode of the miniseries *Holocaust*. I read and reread *The Diary of Anne Frank* and Martin Gary's *For Those I Loved*, whose film adaptation Danièle and I of course went to see. Later, I too would have my heart broken by William Styron's *Sophie's Choice*. Slavery and the Holocaust are the reasons I'm a humanist.

In 1987, Danièle became managing director of FTI, Ivory Coast's radio and television service. As part of her duties, she attended MIP-TV, the international media-content market, in Cannes to purchase new programs. Deeply moved by a screening of Claude Lanzmann's documentary *Shoah*, whose rights exceeded her budget, she arranged for a personal meeting with the director. She convinced Lanzmann to broadcast his ten-hour documentary for free as a three-part special on Ivorian television. In return, she promised to make the airing of his film a major event in Ivory Coast and to devote a TV special to it on which he would appear as the guest of honor. Lanzmann accepted, and Danièle returned home triumphant with the video cassettes of *Shoah*. She declared it a masterpiece. Although I promised myself to watch it in its entirety, in the end I only saw a few parts. Yet again, Danièle was such a good narrator that I preferred to listen to her recount the films, especially the classic scene with the Israeli hairdresser Abraham Bomba, chosen by the SS to cut the hair of victims before they entered the gas chambers.

Lanzmann's trip to Abidjan didn't go well, although Danièle had made sure he received the warmest of welcomes. As soon as he arrived, he became infatuated with a young Frenchwoman determined to show him the real Ivory Coast. So, she dragged him to every slum in Abidjan. Which didn't stop her from coming to our house to sip champagne at dinners my mother organized in the filmmaker's honor. Unlike the elegantly dressed women at these receptions, the wannabe rebel sported a pair of jeans and a stubborn pout to make clear she didn't endorse the luxury around her. Danièle was furious. Georges railed privately against the "little bitch." Lanzmann, I imagine, had a fine time. Things got worse on the set of the TV special my mother hosted, when Lanzmann dug in his heels on the singularity of the Holocaust, on its unequaled horror, insisting that it was the most important of all the crimes against humanity, while refusing any possible parallel with slavery. Ivorians, on the other hand, had been hoping to hear about a shared brotherhood of Blacks and Jews. Danièle was sorely disappointed by the missed opportunity.

Yet even if historians remain divided on the issue, it isn't unreasonable to see a line running through the racial theories that arose in Europe at the time of the transatlantic slave trade, the colonization of Africa by European (and in particular German) powers, and the rise of Nazi eugenics.

The first genocide of the twentieth century took place in Namibia, when the Herero and Nama people attempted to defend their land against the colonial ambitions of Germany's Second Reich. Their resistance was considered an affront to the Kaiser's power but also a challenge to the superiority of the white "race" by an "inferior people" whom the Germans would easily subdue.

On October 2, 1904, General von Trotha gave the order to exterminate the Herero. In his correspondence, he speaks of a "race war."[2] Men, women, and children—everyone must be killed. On April 22, 1905, a similar extermination order was given against the Nama. Those who survived were imprisoned in concentration camps, Germany's first. They were tattooed with the letters GH, *Gefangene Herero*, "captured Herero," and reduced to forced labor in atrocious conditions. They died of hunger and exhaustion or were executed.

The camp administration kept a daily tally of deaths in its carefully kept logs. According to the Belgian historian Joël Kotek, a Holocaust specialist, the mortality rate was higher than in the Nazi's subsequent concentration camps.[3] Forty percent in the latter, more than fifty percent in Namibia.[4] In just a few years, eighty percent of the Herero and fifty percent of the Nama had been killed.

The horrors didn't stop there. "The prisoners [. . .] were forced to boil the heads of those who may have been their own family members or friends, and then, with shards of glass, to scrape the flesh and ligaments off the skulls. They cleaned them so that the skulls could be sent to Germany."[5] At the time, numerous German doctors and researchers were working to establish "objective" differences between races. The anthropologist Theodor Mollison, for example, went to Namibia in 1904 to carry out experiments on prisoners. The most well-known of these researchers, Doctor Eugen Fischer, arrived in 1908. Beyond his experiments on the cadavers of camp prisoners, he studied the effects of interbreeding between German colonizers and Herero women, which led, according to him, to a degeneration of the German race. His work in eugenics inspired Hitler's racist arguments in *Mein Kampf*. Devoted to race purity,

Fischer advocated for the widespread sterilization of "Rhineland Bastards," those mixed-race children conceived by German women and the African soldiers among French occupation forces. In 1937, under Fischer's supervision, four hundred of those mixed-race offspring were arrested and forcibly sterilized. Mollison and Fischer would both have Josef Mengele, the "Angel of Death," as a student, whose experiments on—or, more accurately, torture of—Auschwitz prisoners are well documented.

According to the Ivorian journalist Serge Bilé's *Noirs Dans les Camps Nazis*,[6] the foundations of the Nazi concentration camps were established in Africa in the early twentieth century. But Lanzmann simply refused to hear of it.

Leaving my mother to her disappointment, I sat in my room listening over and over to Alpha Blondy's song "Jerusalem," released the year before. "Baroukh ata Adonai . . . Baroukh ata Yeroushalaim . . ." Blessed are you, Lord . . . Blessed are you, Jerusalem . . . In his video, Alpha Blondy sang optimistically about ecumenism. At each new year, my grandfather, a fervent Catholic, ended his resolutions saying, "Next year in Jerusalem." He didn't fulfill his dream of visiting the Promised Land, but in one of life's ironic twists, when Alpha Blondy played a concert in Israel it was my grandfather's son, my biological father, who was there to greet him. After breaking all ties—at least officially—with Israel out of solidarity with Egypt and other Arab countries following the Yom Kippur War in 1973, Ivory Coast had recently reestablished diplomatic relations in 1986. Jean-Pierre was the first Ivory Coast ambassador to Israel.

I asked the stage manager of Alpha Blondy's band to bring me back a bit of soil from their trip. He kept his promise and returned with a stone from the Dead Sea.

In 1991, I was in Israel at the beginning of Operation Solomon. In the streets and markets, people stopped me to ask if I was a Falasha. Everywhere, on television, on the radio, in the newspapers, all people talked about was the thousands of Ethiopian Jews who had just been repatriated. On the news, they told us that most of the Falasha had never taken an airplane and that some of them had even relieved themselves in the aisles. They described the makeshift shelters constructed along the roadsides to house the new arrivals. They recounted in condescending detail how the Ethiopian Jews had to be taught to use running water. Meanwhile, in the cozy world of the embassies, I attended classical music concerts given by recently repatriated Russian Jews. The contrast was stark, the racism patent, between the image of the Ethiopians and the cultured and elitist image enjoyed by the Russians. Always the same fault lines between Africa and Europe.

Still—and this was the first thing that struck me when I arrived, because it was so different from the idea I had of the country—Israel was multiethnic, a true mosaic of colors and peoples. The second thing, which is what allowed me to spend a bit of time there despite its policies against Palestinians, was that the people there were utterly insane. When I returned to Israel ten years later, I witnessed epic arguments between artists from Tel Aviv and artists from Jerusalem, the former accusing the latter of living in a cult of the Holocaust, the latter calling Tel Aviv a city without a memory. I found I could laugh with Israelis about the "competition of memory" between Blacks and Jews.

My skin color, however, didn't go unnoticed. One night when I was out at a techno club, an orthodox Jewish man, completely drunk, repeatedly pressed his gigantic belly against me while staring at me with an obvious mixture of desire and scorn. His presence in the club surprised no one, nor did his behavior toward me. It was perfectly acceptable, someone explained, for *Hasidim* to have extramarital sex with a prostitute.

# 8 When My Grandmother Married a Black Man

When my grandfather went to university in Toulouse, he found himself back in the company of Black classmates for the first time since he arrived in France. They were Africans like him, or West Indians. Although there were no other Ivorians at the university, he was delighted to be with fellow students of the same color, which eased his sense of exile. He clearly received a warm welcome into the close-knit community. The celebrated Senegalese poet Birago Diop thus speaks for the group when he relates my grandfather's arrival in his memoirs: "Boni [. . .] came to us in the late 1920s, from the Collège Saint-Paul in Angoulême." He reports an amusing anecdote about Alphonse's miliary service some years later: "he [. . .] always had his cap in his hand or stuck in a pocket of his greatcoat, because he'd never found a single cap big enough to fit his head."[1]

Among this happy band of young men from "overseas," as people said at the time—students from the West Indies, Guiana, Reunion, or Africa—there were also those from mainland France. They nicknamed Alphonse "salsify": Black on the outside, white on the inside. Decades later, it still made my grandfather laugh. For my part, I'm not so sure I would have liked being named after a Mounds bar.

It was 1929. Alphonse had just earned his baccalaureate degree a year early. True to his promise to his parents, he enrolled in the law school in Toulouse. It was there, in the hushed setting of the university library, that he met the woman who would soon become the love of his life.

My grandmother, Rose-Marie, was born on April 1, 1910, about thirty miles from Toulouse, in Gaillac, a small town in the Tarn department known for its wine. Her father, Félix Galou, was a wholesale and retail butcher. He lived with his wife, Jeanne, above their shop, in a townhouse where a branch of the family still lives today. Already advanced in age, her parents didn't expect another child. They had had three boys, one of whom died very young. When Félix Galou learned that he was the happy father of a little girl, he thought it was an April Fool's joke. Rose-Marie quickly became his favorite.

My grandmother had a strong character and a fierce independent streak. She felt stifled in Gaillac, where, in her own words, her home life was "divided between a very devout, somewhat Jansenist, mother, a much more liberal-minded father, and brothers who weren't liberal at all." She "resisted," she writes, an upbringing in which the "the word 'protest' hadn't yet entered the vocabulary."

Thanks to the 1924 school reform that finally allowed girls to take the same baccalaureate exam as boys, Rose-Marie took hers in 1928. In terms of schooling, her parents figured that she had done more than enough and that it was time for her to find a husband. But Rose-Marie wanted to attend university.

Her mother was vehemently opposed to the idea. The closest university was in Toulouse, and she deemed it unseemly for a young woman to live on her own outside the family home. Rose-Marie was sufficiently stubborn that they finally settled on a compromise: she would take the train round-trip between Gaillac and Toulouse, returning each night to her parents' house to sleep.

In her manuscript, where she describes the immense joy that overcame her the day of her departure for the Faculty of Arts, Rose-Marie writes,

> It wasn't what my parents had envisioned for me. To them, leaving for the university meant my emancipation. And at that moment I really did have a feeling of liberation [. . .]. Escaping that stifling small-town atmosphere, with its shutters always closed to prying eyes, the curtain edges parting as you pass;

> everything ground me down, just like my parents, whose affection suffocated me. And yet I did love them so.

On the day she left, she marked her newfound freedom by wearing a pair of culottes—but not pants, which would have been much too risqué.

My grandfather told me several times about the first time they met, always with the same happy smile. He didn't give me the exact date. It had to be between 1931 and 1933. He was at the library. But that day, instead of studying law, he was playing games of tic-tac-toe by himself when Rose-Marie, seated next to him and presumably looking to strike up a conversation, asked him what he was doing. Deeply embarrassed, he told her he couldn't answer without being crude. For in French, if you play tic-tac-toe, you *joue au morpion*, and, as everyone knows, *morpions* are lice that live in pubic hair. My grandmother wasn't the kind to let a refusal go unchallenged. She kept at him. With a heavy heart, Alphonse finally whispered the forbidden word, *morpion*. Far from offended, Rose-Marie asked him to teach her how to play right then and there. Such were the joys of flirting in years gone by.

In her manuscript, my grandmother offers several versions of her meeting with Alphonse. In one of them, which seems to share the same starting point as the scene described by my grandfather, she watched him playing tic-tac-toe with his friends, "a secret game that would have meant the end of library privileges for whoever got caught playing it." She asked a girlfriend, another law student, about him. One senses that she was at once attracted to and irritated by this young Black man who had a reputation for being both hardworking and "a regular at the dance hall." She didn't want to pass for an easy conquest. When he asked her out, she was torn between these contradictory feelings and hedged her bets by going on the attack. "I didn't know you were working as a pimp," she said bluntly. A sparring match followed, during which Alphonse called her a "nasty little girl." She struck back with what was most obvious about him, his skin color: "What if I called you a 'dirty *nègre*,' what would you say to that?"

"I'd give you a smack."

Rose-Marie was delighted. "You're starting to grow on me. I imagined you all as apathetic, without any character."

"Subjugated is what you mean."

"Yes, by us."

The confidence of my grandfather's replies reassured her. And later, her friend confirmed it: Alphonse didn't let anyone joke around about his origins. Rose-Marie had found someone proud, someone who, like her, gave as good as he got. They saw one another in secret, with a predilection for the romantic Jardin Royal. But Toulouse wasn't so far from Gaillac, and rumors of their relationship soon got back to Rose-Marie's mother. A bitter confrontation ensued.

> "Rose-Marie, I've heard you're seeing a Black man in Toulouse."
>
> "A Black student, mother. He's doing a doctorate and studying for the magistrate's exam."
>
> "Your father and I forbid you. From what I've heard, you've been seen walking arm in arm."
>
> "Is that really all you've heard?"
>
> "What's the meaning of this intimacy with a *nègre*?"
>
> "First of all, the word 'intimacy' is ridiculous, and this intimacy, since you're so keen on the word, means we're getting married."
>
> "You marry a Black man? Never! You hear me, never!"

Rose-Marie didn't notice the use of the word "*nègre*." But infuriated by her mother's veto, she screamed "damn it all!" and threatened to move out. Jeanne Galou, beside herself at first, then tried to reason with her daughter in the hope she would promise never to see Alphonse again. She used emotional blackmail, arguing that Rose-Marie's father, Félix, whose health was already failing, would fall ill and die from the shock. Nothing worked. Rose-Marie replied with more than a hint of impertinence, "What do you have against the man? His color? Well, what if you found out that God was Black, would you still pray to him? Jesus was a Jew and he didn't look a thing like the statues of him in your colored prints. I'm sick and tired of your hypocritical, bigoted piety."

In the end, a meeting was arranged between Félix Galou, Alphonse, and one of Rose-Marie's brothers, whom she described as an avowed racist: "For him, anything that wasn't French going back to the umpteenth generation didn't count." Félix had never seen an African in his life. There was only a single Black man in Gaillac, a West Indian and, it appears, an alcoholic. But Félix put his prejudices aside and Alphonse quickly won him over. The family then split into two camps. On one side, Rose-Marie's father and grandmother, who trusted her granddaughter and didn't see the issue of race as an impediment to marriage. On the other side, Rose-Marie's brothers and mother, but also her uncles and aunts, for whom a marriage with a "*nègre*" was unnatural.

With the "no" side sticking to its guns and a deadlock on the horizon, my grandfather, in desperation, sought the support of Toulouse's archbishop. Extremely devout, my grandfather had taken theology classes at Toulouse's Catholic Institute, run by Monsignor Saliège. The latter confirmed for the Galou family that skin color didn't make the man, that as Black as his skin might be, Alphonse was a human being no less than themselves, and, moreover, of a highly moral character. A staunch believer, Rose-Marie's mother yielded before the opinion of this lofty representative of the Church.

Looking over Jules Saliège's biography, I can see it was no accident he stood up for my grandfather. From the start of the Second World War, it seems, he had been vehemently opposed to racism and anti-Semitism. Later he joined the Resistance and helped numerous Jews hide or flee to unoccupied France.

Alphonse's first visit to his future parents-in-law's house caused a sensation. Rose-Marie, in a typical show of bravado, made it a point of honor to meet him at the train station and walk across town with him, her arm in his. Deep down, however, she was pained by the crowds that formed along their path, by the windows that opened furtively, and by the murmurs that pursued them as they passed. Hardly 7,500 people lived in Gaillac, so not a soul had missed the news. People poured out to catch a glimpse of the *nègre* who, they'd heard, was going to marry the Galou girl. They felt sorry for the unfortunate parents who had had to resign themselves to the marriage.

But at least the couple celebrated the engagement and Alphonse was officially admitted into his future family. Which didn't mean that the battle had been won. Before Félix Galou ceded his daughter's hand, he expected my grandfather to have a job. And on this point, he made it clear that there would be no discussion.

Alphonse then went through a period of uncertainty about his future. Obviously, he had accepted his family's decision to send him to France at the age of fifteen. He had followed the career path they had laid out for him. He was studying for his doctorate in law and two possibilities were theoretically open to him: becoming a lawyer or a magistrate. But as a subject of the French empire, as a "French native" with neither civil nor political rights, working in the legal profession wasn't straightforward. First, he had to have French citizenship.

Anticipating this prerequisite, as soon as he earned his bachelor's degree, Alphonse applied for citizenship in August 1932. As part of the process, every aspect of his life was gone over with a fine-tooth comb. How long had he lived in France? What was the nature of his conduct and morals? Where did his loyalties lie? Did he still have ties with Ivory Coast? If so, of what kind?

They inquired into his health and income. They noted, and I assume this worked in his favor, that one of his uncles and two of his cousins had fought in the First World War as Senegalese Tirailleurs, that is, as riflemen in the colonial army. On the other hand, he ranked low in "social utility." To the question of whether he represented a significant benefit to the community, the answer was "no," although it was narrowly conceded that his intention to later return to his native country might allow him to provide some service to France. Then came his "level of assimilation," which was dealt with in detail. On that score, Alphonse had hit the jackpot. He was considered "completely assimilated into the French population." He had adopted French customs and his nationalization would even allow him to "create a truly French family." In conclusion, Toulouse's mayor wrote to the prefecture, "Monsieur Boni demonstrates upstanding conduct and morals, he is completely assimilated to our customs and culture. He has asked to enjoy the rights of a French citizen, being already French in all other respects. I therefore issue a favorable recommendation."

Alphonse would nonetheless have to wait two years before being "allowed to enjoy the rights of a French citizen."[2] As he studied for his law degree, he still didn't know what would happen.

Rose-Marie's father wanted Alphonse to become a lawyer and open a practice close to Gaillac. As for Alphonse, he dreamed of only one thing: returning to Ivory Coast. He hadn't seen his parents, his country, or any Ivorian for ten years. Nor had he forgotten the lengths his father had gone through over the years to pay for his education. Alphonse wasn't a French scholarship student; he depended entirely on the money his father sent him.

Despite the years and the distance, his father continued to believe in his son, even when other family members had their doubts. Every telegram Alphonse sent him announcing a recently passed exam raised his hope of seeing his son one day wearing the same black robe as the white lawyers at the Grand-Bassam courthouse.

But in order to practice law in French West Africa, one had to be nominated by the governor general, who had complete and final decision-making authority. Judicial nominations of French citizens of African origin also required a special exemption because the colonial administration above all feared that these university-educated "intellectuals" might get mixed up in politics. In addition to that requirement, one had to build a client base. Africans could, of course, bring cases before French courts, and my great-great-great-uncle had had the means to hire a French attorney, but how many French people would accept being represented by an African lawyer?

All the same, Alphonse found an internship in a law firm. The profession scarcely appealed to him. He wavered: what if, instead of the black robe of an attorney, he opted for the red robe of a magistrate?

The colonial judiciary suffered from a lack of prestige—being a magistrate in mainland France was markedly more distinguished. Yet it had the reputation of being less discriminatory than the world of attorneys. Furthermore, no doubt because of their insufficient number and distance from France, colonial magistrates enjoyed greater freedom than their European French counterparts. A conversation in Toulouse with a French Guianese magistrate finally made up Alphonse's mind not to become an attorney.

Thus, in addition to working as an assistant in the Toulouse prosecutor's office in 1935 as well as fulfilling his obligatory military service twice a week, Alphonse studied relentlessly for the magistrate's exam.[3] At the time, the French National School for the Judiciary didn't yet exist. To become a magistrate, one needed at minimum a bachelor's degree in law and to pass a cumulative professional exam, whether one chose to work in the judiciary in France or overseas. Those who knew they wanted to be a "colonial judge" could also, depending on the results of a competitive entrance exam, attend the National School of Overseas France. Over the course of the two-year degree there, they would bolster their knowledge of the political, administrative, and judicial organization of the colonies. At the end of their studies, they would take two exams, the school exam and the professional exam specific to the judiciary.

Alphonse took the colonial magistrate's exam in 1937. It was held in Paris. Of the 108 students who took it, only the top three were selected. Alphonse was on pins and needles; he came in first. He was given the option of Indochina or Africa. Obviously, he chose Africa, never suspecting that during his twenty-year career as a French magistrate, the colonial administration would never sign off on his working, let alone living, in Ivory Coast.

Alphonse now had a career, although he still had to wait for his first posting. Félix Galou had to yield: nothing now stood in the way of my grandparents' marriage. And so, Alphonse and Rose-Marie were married on July 19, 1937, at 5:30 p.m., at Gaillac's little town hall. The religious service took place at midnight.

Why so late?

Jean Galou, my grandmother's nephew, reassured me that the intention hadn't been to hide the wedding. It was simply a family tradition. Rose-Marie's older brother had also been married at midnight. There had just been a death in the family, and the family thought it more appropriate for the wedding to remain discreet. No similar excuse came from Rose-Marie, whose parents, according to her, feared that if the ceremony were held during the day, the church would be overrun with tactless onlookers. My grandmother felt somewhat bitter as a result, sensing that her family hadn't entirely accepted her marriage to a Black man. Even so, the ceremony moved her deeply.

> During the mass, she [Rose-Marie] had to dispel a certain nagging anxiety. Her childhood, her life as a pampered, spoiled young girl, was over. What would her new life bring? She was entering the unknown, something that attracted and frightened her all at once. The Languedoc adage that her grandmother had translated for her before she left for church hammered in her head.
>
> "Rose-Marie, when the priest puts on his cope, you'll say: Farewell sunny days, slipping away forever."
>
> And what if it were true? She knew what she was leaving but not what was next. A flood of memories flashed before her eyes. She felt herself taken by the arm; she started. The ceremony was over. She looked at her wedding ring, the flowers, listened to the rich voice singing Gounod's "Ave Maria." The reassuring presence of her girlfriends chased away her apprehensions, and she calmly left the church on Alphonse's arm, having just become Madame Alphonse Boni, for better or for worse.

For their honeymoon, my grandparents chose Italy, a place Rose-Marie had long dreamed of visiting. They stopped in Alassio, a small seaside resort in the country's northwest, not far from the French border, the first leg of a journey that would ultimately take them to Venice. After dropping off their luggage at the hotel, they left to explore the old part of the city.

> Rose-Marie felt Alphonse's powerful, protective arm around her waist. She slipped her arm in his as they arrived at a magnificent dry fountain in the middle of a cobblestone square. It was

> bordered by old hotels that the passage of time had transformed into slums. Street urchins were playing with homemade wagons. Like a flock of sparrows, the children scattered at first, then doubled back and surrounded the young couple. A few stones rained down on them. Rose-Marie and Alphonse managed to open a path and leave, assailed by the children's echoing jeers, among which they made out "nègre, nègre, Ethiopia!" repeated again and again.
>
> "Why did it never occur to me?" Alphonse roared. "Ethiopia and Italy are at war. Anyone Black is Ethiopian for these miserable kids. Let's leave, Rose-Marie, let's go back to France. It's the sensible thing to do. We'll avoid an incident we might just regret."

Thus ended their honeymoon, having barely begun. The experience foreshadowed the hostility they'd encounter when they went to live in colonial Africa.

# 9 An "African Girl" in Bordeaux

Just as I was starting to find my place in Abidjan, my parents decided it was time for me to return to France, thus setting me on the opposite path of my grandfather's. They wanted me to do my baccalaureate in a French school, thinking that by doing so I would have the best chance of getting into a good preparatory program for the competitive entrance exams to one of France's Grandes Écoles. That was the future they had mapped out for me: Sciences Po, the Grande École for political science; HEC, the Grande École for business; Normale Sup, the Grande École for the humanities; or perhaps ENA, the Grande École for the French civil service.

But the most prestigious Parisian high schools didn't want anything to do with me. They told us I needed to have taken all my secondary courses there from the start. Georges ultimately settled on Bordeaux, where he was born and had attended university. He asked my grandfather to intercede to get me admitted to one of the city's most prominent private schools, run by the Jesuits. Like Alphonse sixty-five years earlier, suddenly I was among the "Jez." Like him, sixty-five years later, I was the school's sole Black student. Unlike for him, it wouldn't be much of a culture shock for me. At least that's what I thought.

When I arrived in Bordeaux, I was officially, and in the eyes of everyone else at the school, a foreigner. I had an Ivorian passport; I had to check in at the prefecture, but I was lucky because the process was quick, a mere formality. In any case, I couldn't have imagined it happening any other way. Yet I still didn't consider myself French.

"A little Ivorian girl." "A little African girl." These were the terms my parents used to talk about me, so that was how I referred to myself with others. And that was in fact how other people saw me: as a little African girl in France to do her baccalaureate.

But this story about me wasn't really true. Although my parents hadn't worried about getting me French papers, I could claim either French or Ivorian nationality by birth.

I spent the first part of my childhood in France, where I came two or three times a year when we lived in Ivory Coast. During winter vacations, I joined my father on the foxhunts he relished so much. Since 1976, he had been master of a team of English hounds in Pau, and I followed the hunts from the age of three. At home, posters announcing the dates for the season's hunts hung in our hallways and stairs, duly framed and hard to miss. Decorated with old drawings and the initials of the hunting teams, the posters were simply magnificent. As a little girl, I learned to read by sounding out their words.

When I was fourteen, I hunted for the first time. At the end of the hunt, after the pack had caught a fox but before the hounds had time to eat it, the huntsman intervened and cut off its tail and head. The animal was already dead. My father took the bloody tail and drew the sign of the cross on my forehead. The hunting horns rang out across the frozen fields: I had earned my hunt button and could now call myself a member of the Pau Hunt Drags. Georges beamed with pride. I was happy.

From the outside, the scene may have seemed incongruous. A Black teenager on a horse completing her initiation into one of the most elitist traditions in France, and one of the traditions most anchored in the notion of Frenchness. For the people present that day, it made perfect sense. I was Isabelle, Georges and Danièle's daughter, whom they had all known since I was knee-high to a grasshopper. Everyone was kind to me; they had seen me grow up from one hunting season to the next. They doted on me. I was the daughter of the Master of the Hunt. But if someone had asked them "Is Isabelle French like you?" they would have spontaneously said no. I was part of their French friend's Ivorian family. I was a "little African girl" who rode horse. Surely, the only one they had ever met, although I doubt that that was something they were conscious of. Nor was I, for that matter. Not at that time in my life.

Similar memories come back to me now. As a little Parisian girl, I spent part of my winter and spring vacations with my grandmother. She brought me skiing in Font-Romeu in the Pyrenees. We stayed in Toulouse. Despite the forty years she had spent in Africa, Rose-Marie still had her southern-French accent. She said "adieu" instead of "bonjour," and gave violet-flavored candy for a treat, dolls in the form of violet-selling shopgirls as a gift, and garnet crosses for First Communion jewelry. Her intention seemed clear: she wanted to pass down some of her own culture to us, her mixed-race grandchildren.

I was once on vacation at her place with two of my first cousins. We were behaving so badly that she put us on a plane back to Paris. By chance, Georges was on the same flight. That evening, amused, he told Danièle the story: Just imagine, he said, the hostesses' look at the airport, seeing me with three little Africans registered as "non-accompanied minors," and me having to explain that one of them is my daughter and the other two my nephews.

The whole paradox of my situation was summed up in that remark.

In reality, like Monsieur Jourdain in Molière's *The Bourgeois Gentleman*, overjoyed to discover he has unwittingly been speaking prose his entire life, I was, unbeknownst to me, French. I'd go even further: I embodied, without really knowing them, the very principles of French republican universalism. I was the fulfilment of the republican ideal, and that included its ambiguities.

"France shall be an indivisible, secular, democratic and social Republic," we read in Article 1 of the French Constitution. "It shall ensure the equality of all citizens before the law, without distinction of origin, race or religion." That was me to a T. I had no awareness of class or race. I sincerely believed that everyone was the same, that everyone was equal. I didn't see that I was Black and others white. I wasn't a practicing Catholic, but I had the good taste to be part of the Catholic culture, which, although the Constitution doesn't say so, put me on the right side of French secularism. And of course, I had zero awareness of the ethnocentric biases on which my universalism was based.

While I certainly noticed that some people around me were poor and others rich, I didn't judge them on that basis. I had the luxury of being ignorant of the value of money. Somewhat hypocritically, Georges kept me far removed from conversations touching on material concerns, considering them unsuitable for the education of a young girl from a good family. And I was indeed from a good family, that much I knew. On the other hand, when Danièle got angry, she would scornfully trot out my birth mother's humble background. Making it out to be worse than it was, she spoke as if it were a blight that would sully me forever, a kind of congenital defect that explained my flaws or, at least, my incapacity to fulfill the demands for perfection she placed on me.

One day, I asked Georges if he was rich. He said he was comfortable. Until his death, I never had the foggiest idea of how much our lifestyle cost. Yet all the signs were right there in front of me.

My parents had an intensely active social life. Not a week went by without our hosting a dinner at home. When I returned from school, there was a steady stream of lavish flower arrangements addressed to my mother. She took advantage of my stays to refine my skills as the future lady of the house. We drew up the seating arrangements together: to her right, the most important male guest, to my father's, the guest's wife.

I picked flowers in the garden to decorate the table. There were the soup spoons, teaspoons, dessert spoons, demitasse spoons, cutlery for fish versus shellfish, etc.—we did a full tour of the silverware. The butler ironed his white gloves. The chef promised to send a tray up to my room with a little bit of every dish he served. I helped Danièle with her clothes. When, more than once, I was surprised that she wasn't wearing a more flattering necklace or dress, she explained to me that, as the host, she had to dress more modestly to avoid making the less fortunate invitees feel ill at ease.

Then came what was a real drudgery for me: the times I had to go downstairs to greet the guests, all sorts of supposedly important people. Quietly seated on a footstool during the aperitif or crouched in the stairwell if I had managed to extricate myself sooner, I observed the social comedy afoot in the living room. The power struggles, the games of seduction, the glasses certain guests emptied too fast, the dead eyes in glittering gowns, the cutting remarks between longtime spouses, the compliments that slipped into fawning, everything that scuffed the apparently perfect veneer of my mother's society dinners. As an only child, or at least raised as one, I spent most of my time in the company of adults. I heard private conversations about French politics (my parents knew I would never repeat a thing), and I learned how to decode the way rich and powerful people spoke and behaved.

Nor was I unaware of my parents' most obvious flaws or the self-doubt that preyed on Danièle. When I was barely twelve years old, if my father wasn't free, I was the one she asked to correct her speeches. I helped her rehearse until she knew them by heart, because Georges had decreed that a good speaker didn't read notes. No one had to tell me that, despite her public and political successes, my mother wasn't happy. I concluded early on that fame and money are worth nothing in themselves.

The only qualities I admired came from the heart—or from good sense—and neither required social status or a diploma. I chose my friends solely based on the affection and affinities I felt. Already in Paris, where social barriers had been less porous than in Abidjan, I was just as comfortable spending time at the school caretaker's lodge—her daughter was my best friend for a time—as I was hanging out with kids my age at my mother's friends' manor. I didn't judge, and I didn't jump to conclusions.

For example, when I was around fourteen years old on vacation in Paris, a girlfriend thought it wise to forewarn me that her best friend, from an aristocratic family like herself, had a building caretaker's son for a boyfriend. She hastened to add, "But he's really very nice!" These last words gave me a start. Clearly, there were some poor people, just as there were some Black people, whom it was okay to be seen with.

My parents were snobs, a term Georges would never have countenanced, since in Latin it means *sine nobilitate*, "without nobility," his worst nightmare. Nonetheless, despite their prejudices, they did me the favor of not interfering in my relationships, letting me see whomever I wanted, greeting all of them with the same politeness, and maintaining my illusion that class had no role in my friendships. It was only later, much later, as my mother was despoiling me of my father's estate, that I discovered what that estate consisted of, and finally understood why certain of my friends never invited me to their homes or sometimes invented a fake address down the block from mine.

At home, as I mentioned, we ate, breathed, and bought French. Without knowing it, I grew thoroughly convinced that culture—the culture that mattered—was French or, at the very least, European.

I must have been ten years old when I first set foot in a museum. Georges took us to the Prado in Madrid. It was a shock to my senses. I was entranced standing in front of El Greco's paintings. I rushed from Goya to Velasquez and back again. My parents found it amusing, they laughed, then, after a few hours, they were worn out. But I wanted more. To persuade me to leave, they promised me that in Toledo, where El Greco had lived, we would see his other paintings. (Since then, whenever I find myself in a new country, I always visit the museums.) It never occurred to me that there might be something unusual about not finding anything equivalent in Ivory Coast.[1] There was the National Museum in Abidjan,[2] created during colonialism, which mixed archeology, ethnography, and classical Ivorian statuary. But Danièle discouraged me from going, assuring me that the dusty place wasn't worth the visit.

The first time I finally saw African art, let alone classical Ivorian art, in a museum was in 1989 at the Grand Palais in Paris, during its magnificent exhibition "Corps sculptés, corps parés, corps masqués."

I still couldn't name a contemporary African or Black artist. If I had read a certain number of classics of African literature, it was because they had been on the nationwide mandatory reading list of Ivory Coast's Department of Education. But as we know, school isn't life. Day after day in Abidjan, I was taught that knowledge and civilization were white. The message was reinforced by my teachers at school. All of them were European. It was only in middle school that I had an African teacher for the first time. Monsieur Maga taught history and geography. He was a brilliant man and outshined most of his colleagues, as if he had to be better than the others to be hired in our prestigious school. One day after class, he told me that his father and my grandfather knew each other well, and that he had been to my grandfather's house several times. That's how I discovered that he was the son of Hubert Maga, the first president of the Republic of Benin.

Unlike Georges, Danièle had no inherent prejudice against African or, broadly speaking, Black culture. One of her friends was very close with Amadou Hampâté Bâ, who lived in Abidjan, so one afternoon my mother sent me to visit him. The famed author planned a special reading of the adventures of *Leuk le Lièvre* (Leuk the Jackrabbit) for me and my mother's friend's daughter. Danièle made sure we understood that it was a great honor for us girls. She told us to keep silent and only speak when Hampâté Bâ asked us to. I was eight years old, I had just arrived from France, and I didn't know the African rules of respect. Quickly forgetting her instructions, I let my normal personality take over. Again and again, I interrupted the old storyteller with my questions, occasionally predicting what would happen next. He didn't appreciate it.

Nine years later, my mother took me to see my first Spike Lee film, *Do the Right Thing*, in Dolby Stereo, on the Champs-Élysées. Public Enemy's "Fight the Power" blasted in my ears. Rosie Perez transformed her rage into dance in front of a graffitied wall. A pure shot of adrenaline. From the opening scene I was glued to my seat. At the time, I didn't realize it was the first film I had seen directed by a Black person. *Do the Right Thing* was the epitome of cool, no question. I left the theater galvanized. Danièle was just as enthusiastic. She thought the film was great.

The rest of the time, on other, less special occasions, she shared what she herself had learned to appreciate, Greco-Roman European culture. She had been thoroughly fascinated from her childhood by Greek and Roman antiquity. This was a woman who, at twenty years old, dreamed of becoming an actress but, instead of accepting the leading role in a play, preferred a trip to Greece my grandfather proposed.

I have to say, however, that even if the play was a hit in France, the role was hardly top-notch and reprised a load of exoticizing tropes. The play was the François Campaux comedy *Chérie noire*, played in its theatrical production by Marpessa Dawn, the unforgettable actress in Marcel Camus's *Black Orpheus*. Yet the mere idea of playing a maid irked Danièle. On the other hand, she returned from Greece disappointed. She had forgotten that between antiquity and the present day, the archipelago had been invaded by the Turks. The Greeks she came across didn't match her Hellenic ideal. Too Eastern, not Western enough.

In reality, the only field in which the people I admired were unmistakably Black was—an eye-watering cliché—music. In this respect, I was just like any French kid today, able to quote ten rappers or R&B singers but ignorant of the mere existence of writers or artists of African descent.

My blindness was such that, every month during my teenage years in Abidjan, I bought all the French women's magazines without ever being surprised or even noticing that I wasn't, or very rarely, represented in them, or that they never showed Asian or North African models. Like all budding young women, I looked to these magazines for the material from which I would construct my own sense of what being a woman meant. I didn't realize that the hair and makeup advice they doled out weren't feasible for someone with my complexion and hair texture. I imagined that I simply needed to straighten my hair to look like the models in the pictures. As for makeup, I always saw Danièle use the same products as the ones in the magazines. I thought they were for everyone, universal.

From time to time, a photograph showed Naomi Campbell or Iman. I found Naomi Campbell's beauty all the more exceptional because I thought her long straight hair and bluish eyes were natural, even though I had gotten used to seeing colored contact lenses around Abidjan. Naomi Campbell had Jamaican origins; she was from mixed-race people. Why wouldn't she have mixed features?

It's true, I was living in a land of make-believe. Even so, I didn't end up disliking who I was. I didn't tell myself it was ugly to have Black skin or kinky hair. I wanted to be cool. But from what I could see, cool wasn't African. It was European.

The same went for high culture. I constructed my identity around cultural references that didn't include me, while firmly believing that they were meant for me. As for my parents, they told me I was African but did nothing to nourish a sense of my Africanity. Inevitably, I was rather confused about who I was.

In Bordeaux, I lived in a girls' dormitory run by nuns. They put me in a room with a girl who had arrived from Senegal to do her final year in the same high school as mine. I found the coincidence of the two of us together reassuring.

When it was time for me to leave for Bordeaux, Danièle told me in a very serious tone to be careful. Seeing a young African girl, she said, the men were bound to misbehave or say inappropriate things. I was surprised. My mother had never spoken to me that way. I sensed her own past experiences in what she said. I connected them with the long, very long day we had just spent together in a Parisian boutique near the Champs-Élysées where she usually bought her clothes. With the saleswomen's help, she picked out a wardrobe for me that was far too pricey and elegant for a teenager. I suddenly understood that her point had been to fend off the image that certain people in Bordeaux might have of me because of my ethnic origins. But where did that image come from? Danièle didn't elaborate.

I got my first clue when I started at my new high school in Bordeaux. I received a warm welcome at Saint-Joseph-de-Tivoli. A little too warm, even. The teachers came to see me at the end of the day to urge me to ask them for help if I had any trouble with their lessons. Ultimately, I found their kindness suspect. They had seen my academic record; it was excellent. Were they honestly worried about the impact that culture shock and living far from my parents would have on my schoolwork? Or did they assume that, coming from Africa, I would struggle with the more demanding academics?

I thanked them and promised to seek them out. I did no such thing. The first semester ended and out came my grades. I was second in my class. The way my teachers looked at me changed. Some of them couldn't hide their surprise, which only confirmed my intuition. They had thought that an African "A" would never equal an "A" in France.

I soon discovered one not-insignificant benefit of my new school. Unlike the practice at my strict high school in Abidjan, in Bordeaux the front gates were always left open. I came and went as I pleased. Shortly after my arrival, I joined a modeling agency. Between going to class and going to auditions, my mind was quickly made up.

The agency's director found my name and the pseudonyms I proposed too traditional. So she renamed me Ebony—not *Ébène*, as we say in French, but the English *Ebony*. Did she consciously make the connection between my skin color, my African origins, and the blackest of black wood? Or did she simply give in to the dyed-in-the-wool exoticism of the new alias without digging any further into the associations behind her choice. As a consolation, I reminded myself that *Ebony* was the most venerable publication among African American magazines, that my mother had been a subscriber for many years, and that, as a little girl, I loved to leaf through its pages, even if I didn't always understand what they meant. Despite my efforts, it was no use. Ébène. Ebony. Ebony wood. I felt like I had been given a slave name. But in the little world of the Bordeaux designers and shopkeepers that hired us, a world in which there were very few Black girls, people liked Ebony. I was usually alone; sometimes, there were two of us. Our presence literally added a touch of color that enhanced the monochrome setting. Everyone was very nice. No one required me to be the size of a supermodel. A size 4 or 6 was good enough. People made sure I looked as pretty as possible. My hair wasn't a problem; they straightened it.

On the other hand, for reasons that I couldn't explain at the time, I always walked out of makeup the color of moon rock, which didn't at all match my complexion. One day, a makeup artist, wanting to be sure the colors could really be seen on me, applied very pale blush. Dismayed by the result, he turned to ever lighter shades. In the end, it was a disaster. I was completely gray. My inexperience meant I couldn't tell him that the darker the skin, the more pigmented the colors had to be.

To excuse my repeated absences, or to cover for the times I simply wanted to read or listen to music in my room, I had struck on a watertight alibi: tropical illness. The idea came to me thanks to a bottle of the antimalarial drug Nivaquine I found among my things. Because I had once had malaria, the disease could remain dormant and recur without my getting bitten again by a parasite-carrying mosquito. I explained to the dormitory's nuns that my illness was chronic and, alas, so frequent that I could manage without a visit to the doctor.

Tropical illness quite appealed to the sisters. It must have awakened a familiar fantasy in them, one of a dark and mysterious Africa, with its hostile natural environment, unexplained diseases, and sudden and devastating fevers, popularized by the tales of missionaries and colonial explorers. They completely bought my story and signed my absence notes without further ado. At the end of the second semester, the school sent my mother the tally of my absences. But no one was in a position to say much: my grades were excellent.

After several months, a classmate invited me to spend the night at her place. We weren't especially close and the intense attention her parents focused on me led me to believe that the invitation had come from them. They must have thought that I was all alone—which was true—far from my home and country, that some time in a family setting would do me good. All very commendable, in short. But at meals, people have to talk. We didn't know each other and didn't really have much to say. They asked me about Ivory Coast. If I had been Japanese, we would have spoken about Japan. I played the game and told them about Abidjan, about the country, etc. I lingered on the Basilica Notre-Dame de la Paix in Yamoussoukro, which had just been completed and was larger than Saint Peter's in Rome. I thought it would flatter their Catholic sensibility. To offset the megalomania underlying the construction of a building Houphouët-Boigny considered an ultimate testament to himself before he died, I proffered the usual criticisms about the money it had cost an otherwise impoverished country. My classmate's parents were very pleased with our time together. I sensed that thanks to their invitation, they had ever so slightly but quite tangibly burnished their image of themselves, an image of benevolent paternalism fringed in Christian charity. I doubt that they ever imagined the effort it took me during those twenty-four hours to go along with their peculiar outlook while concealing anything that might have made them feel socially inferior.

In Bordeaux, I also had to adapt to my new way of life. Specifically, I learned how to do housework. That was part of the dormitory rules: we had to clean our own rooms. I copied my roommate as best as I could. I hadn't ever used a vacuum or a mop, held an iron or a sponge. Despite my mother's theoretical—and very bourgeois—lectures about needing to know how to keep house oneself in order to oversee the work of the help, she had never taught me how to make my bed. As for Georges, he obviously had no idea how to cook a steak. At all.

The first time I ironed a blouse in the dormitory's laundry room, I felt thoroughly proud of myself, positive I had intuitively discovered the right way to do it. I was so flagrantly wrong that a girl took the iron from my hands and ironed my clothes for me. Otherwise, she said through a fit of laughter, you'll be ironing all night. She became my only friend that year. My head and my heart were elsewhere, somewhere between Paris and Abidjan, between hope and nostalgia. The baccalaureate exam had hardly finished when I left for Paris, without waiting for my grades. My parents had enrolled me in a private preparatory program for the Grandes Écoles. At the end of the summer, I would take the entrance exam for Sciences Po. A classmate told me over the phone that I had passed my baccalaureate with honors. I was relieved and disappointed at the same time. I was hoping for high honors.

The preparatory program I had enrolled in was in the sixteenth arrondissement, near the anthropology museum, the Musée de l'Homme. The school was filled with daddy's boys and girls like me. As usual, I was the only Black student. Conversations were scarce; everyone had their nose in a book. It was summer outside, but we were all deathly pale, me included. I was stuffing myself with over-the-counter pep pills to work until all hours of the night, and the lack of sleep began to catch up to me. One morning, at the time I usually took the metro, I stayed home. I was living in a little studio, again in a dormitory, although this time run by Lebanese nuns. I put on a reggae cassette, opened a package of cookies, and threw myself into a book that had nothing to do with the entrance exam. That was when my brain finally registered what the problem was: I didn't have the least desire to study at Sciences Po or at any of the prestigious schools my parents thought I was destined for.

A few weeks earlier, to celebrate my success on the baccalaureate, my grandfather had given me some money to buy a typewriter. Flouting my parents' inevitable disappointment, I shut myself up in my studio for several months and wrote what would become my first novel, *La Grande Dévoreuse* (The Great Devourer). I was seventeen years old and, at the cost of exploding all my youthful certainties, my calling had just become crystal clear.

Danièle was furious. She predicted that writing would make me crazy and that I would end up as a supermarket cashier. I told her that that was fine by me. I would live in an attic somewhere and write. My father, who wasn't one to beat around the bush, asked me if at the very least I was a genius.

Realizing that they couldn't talk me out of it, Danièle decided to do something with my latest whim. From Abidjan, she sent my manuscript to the prestigious Young Writers Award. At the time, it had two categories: one for Young Writers and the other for Young Francophone Writers. It was in the latter group, reserved for non-French French-speaking authors, that Danièle entered me.

# 10 What Color Is the French Language?

My novel *La Grande Dévoreuse* takes place in Abidjan. A teenage country girl falls in love with a boy from the streets determined to avenge the death of his father, an ex-gangster. With nothing but the clothes on their backs, the strength of their love, and a saxophone from a Jamaican Rasta who longs to discover the "land of his ancestors," the two heroes set off to fulfill their dreams. Along the way, they confront the barriers of a world bent on keeping them out.

Why do certain stories take root in us? Perhaps because *La Grande Dévoreuse* corresponded to my own—undoubtedly subdued but nonetheless real—rebellion, its story reflected the immense feeling of injustice that, several months later, would push so many Ivorian young people into the streets and make Ivory Coast's political class tremble.

In the early 1990s, student protests erupted on the campus of the University of Abidjan. Frustration over Ivory Coast's ten-year recession, President Houphouët-Boigny's plan for drastic austerity measures, and a general lack of political freedom had finally come to a head. Although the protests challenging the Old Man's power were violently suppressed by the army, the spirit of revolt spread among the country's disaffected youth. Not only students but young people from the poorer neighborhoods of Abidjan and other large towns flooded the streets, soon followed by the country's public- and private-sector workers. It was chaos. Schools and universities closed. The government cancelled the school year.

On April 30, 1990, Houphouët, his back against the wall, yielded to the pressure and, after thirty years of autocratic rule, reestablished a multiparty system. It was in this tumultuous context, albeit from the safe distance of my Parisian studio, that I received the news that I had won second place in the Young Francophone Writers Award. Thrilled at first, I quickly grew anxious. What if the organizers discovered that I didn't actually live in Ivory Coast but in France like them? What if they took the award back?

Other considerations—more pragmatic or more romantic, or both, depending on your temperament—stoked my fears. I was in love with a young man living in Abidjan and planned to visit him over the summer, with or without my parents' approval. If Georges and Danièle refused to cover my Paris-Abidjan round trip, the flight from the award would be a windfall I simply couldn't pass up. Today, I imagine I'd have enough self-confidence to tell the truth. At that age, I preferred to let everyone believe I lived in Ivory Coast. But on May 16, two days before my arrival in Toulouse—the award ceremony was taking place in the nearby town of Muret—a mutiny broke out in Abidjan. Young conscripts occupied the airport and were heading for the offices of the publicly owned radio and television authority, where my mother was then CEO. My father was at our home on the Basque coast, I was in Paris, and Danièle was alone in Ivory Coast. Although we were very scared for her, thankfully the mutineers weren't violent. On the other hand, the airport was closed. Under the circumstances, getting to Abidjan wasn't going to be easy.

I went to the post office closest to my Parisian studio. I knew from experience that it had a dilapidated telephone booth whose line always crackled—perfect for corroborating my very long-distance call. I rang Marc Sebbah, the award's organizer, and told him I was stuck in Lomé where I had been visiting friends. Given that the Abidjan airport was closed, it was impossible for me to return home to take the flight to Paris and on to Toulouse. I was crushed. I was going to have to miss the ceremony. Except that . . . One of my mother's best friends worked at Air Afrique. I told him that I could ask her to help me get a free ticket from Lomé to Paris. In which case, the Young Francophone Writers Award would have to transfer my ticket to an agent in Paris so that I could make the connection for Toulouse and afterward return to Ivory Coast. Marc Sebbah very graciously promised to take care of it. On the morning of May 18, I calmly left my studio in the sixth arrondissement and took the plane from Paris to Toulouse.

The most plausible stories aren't always the most realistic; they're plausible because they reflect the belief systems of the people to whom they are told. French media had been extensively covering the turmoil rocking Ivory Coast for the three previous months. Anyone reasonably informed knew that things weren't going well. Most important, like my tropical illness with the Bordeaux nuns, violence, political instability, a society structured on favoritism, in which as if by magic a family friend would find me a free airline ticket—all this was in keeping with a very "believable" image of Africa. My feigned determination to get to France at all costs, besides it being flattering to the organizers, reinforced the impression in many French people's minds that France held a kind of magical allure for Africans.

My tale was so compelling that the local press picked it up. Marc Sebbah himself would later recount my harrowing trek from Togo before calling me up on stage for my award.

At the Toulouse airport, I arrived so much later than the other award winners that I ended up in the same van as several of the writers serving on the awards committee. Although its full cast of writers couldn't make the trip, those who could comprised a no less impressive list. René Depestre, Hector Bianciotti, Pierre Mertens, Rachid Mimouni, to name only a few. Plus, for the obviously-French-(not-Francophone-so-no-need-to-mention-it) Young Writers Award, there was Jean Vautrin, Georges-Olivier Châteauereynaud, and Roger Vrigny. At the restaurant we were taken to, I made myself small. Intimidated at first, then somewhat bemused, I listened to these literary figures, the first I had ever rubbed shoulders with, as they tried to outdo each other in a flurry of erudition and wit, quotations and wordplay, that suddenly devolved into a long discussion of the best way to keep one's feet warm while writing. One of them boasted about the thickness of his socks, another described his space heater, and still another marveled that only one of his feet ever got cold. All of this without showing the slightest interest in the young woman they had chosen for their award. So that's what a writer is, I wondered, a mixture of vanity and cold feet?

Over my two days in Toulouse, my uneasiness steadily grew as the gulf widened between who I was and what people wanted me to represent.

Rachid Mimouni shared his reservations about the term "Francophone" in an interview in the regional newspaper *La Dépêche du Midi*. "We don't like the word; it smacks of colonialism. Actually, we African writers have the advantage of being bilingual. For my part, I 'naturally' write in French."[1] Daniel Zimmermann, one of the judges for the Young Writers Award, went a step further in his interview. He thought there was definitely something colonial about the Francophone award and expressed his shock at the age difference in the rules for the two groups of writers: "Twenty-five years old for the Belgians and Congolese, twenty years old for the French—it's outrageous."[2] Yves Marek, representing France's Minister Delegate for Francophonie, had no such scruples: "The award lifts up young French-speakers, it's a golden ticket for when they return to their home countries."[3] My goodness! Is that all?

I wasn't bilingual and French was my native language, but Mimouni, like Zimmermann, partially conveyed the uneasiness I felt once I was there, the impression that I was the poor provincial cousin at the party, seated with her peers at a table in a back room while the actual banquet was taking place in the main hall. The icing on the cake had actually come in an article about the judges' deliberations I discovered the afternoon I arrived: "The judges' initial impressions very quickly single out the best writers. *La Grande Dévoreuse* by the young African (Ivory Coast) Boni-Claverie evokes vivid cinematic imagery. Its prose is vigorous and raw. Africa simply does nothing by halves."

Africa does nothing by halves . . . So, all by myself, I was supposed to embody an entire continent reduced to a single characteristic. Giving free rein to her fantasies, the journalist concluded:

> I imagine Boni living her life of a young African girl. What does she do? How does she live in a country at war against its own upstart generation? Does she write at night in the glow of streetlights like that young man from Togo doing his homework

> one evening last May, the young man to whom I humbly dedicated these words?[4]

I felt doubly offended. Beyond her bleak view of Africa, the journalist denied me the right to have had enough imagination to create protagonists who weren't me. Being relegated to some dreamed-up elsewhere was all the more absurd because everything—the awards ceremony, the newspaper articles—occurred in Toulouse, a city close to my heart if ever there was one. Toulouse meant my grandfather, who attended school there; it meant my grandmother, who never fulfilled her own desire to become a writer; it meant Georges and Danièle, who met there. I started school in Toulouse at two years old. I visited on vacation as a little girl. Several months before the awards ceremony, I had returned for my grandfather's funeral. Georges still had very close friends from there, including one, a witness at his wedding, who was none other than the editor-in-chief of *La Dépêche du Midi*. But how could I convey my closeness to the place when people expected me to represent Africa? And when I myself, because of my lies, had contributed to that representation of me?

As if the whole situation weren't already complicated enough, Georges decided to join me. Although I was supposed to stay with a neighborhood family like the other award winners, he declared it out of the question for me to spend the night with strangers. He reserved us two rooms at a hotel, the same hotel, it turned out, where the judges were staying. The latter watched with unabashed surprise as I entered the lobby with them after our lunch and walked toward the reception desk to pick up my key. In this context, clearly, one's lodgings gave tangible form to the hierarchy of talent and social status. For the famous authors, the comfortable hotel; for the writer-apprentices, the foldout beds of the volunteer hosts. Once again, I had strayed from the role they wanted me to play. And who was this white man by my side, with his impeccable three-piece suit and hint of a regional accent, whom I called Papa?

In the evening, the epic muddle continued. During the awards ceremony, an actor read two passages from my manuscript. He led with a particularly detailed love scene. My father, sitting next to me, stared wide-eyed. I wanted to crawl under my seat. Not that Georges was prudish, but this wasn't exactly the prose he was expecting from his barely eighteen-year-old daughter, nor the kind of writing I wanted to share with him. In short, things were a mess all over. As if every mixed-up part of my identity was colliding all at once.

Several days later, *La Dépêche du Midi* wrote a profile of me that was light years from the third-world fantasies of the journalist who had imagined me writing under the glow of a streetlight. In this case, the article resembled a high-society column gussied up with three generations of my family's curriculum vitae. I immediately suspected Georges of using his friendship with Fernand Cousteaux, the paper's editor-in-chief, to slip his own notes to the journalist. It was typical Georges.

Faced with the jumbled puzzle of my origins, my father continued to impose his own personal mythology—no doubt the only one he had to give me. The fact that I belonged to the upper class would cover over my imperfections, provide me with an identity, and open doors for me in society. Besides the fact that I didn't necessarily want to fit myself into this mold, he didn't realize that what worked for him simply wasn't feasible for me.

# 11 Why Race Trumps Class

September 1990. No more dormitories, no more nuns. Now that I was an adult, my parents accepted the reality of my living alone. I moved into my first apartment, a studio near the Porte Maillot, in northwest Paris. The rental was arranged without an agency, through one of Georges and Danièle's very close friends who knew the landlords, a retired couple living a street away. My parents' friend spoke of them with a hint of condescension, as the bourgeois do when speaking of their social inferiors, even if it wasn't nearly the same condescension used to express the paternalistic indulgence reserved for the poor or "deserving." Which didn't stop the residents of this part of the seventeenth arrondissement, albeit less chic than where I had grown up, from taking themselves very seriously.

There were just minor details. At first, I didn't pay attention. Then I noticed that the old lady living, like me, on the first floor of this beautiful nineteenth-century building, never thanked me when I took out her trash bins. Nor did the pretentious bourgeoise who seemed to find it normal for me to open the door for her as she passed, nose in the air, with hardly a look in my direction. One day, on a walk to a nearby open-air market, I had a sudden hankering for chocolate. The manager of the little bobo chocolate shop didn't hide her displeasure when I entered. I asked her for a chocolate praline. She told me they didn't sell them and suggested I buy a Kit Kat at the corner store. Stupidly, I thanked her, and only realized once back on the sidewalk that she had just run me off, insinuating that I wasn't good enough for her hand-crafted chocolates. But instead of drawing the obvious conclusion from these incidents, I kept asking myself the same question: had I unwittingly been so impolite with these people that I'd made them react like this?

The eye-opener came one night when I went to the dance club La Main Jaune, at the edge of Paris in the seventeenth arrondissement. La Main Jaune had cult status for me, the place where the roller-skating protagonist Vic, a young Sophie Marceau, hangs out in the film *La Boum*. I watched and rewatched the movie at least ten times when I was in Abidjan. Like millions of young girls, I dreamed of a slow dance in the arms of the beautiful Mathieu. So it didn't matter if La Main Jaune was already out of style; I lived so close, I went as a kind of pilgrimage. Over the course of the evening, a preppy-looking boy came up to me in the most humdrum way imaginable, asking if I liked the music that was playing—a banal love song. I answered him honestly: no, not so much. He stood back, looked me up and down, then snapped at me scornfully, "Oh yeah, of course not. You like rap." Do I even have to say it? He was white.

This time around, the hostility was so obvious that it registered. Black = rap = the suburbs, the *banlieue*. Out of spite, in a single, apparently insignificant remark, this stranger had excluded me from his world and expelled me into what he judged to be an ugly periphery. It shouldn't have gotten to me. I wasn't interested in him and, yes, I liked rap, just as I liked other kinds of music. But I discovered a way of thinking that until then had remained foreign to me. I finally understood the reactions of my neighbors, of the chocolate shop manager: they wanted to make me feel that, although I might live in the same neighborhood, I didn't belong to their world. I could make no claim to being their equals; my place was necessarily beneath them. Or, preferably, somewhere else, where my kind must of course be under house arrest in the *banlieue*, the Parisian suburbs of housing projects and immigrants, as I learned thanks to the young man in the dance club. A good part of my naïveté suddenly vanished. So that was racism? I finally understood in my bones what it was, but I didn't know how to react. It was easy for me to reply to someone calling me a "dirty *nègre*," as would happen to me later on in the same neighborhood, because at that level of insult, the words had no more effect on me than if someone had called me a bitch. But I was helpless against the racism of rejection and exclusion expressed in such an insidious way. Since I was a young girl, my education consisted of mastering social codes and acquiring the intellectual and cultural knowledge that would supposedly open every door, regardless of where I was and regardless of the social hierarchy. That was my parents' implicit promise to me. It worked relatively well as long as I lived with them and as long as it remained easy enough for others to "situate" me. My parents' way of life left no doubt about their belonging to the world of the powerful. Now that I was living alone, without my pedigree on display, I was no longer Isabelle Boni-Claverie, daughter and granddaughter *of* . . . nor even an African in France to study, with all the fantasies that might entail. I was a Black woman.

And although I had only just made this discovery, I would have plenty of time to experience what it meant over the long haul: being Black in France means enduring a constant process of social inferiorization.

When it wasn't the neighbors who snubbed me or the shopkeepers who only grudgingly served me, it was the customers and managers at stores in other chic neighborhoods handing me piles of clothes to reshelve. It was the immediate use of the inappropriately familiar "tu" with me. Years later, it was the screenwriter who imagined that I was there to fulfill the writing team's diversity quota and wanted to crawl under a rock when she discovered where I had gone to school. It was the subtle way at certain dinners or parties that people with high opinions of themselves steered their gaze from me to avoid engaging in conversation. It was the grandmother in the waiting room of a music class who was shamelessly surprised by my ability to explain to my son the meaning of an otherwise commonplace French word. It was the schoolteachers who spoke in something bordering on pidgin to African parents who were just as—if not better—educated than them. It was the school director who called in the mother of a little girl of Congolese descent because the latter had written on her information form that her father had attended the prestigious École Nationale d'Administration. She had refused to change it, despite her teacher insisting that what she had meant to write was that he was a security guard there. It was all the human stupidity.

These people's minds were already made up. It was automatic. They didn't have to think about it.

A Black woman in France doesn't live in an upscale neighborhood.

A Black woman in France doesn't go foxhunting.

A Black woman in France only goes to a fancy restaurant if she works there—unless she's a celebrity or high-end prostitute.

What were the factors on which these judgments were based?

With the exception of a somewhat eccentric period in my life, when I wore a leopard-print sheepskin jacket, yellow dreadlocks, and lace pants, I dressed relatively conservatively and, I hope, rather stylishly. Whether I liked it or not, it seems I had the good manners and diction that betrayed the social environment in which I had grown up. In general, people are sensitive to those social markers. In order for the latter not to have an effect when it came to me, there had to be something more decisive that superseded everything else. Besides my skin color, I had no idea what it could be.

"My skin is black," Nina Simone sings in her song "Four Women." "My skin is black / My arms are long / My hair is woolly / My back is strong / Strong enough to take the pain / Inflicted again and again / What do they call me? / My name is AUNT SARAH / My name is Aunt Sarah."[1]

Slavery . . . Lashes meted out for the smallest act of disobedience . . . In her powerful song, Nina Simone reminds us of one aspect of the Black condition. Of a history, in principle, now past. Slavery was abolished in the United States in 1865; in France, in 1848. In reality, many of its same structures remained into the early twentieth century. In French dictionaries, "Noir" is no longer synonymous with "slave," even if the dictionary of the Académie Française still can't help but mention it: "Un Noir, une Noire. L'esclavage, la traite, l'émancipation des Noirs," that is, "A Black man, a Black woman. Black slavery, the Black slave trade, Black emancipation."[2] The Larousse dictionary more prudently refrains from offering examples and provides a relatively neutral definition. Persons referred to as "Noirs" are those "whose pigmented skin is high in melanin." A definition general enough not to offend a soul.

But does that mean that we have actually stopped being symbolic slaves in the minds of white people? Indigenous people subjected to forced labor? "Body-machines"? Subaltern workers? Socially inferior beings?

Nina Simone wanted to be a classical pianist. She practiced seven hours a day, starting at four years old. She had to take up jazz instead. A Black woman simply didn't do "high" art. She ought to have known: in musical notation, a black-filled note is never worth more than half of an unfilled—white—one.

# 12 Alphonse and Rose-Marie: A Mixed-Race Couple in the Colonies

If a white note is worth at least as much as two black-filled ones, then what is a white woman married to a Black man worth? As much as, or perhaps less than, a Black woman? The harsh reality of race-based inferiorization would soon become part of my grandparents' experience.

On June 2, 1938, Alphonse received a telegram with the news he had impatiently awaited for over a year. He had been named to his first posting in Africa: a deputy judge at the court in Lomé, the capital of Togo. After a fourteen-year absence, he would finally return to the continent of his childhood.

So much had changed since his arrival in France in 1924. As he rode the train to Bordeaux to catch the boat for the Gulf of Guinea, retracing a journey he had made from Ivory Coast long ago, his past came rushing back to him. He saw himself again, my grandmother writes, as

> a quivering little boy in his cotton-drill suit, lost, wide-eyed, having formed a picture of France so different from the reality. He saw himself landing in Bordeaux, astonished by the illuminated streets, then his arrival in Angoulême, his five years of boarding school, his life as a student, and finally accomplishing

> the goal that he set for himself. He saw his entire life again with the optimism of his youth.

Alphonse could indeed take pride in how far he had come. He had kept his promise to his parents. He was now a magistrate. Despite the obstacles, he had married the woman he loved. And he had just become a father. Jean-Pierre, my biological father, had been born several months earlier in Gaillac, in the same little house where Rose-Marie herself was born. But his joy was clouded by apprehension.

> They would have to confront the issue of skin color, which he had never had to deal with before, neither in secondary school nor at university. He dreaded it, for Rose-Marie's sake. How would she react to these new difficulties? He reminded himself that she had managed quite well with her own family. Except in that case, she had settled things at a single blow. How would she hold up against the daily wear and tear of the petty slights she was bound to be subjected to? A couple in half-mourning, as she delighted in calling the two of them, was bound to be a rare sight where they were headed.

"Half-mourning": after full-mourning attire, all in black, there was half-mourning, in which white and black could be worn together. That is how my grandmother referred to her and her husband.

The racism that Alphonse feared for his young wife revealed itself even before they set foot on the ship for Africa. As they edged their way up the gangway, Rose-Marie's attention was drawn to two old colonials speaking loudly enough for her to hear.

> "Look at that *nègre* heading for the first-class deck."
> "Must be a West Indian. You see them everywhere."
> "No, he looks African."
> "A Senegalese?"
> "No."
> "If the *nègres* get an education, what'll become of us?"

Fortunately, Alphonse, too busy protecting his son from the pushing and shoving in line, didn't hear a thing. Rose-Marie preferred to keep quiet. But that evening, in the ship's dining room, "the passengers, comprised mostly of colonial administrators, military doctors, and officers, were arranged by rank." She and Alphonse were seated at a table of non-commissioned officers, which didn't reflect my grandfather's status. They were there, of course, because he was Black.

Bothered by the exchange of barracks jokes at her own table, Rose-Marie observed the social comedy playing out around her. As she put it herself, she felt as if she were in one of the French writer Georges Courteline's satires.

> The civil servants of various ranks eyed one another scornfully. Madame Chief Administrator, who found herself seated to the right of the ship's captain, haughtily surveyed the unfortunate ladies whose lesser-ranked husbands had never had the singular honor of having a place at the Official Table. The wife of an infantry colonel inspected through her lorgnette the troop of blushing student administrators, among whom she might find husbands for her three daughters accompanying her, the three girls making a noisy show of their stupidity.

When Rose-Maire later expressed her surprise at such behavior, Alphonse explained that "'as soon as these people are on the boat, they already have one foot in the colony and enjoy the prestige of skin color and their husbands' rank.'" To which my grandmother sharply replied:

> "Ah! Because there's something prestigious about skin color? [. . .] The scales have fallen from my eyes! Now I see what racism is. Does skin color give a man worth or is it the goodness of his heart? [. . .] I'll never spend time with people who think such things. Never."
>
> And her voice grew hoarse from sobbing.

Throughout their journey, Rose-Marie endured her compatriots' scornful looks; in them, she perceived the "contempt reserved for a French woman married to a Black man." The ship's captain seemed to be the most disapproving of the lot.

> Rose-Marie had seen him give a courteous bow to everyone who passed to greet him. When it was their turn, she felt him scrutinizing her from head to toe. She followed his gaze defiantly. A sensitive woman, she felt the blood rush from her heart to her head, her eyes grew misty, and rather than sitting, she simply collapsed in her chair [. . .]. How terribly their looks cut her to the core! She would have preferred harsh words, which would have at least given her the opportunity to say something in response to a contempt that threatened to completely undermine her happiness.

To spare Alphonse, she kept these humiliations to herself. But she also promised herself never to forget how proud she was of her husband, and to steel herself so that one day she would be indifferent to what people thought of them.

What did these disdainful French people reproach her for if not degrading the race by allowing a Black man into her bed? She had failed to live up to the superiority accorded to her as a white woman. She had debased herself in the eyes of the colonizers. Still worse, she was leaving France to set a bad example in the colonies, instilling in every native who crossed her and my grandfather's path the idea that white women, fallen from their pedestal, were now accessible.

I have often wondered about the uncompromising rigor with which Rose-Marie maintained her grace and elegance, her need to look impeccable regardless of the temperature—and even though she couldn't stand the heat—a rigor she likewise imposed on her children, demanding that their manners always be beyond reproach. I have wondered if this severe form of intransigence, which I never noticed in any other members of her family, was in fact her response to her compatriots' contempt. My grandfather had his professional status, the power and, despite everything, the prestige that went with it. Rose-Marie hadn't finished university. She didn't work. She could only assert herself through her control of the domestic sphere and perhaps in high society. Her children said that she was tough. Would she have survived if she hadn't been?

The first stopover was in Dakar, July 14. Alphonse went to pay his respects to the Attorney General of French West Africa. For reasons that escape me, Senegal's capital, Rose-Marie's first exposure to Africa, disappointed her. They then went to Conakry, and finally the shores of Ivory Coast. They stopped first in Sassandra, a town my grandmother loved. "The setting sun plunged into the sparkling smooth blue sea," she wrote. "Coconut trees bent toward the water to hear its murmuring waves. In the distance, nestled among the greenery covered in beautiful purple-blue bougainvillea, several white villas could be seen. The sea seemed to caress the sand with its foam." In Sassandra, they received a telegram signed by one of my grandfather's former classmates, Jean Delafosse, the mixed-race son of the colonial administrator, Maurice Delafosse: "Wish family and friends good last leg of trip await you in Port Bouët."

Rose-Marie was anxious. She was finally going to meet her husband's family. She dreaded introductions. A year and a half earlier, when their wedding was announced, Tano Ehouman, Alphonse's father, had made it clear he disapproved of his son's marriage to a white woman. In a letter, he had written acidly that "a tree that falls in the river may stay there for a hundred years, it will never become a crocodile." Whatever she did, Rose-Marie would never be like them. She feared not being accepted. Alphonse, on the other hand, wasn't worried. He came with a son, and he knew that the child's presence would quell whatever misgivings his family had. And he was right. It was the warmest of welcomes.

Jean Delafosse was the first to greet my grandparents on the boat. He and Alphonse hadn't seen each other since primary school in Bingerville. "They stood at arm's length to get a better look, to see if they still recognized each other. Fourteen years apart had transformed the boys into men."

Once Jean Delafosse stood aside, Rose-Marie, according to her own petrified words, perceived the proud figure of my great-grandfather advancing toward them, dressed in his imposing traditional attire of chief. Tano Ehouman didn't speak French. Alphonse would have to reacquaint himself with his mother tongue. He spoke it with difficulty, although he still understood the language. Spontaneously, words from his childhood came back to him, words from the heart. "Man," he said, using the diminutive for Ehouman he had used as a boy, "where is my mother?"

Only the patriarch and his entourage—a chief never traveled alone—were authorized to come aboard. Intimidated, Rose-Marie embraced her father-in-law and held out her son to him. Then they disembarked to the customs office, where they were greeted by Akissi Ba, Alphonse's mother, the rest of the family, childhood friends, and even two young colonial administrators who had studied law with my grandfather in Toulouse. Alphonse threw himself into the open arms of his mother, who had a hard time recognizing her little boy at first. Rose-Marie met family and friends, embracing each in turn, when suddenly she overheard a young Frenchwoman in the customs hall say, "A white woman kissing *nègres*. She's not a fussy one." My grandfather heard the remark as well, and knowing my grandmother's temperament, he worried how she would react. He didn't like scenes, so he quietly asked her not to respond: "Don't stoop to their level." Rose-Marie kept her cool. Once again, she felt the same burning contempt directed at her. But one mustn't spoil a homecoming.

From Port-Bouët, they took the train to Abidjan where a coach was waiting for them. Jean Delafosse had arranged things well. They rode past the notable buildings that existed then, the post office, the governor's palace, the ministry of finance, the treasury. My grandmother described the administrative center of Abidjan, which wasn't yet Ivory Coast's capital, as a large village, with shaded avenues and tile-roofed villas, connected to Treichville, the African town, by a dilapidated bridge and little in keeping with the beauty of the lagoon that stretched farther than the eye could see.

They arrived in front of a new building where a reception was planned in their honor. Everyone who hadn't been able to meet them in Port-Bouët was there. A large banner hung across the room's entrance: "Honor to Our First Magistrate!" Indeed, Alphonse was the first Ivorian to reach such a position.

But it was soon time to say goodbye. The boat departed the next day for Lomé. A fourteen-year absence, a twenty-four-hour port of call. That was all the colonial administration gave my grandfather for this first return to his homeland. Denied assignments in his own country, Alphonse thus traveled Africa. Lomé. Bamako. Conakry. Dschang. Ziguinchor. Brazzaville.

My grandparents were well received in Lomé. The country's "legal family" came out in force to greet them: the court president, the dean of attorneys, a woman attorney, the head of court clerks, and the "little people." The president's wife took Rose-Marie under her wing and initiated her to the mysteries of her new life, discovering a substitute daughter in the process. Things didn't work out so well everywhere.

My mother thought she recalled a large Corsican community in Ziguinchor. It was 1948. Mistaking the origin of the namesake "Boni," all the town's Corsicans turned up to welcome their new justice of the peace. When they found out he was African, their welcome cooled. Yet my grandparents' oldest daughter, my aunt Marie-Françoise, assured me that they were never victims of racism by the colonial French. "My father was Black and that was that." According to her, the positions that Alphonse held made him an important person in the small world of the French colonies and shielded the family from any overt displays of racism. As for Rose-Marie, my aunt told me, it was her good manners that set her apart.

Danièle's memories are very different from her older sister's. As an adult, she still remembered the bitter humiliation she endured in one of the colonies she lived in as a young girl with her parents, probably in Brazzaville, given her age, or during a stay in Abidjan. It was very hot that day and she wanted to go for a swim at the city's private pool. An employee stopped her at the entrance: the pool was for whites only.

In Brazzaville at around the same time, Alphonse had ended his career as a French Overseas judge and was now a prosecutor. A chain smoker, he left his office to light a cigarette in front of the courthouse when a French colonist approached him. Taking Alphonse for a porter—obviously, because here was a Black man standing near the building's entrance—the man began speaking to him in pidgin, demanding in an overbearing, degrading way that he show him to the prosecutor's office. Complying with the man's request, Alphonse threw down his cigarette and led him into the courthouse. When they arrived at his office, my grandfather calmly sat down in his chair, returned to his usual French, and asked the colonist what he could do for him. The guy was white as a sheet. He had come to request a favor in a criminal case in which he himself was the defendant.

Omar Bongo, Gabon's deceased president-for-life, relates a funny anecdote from the time he still went by the name Albert-Bernard.

After finishing high school, he found an internship at the Postal and Telecommunications Authority in Brazzaville. He was working in transmission services. One day, he saw a confidential telegram come through from the colonial governor addressed to the heads of the administrative districts. The telegram gave specific instructions about the people France wanted to see elected in the upcoming elections.

> I screamed. I yelled. I told all Brazzaville about the scheming of the colonial army and how it had rigged the elections [. . .]. My revelations created one hell of a fuss. All the newspapers talked about it. So, sure enough, I was arrested. They brought me to the courthouse. And there, I happen to get a judge who's as Black as can be. I was scared because I thought he was Martinican. His name was Alphonse Boni. As it turns out, he was Ivorian . . .

Because he was a sworn official, Bongo was charged with violating state secrets. He defended himself: "I'm just an intern and I've never sworn an oath to anyone."

With that, the judge Alphonse Boni lost patience with the prosecution: "If Albert-Bernard Bongo hasn't sworn an oath, what is he doing here? Free him at once!"[1]

What the end of this story doesn't say is that the agitator-intern would go on to become a spy in French pay in the very same Postal and Telecommunications Authority before entering politics and rising, thanks to Jacques Foccart and Charles de Gaulle, to the Gabonese presidency. After becoming one of the most indispensable pillars of Françafrique, he would confidently declare in 1996 that "Africa without France is a car without a driver. France without Africa is a car without fuel." True enough, Bogo would unstintingly fuel the French economy over his forty-year rule, whether with oil or (millions of) low-denomination banknotes.

# 13 A Little Story About Discrimination

Perhaps it was excusable in the 1950s, given the small number of judges and prosecutors of African descent, if not exactly to speak pidgin to an African, then at least to assume that Alphonse was a porter or, for that matter, a West Indian, that is, higher up on the socioracial hierarchy of the day. What is remarkable is that sixty years later in France, a Black man in a suit continues to be a security guard, whether he is West Indian or not. Afrodescendant business executives frequently encounter this kind of mistake, as once happened to my cousin, who had a high-level position in one of the largest companies on the French stock exchange. One morning, he arrived earlier than usual at work and found the doors to the building locked. He was patiently waiting to enter when two secretaries arrived. One of them curtly asked him what was taking him so long to let them in.

In France, the fact is—and discrimination is definitely a part of this—you are more likely to meet Black security guards than Black businesspeople. But must we then conclude that every time we see Black people in suits, they're security guards?

If she had seen anything other than his skin color, the secretary would have noticed that my cousin had documents in his hand and was wearing a gray suit instead of the typical black suit of security guards. But the woman wasn't standing in front of a man whose specific features she had the patience to scrutinize. She was standing in front of a Black man. Whether it was utterly rational or, for that matter, grotesquely rational of her, all she could see was skin. That was enough for her to draw her conclusion.

In the world of French business, Black people—when they aren't perceived as coming from disadvantaged (that is, "bad") neighborhoods—are considered "nice" and "friendly." People find them relatively "effective" and "competent" but criticize them for their "apathy" and "slowness"[1]—the well-worn stereotype of Black people's nonchalance. Is that why the secretary grew impatient with my cousin? Had she decided she was dealing with a lazy security guard?

She could have politely asked him to open the door, but she was curt and peremptory. I doubt she would have used the same tone if she had been addressing a white security guard. A woman who spent her days subjected to the orders of her mostly male bosses had found herself in front of someone she considered doubly inferior—a Black security guard—on whom she could unleash a bit of the high-handedness she endured or thought she endured at work. An unmitigated joy. How incredibly useful it is to have Black people around to give white people, regardless of their social status, the opportunity to experience their superiority first-hand.

Thanks to a Black man, a white woman can finally take her revenge for the sex discrimination she experiences against her. And white women also have an absolute inferior, Black women, who suffer discrimination based on both race and gender, when they are lucky enough to escape the yoke of class.

The history of the social inferiorization of Black people in France is a long one. It is intrinsically tied to slavery, which is itself the consequence of the European colonization of "new" and geographically distant lands that required an abundant labor supply for their exploitation. Before that time, the few Black people present in France were simply Black. Starting in the seventeenth century, officially in 1643, when the first authorized slave ship landed in the French colony of Guadeloupe, they became slaves.

In European France, the status of Blacks was more nuanced. Slavery was illegal and slaves arriving in the country could ask a court for their freedom. In practice, of the four to five thousand Black and mixed-raced people in France in 1738, the majority were slaves.[2] Forty years later, half of them were emancipated. One of every two were from the West Indies. However, whether emancipated or not, two-thirds worked as domestic servants for white employers.[3]

The abolition of the slave trade could and should have changed the situation. But the structures of sub-Saharan colonialism took over from there, with France moving from the Code Noir, which governed the status of slaves, to the Code de l'Indigénat, or the "native code." Forced labor—merely another form of servitude—was introduced. To keep a clear conscience, people took pride in knowing they were part of France's civilizing mission. In French cities, and indeed throughout Europe, it became customary to exhibit "savages" at local fairs and in the universal and colonial exhibitions that proliferated in the late nineteenth century. These ostensibly ethnographic exhibits drew large crowds to places like the Jardin Zoologique d'Acclimatation[4] or, for another telling example, to the Paris Colonial Exhibition of 1931. Spectators were especially keen to see the Africans, penned up like animals, without ever suspecting that these human specimens were actually paid extras. Seeing them was enough to persuade oneself of the superiority of European, and thus of white, civilization.

A new opportunity for greater equality arose during the world wars, which brought a new category of Africans to French soil, the "Senegalese Tirailleurs," riflemen of the colonial army who, despite the name, actually came from throughout France's African empire. They were extremely popular. Witness, for example, the Tirailleur "Bamboula," the mascot of the chocolate drink Banania, with his iconic "Y'a bon" (*'t's good*), supposedly reproducing the pidgin of African people, to whom, it was thought, only the rudiments of French needed to be taught, just enough to understand orders. The savage's primitive strength was in this context viewed as a positive. Properly channeled and carefully supervised, that strength would help protect the French and fight the Germans. The Tirailleurs nonetheless remained locked in a colonial relationship that maintained their inferiority.

When I was a child, I drank Banania every morning, completely ignorant of this history. How many French children, or even their parents, know anything about it?

My grandfather did his military service between the two world wars. He had just obtained French nationality so wasn't part of the Senegalese Tirailleurs. Instead, he got stuck with a "colonial army officer," my grandmother writes, a "rempilé,"[5] who, catching sight of my grandfather, insisted on having him in his company.

> "Just my luck," he thought. "And why exactly is this officer so interested in me?" He would soon find out. Alphonse would pay for the years of frustration this man had bottled up while earning his stripes with the Senegalese Tirailleurs. Long prevented from tyrannizing the latter, he now turned his ire on Alphonse. Petty indignities, tongue-lashings, drudgery, and insults—he was spared nothing. His grades sabotaged, Alphonse completed his military service dead last, with only sergeant stripes to show for it.

The officer no doubt considered my grandfather an exceedingly arrogant man who needed to be reminded that his status was first and foremost that of a *nègre*. Indeed, their first clash occurred over my grandfather's education. The officer had asked the new recruits to form two lines: one for those who had their upper primary school certificate, the other for those who didn't. Although he had a doctorate in law, my grandfather joined the second line. The officer took this as a provocation. The truth was simpler. The certificate didn't exist in Ivory Coast at the time Alphonse left primary school. It was imported by the colonial administration in September 1924, when Alphonse was already on his way to France.

One would have thought that after the abolition of slavery in 1848, life would be better for those with French citizenship living in African colonies. Such was rarely the case. They were citizens but continued to live under the colonial regime. In 1946, Martinique, Guadeloupe, Réunion, and Guiana were granted the status of French departments. They were freed from the yoke of empire, but the change of status didn't create fully equal citizens.

In the early 1960s, African countries gained independence. At the same time, to fill French labor needs in construction and manufacturing, unskilled workers from sub-Saharan Africa were brought to France. They were also heavily employed in sanitation work. Hence the stereotype that became ingrained in France of African garbagemen and streetsweepers, spending their nights closed up in state-sponsored immigrant hostels.

In 1963, the French government established the BUMIDOM, an agency created to promote the migration of West Indians to mainland France and to oversee their transport, education, and job-placement.[6] "The Sorbonne of the toilet brush," some said. The West Indians who accepted BUMIDOM's free ticket to come work in France believed in the dream of upward mobility that the agency was selling. The mere fact of moving to the mainland, and especially to Paris, seemed a mark of rising social status. Once they were there, however, they realized that their futures were limited to being housekeepers, hospital orderlies, and warehouse and postal workers. In other words, to the menial ranks of the public sector to which immigrants without French nationality weren't entitled. They faced the hardships of exile, prejudice, and racism. They were French and yet considered foreigners in the same way as non-citizen Africans. It was a rude awakening, but it was too late for them to change their minds. The BUMIDOM only provided one-way tickets.

The French cliché of the West Indian postal clerk or hospital nurse often makes people laugh. We forget that this disproportionate representation in the public sector is the result of a government policy that created deep trauma within the West Indian community, one that endures among the descendants of the 80,000 to 160,000 (estimates differ) BUMIDOM migrants.

Today, a new face of inferiority now prevails in France: that of *banlieue* youth, actual or soon-to-be delinquents, who can't be integrated into French society. Add to that the relatively recent caveat that, if these youth happen to be Muslim, they may also be terrorists.

This history, so deeply anchored in our collective unconscious whether or not we know all its details, has created such powerful stereotypes that it's become very difficult to see past them. Yet Black people have played a remarkable role in France throughout the ages. One naturally thinks of Senghor and Aimé Césaire, who were deputies for Overseas France during the Fourth Republic, world-renowned authors, and founders, with the French Guianese Léon-Gontran Damas, of the Negritude movement. But already in the eighteenth century, there was Joseph Bologne, Chevalier de Saint-Georges, born a slave in 1745 from an African mother and French nobleman, who won fame at court thanks to his successful military career and talents as a composer.

There was Jean-Baptiste Belley, deputy from Saint-Domingue (Haiti), the first Black man elected to a seat in the French National Convention in 1794. In 1898, Hégésippe Légitimus, the great-grandfather of the well-known French comedian and actor Pascal Légitimus, was elected deputy of Guadeloupe and, a year later, that country's President of the Council. His arrival in the French National Assembly was met with vicious articles in the press: "He is primitive man in all his amiable artlessness. His are, one might say, the heartfelt proclamations of an orangutan descended from his palm tree."[7]

This notable history continued, of course, into the twentieth century. For example, Paulette Nardal, who in 1920 was the first Black woman to study at the Sorbonne. With her sister, she created *La Revue du monde noir* in 1931, in which she published writers and intellectuals from both sides of the Atlantic. In 1929, Raphaël Élizé was one of the very first Black mayors elected in mainland France. And Gaston Monnerville, also a West Indian, was President of the Senate from 1958 to 1968.

I could cite many more examples. Yet either because there aren't enough of these illustrious Black people or because they haven't sufficiently entered French national consciousness, their story hasn't left its mark. Except, that is, when they have distinguished themselves in the world of sports or the entertainment industry, two areas where, from time immemorial, Black success has been deemed acceptable. On the other hand, the very few times a French Black or mixed-race person attained the status to merit a national monument, no one spoke about their skin color.

# 14 My First Black Role Models

Throughout my childhood, Alexandre Dumas was my favorite novelist. I read and reread *The Count of Monte Cristo* and *The Three Musketeers*. I studied Dumas in school. I watched numerous adaptations of his work on television. At no time did I know that he was mixed race, that his father was France's first Black general, that his grandmother was an African slave deported to Haiti, and that he vigorously defended himself against those who mocked his "*nègre*" ancestry. The height of irony: as a little girl in Paris, I lived just next door to his monument. But it took the transfer of his remains to the Pantheon in 2002 and French President Jacques Chirac's speech on the occasion for me to discover that Dumas was mixed race. Why didn't we hear more about it?

When I was a child, an adolescent, or when, as a young woman, I was trying as best as I could to come to terms with my mixed identity, I would have liked for someone to tell me that people who looked like me had written considerable parts of France's cultural history—including those parts we take to be the most emblematically French. It would have given me some points of reference, some figures to identify with, a sense of legitimacy. Instead, at the age of ten, fifteen, and twenty years old, when I turned on the television, I came across the comic Michel Leeb's skits about Africans in which he grotesquely imitated their accents or compared them to monkeys. When it wasn't him, it was Éric Blanc, whose comedy revolved around his being Black, his name being Blanc (White, in English), and an unrelenting self-deprecation that reinforced Black stereotypes. French audiences had a good laugh: at least when such stupidity came from a Black man, no one could claim it was racist.

The only Black woman I saw on television was the advertising model Michoko, who exemplified the tired analogy between skin color and chocolate. What there was to watch about the West Indies began and ended with the French Guianese pop group La Compagnie Créole. As for mainstream political discourse, Jacques Chirac summed it up in 1991:

> Our problem isn't foreigners, it's that we have an overdose on our hands. It may be true that there aren't more foreigners now than before the war, but they aren't the same, and that makes a difference. It's clear that having people from Spain, Poland, and Portugal working here is less of a problem than having Muslims and Blacks [. . .]. How do you expect a French worker [to react], someone living in the Goutte d'or neighborhood—where I was walking with Alain Juppé last week, three or four days ago—someone who works with his wife, and together they make 15,000 francs, who, in the public housing where he lives, sees a family all crammed together, with the father, three or four wives, and twenty or more kids, and who makes 50,000 francs in welfare—all without working, obviously! If you add in the noise and the smell, well, now, the French worker, standing there, goes crazy. He goes crazy! That's how it is! And you have to understand, if you were there, you'd have the same reaction. And it's not racist to say so.[1]

No more racist, I suppose, than when the National Front proclaims on its posters: "France is for the French."

There was, of course, the tennis star Yannick Noah, but he hadn't won in a while. And the joke doing the rounds was that he was only French when he won.

Without strong role models who were both French and Black, and lacking any theoretical framework, I flailed in a whirlwind of questions to which I had no answers. I grew up believing that I was part of universal humanity. I discovered that my skin color was grounds for exclusion. I had no counterargument to this. French public opinion calls for assimilation. If I wasn't accepted, then that was my fault. Nothing I did could make me any less of a black sheep.

It was a trip to New York in 1991 that gave me my first tools for understanding the world around me.

Before New York, when I was fifteen, I had visited the United States as part of a language-immersion program: one month with an American host family to improve my English. Since the family's background wasn't specified, I assumed that they would be white. But the program we went through informed my mother that they preferred to place me with a Black family. They wanted to avoid potentially racist reactions from the host family. Perhaps, without telling us, the families they usually worked with had refused to take me.

The image of the United States we were sold back then was of a melting pot, of a great multiethnic stew. I abruptly discovered that the reality was one of racial divisions.

The other French teenagers leaving at the same time for Melbourne, a small town not far from Orlando, Florida, were all white. Their white American families came to pick them up at the designated meeting place. I waited alone. The time passed. "BPT," Americans say, "Black people time." My host family finally arrived, very late. Relieved that at least they hadn't forgotten about me, I completely neglected the advice that we'd been given not to kiss our hosts on the cheeks, especially if they were men. It would be perceived, the program's organizers told us, as an awkward display of affection. In a rush of excitement, I kissed everyone. The boy of the family recoiled in horror. No one could say that my first experience with Black Americans was a particularly warm one.

When I arrived at my host family's home, I thought I had landed on another planet. Their little house was in an exclusively Black neighborhood. They themselves only visited other Blacks, particularly for never-ending barbecues at which I died of boredom. On Sundays, we went to a Black church. I did my best to explain to them that I wasn't religious. To no avail. Sunday service wasn't optional. And despite my protests, and despite it being the middle of summer, the mother forced me to wear tights to cover my legs.

Both parents worked. They didn't get along and lived parallel lives in an atmosphere of latent hostility. I spent my time with the children, two teenagers who were about my age and did little else with their time but watch television and roam around the neighborhood. The trips we took with their mother to the mall, accessible only by car, were a major event. The rest of the time, they deluged me with idiotic questions about Ivory Coast. Did we have electricity? Did we ride elephants to get around? Did I have a refrigerator? A TV? Faced with such ignorance, I quickly decided to limit our exchanges to the bare minimum.

After several weeks, in a break from routine, we left Melbourne. It was for the funeral of a senile grandmother, in who knows what tiny Florida town, and included the same interminable masses and meals. My animosity toward my American family began to soar. It was then that my host mother delivered the coup de grâce. She wanted to know what my parents looked like. I showed her a picture. A horrified expression swept over her face. She looked at me in shock and exclaimed, "They're a mixed couple! How could your mother marry a white man?"

At that point, I began counting down the days to my departure.

Not once during my stay did it occur to me that in France I only spent time with white people, who lived in neighborhoods where only white people lived and who only married and socialized with other white people, save for the notable exception of my mother and me. That exclusivity was something that I simply didn't see. It seemed natural. Without realizing it, I too had internalized the idea that France was a country "of the white race." So it made sense that my presence, or the presence of people like me, remained an exception.

Nor was I in a position to grasp the connection between this Black American mother's rejection of whites and the still persistent racial divide caused by segregation. She was in her early forties. She was born and had grown up under Jim Crow laws, when a dog was treated better than a Black person.

Ignorant of this history, I returned home with the feeling that, although the United States offered a distinct change of scenery, we were certainly far more enlightened in France and Ivory Coast.

My trip to New York in 1991 was altogether different. Perhaps relieved to see me ready to go back to school—that fall I would begin a program in art history at the École du Louvre—my parents loosened the reins. This time, I stayed with a friend from Abidjan studying at NYU. No one served as chaperon or made me do anything I didn't want to do. It didn't matter that our Manhattan apartment was a borderline health risk and that at night the white kitchen tiles turned black with cockroaches. I was free. Once unpacked, I headed for a phone booth to let my mother know that I'd arrived in one piece. It was a little after noon, as bright as can be outside. In the booth next to mine, a man plunged a needle into his arm. I stared wide-eyed as he shot up. Welcome to New York, a city where anything can happen!

In the evenings, my friend DJed at parties that brought together Africans and African Americans, as American Blacks were then beginning to be called. It was at one of these parties that I met Gerome. He was a law student. From Detroit. Grew up in the ghetto. His older brother was dead, murdered. He was the first in his family to attend college. One afternoon, he came by to take me for a walk in the city with his best friend, a Haitian American. They were waiting in front of my apartment building. It was terribly hot outside. They wore Bermuda shorts and tank tops, with baseball caps on backward. I was struck by their outfits, by their tall figures that stood out against the concrete walls, by their way of being at once so relaxed and so self-assured. But as I went to greet them, I stopped in my tracks, speechless. On their left forearms, they each had a large puffy scar in the shape of a Greek letter: the sign of their fraternity. To join their exclusively Black student society, they had been branded. Like slaves.

I thought about the pain they must have felt. The burning flesh. The lumpy growth that formed after the iron was pressed. I shuddered imagining how barbaric it was. They were proud of the branding, which not only proclaimed their membership in a Black frat but, quite simply, their pride in being Black.

Unlike the mother of my host family in Melbourne, Gerome wasn't hostile toward whites. Yet for him and his friend, the world was clearly divided in two. On one side, there were Blacks, on the other, whites. Distinct entities with competing interests.

One day, the three of us went to Long Island for a picnic organized by the law firm where Gerome was an intern. His friend, who owned a car, a massive, air-conditioned thing in the American style, drove us. At a certain point, we got lost in a residential area. As we waited at a red light, Gerome asked a young blonde woman in a convertible next to us for directions. She answered politely. Gerome thanked her. Then, after he had closed his window and relayed the woman's directions, his friend blurted out, "Never trust a white woman in a convertible!" With a knowing look, they both burst out laughing.

It was the first time I had heard anyone talk like that. A line that seemed straight out of a Tarantino movie summed up everything separating these two young Black men from this white woman: gender; race; economic background; the legacy of segregation, a time when it was enough for a white woman to accuse a Black man of whistling at her for him to be lynched; the idea that, American history being what it is, even when they coexisted, they would never belong to the same world.

I was becoming aware of a racial dynamic that structured, whether we liked it or not, a large part of our social relationships. I started to see that things weren't what they seemed. Perhaps the white universalism I had grown up with wasn't the only norm. There existed a political and historical subtext that, were I to understand it, would allow me to better grasp the reality around me.

Before I returned to Paris, Gerome and his friend sat me down. They knew that in the fall I'd be studying art history. They spoke to me in a grave tone, trying to impress on me the seriousness of the studies I was about to undertake. "At school," they explained, "they're going to make you believe that everything started with the Greeks and Romans. They're going to teach you that civilization is European. But don't you ever forget, before all that, there were the Egyptians."

They recommended I read Cheikh Anta Diop's *The African Origin of Civilization*. Until then, I hadn't even heard the renowned Senegalese historian's name, even though his work provided the framework for a great swath of Africanist thought. I bought the book's two volumes in French when I returned to France. But what happened at the École du Louvre was the exact opposite of what the boys had predicted.

The national museum curators who taught our classes told us that our modern civilization was born in Mesopotamia, in what is modern-day Iraq and Syria. It was in the Middle East, eleven thousand years ago, that agriculture was invented, then, about three thousand years ago, that the first towns arose, and that, in the same region, the first text of a truly historical nature was discovered, the Code of Hammurabi, the king of Babylon.

I plunged with delight into the *Epic of Gilgamesh*—actually of Gilgamesh and Enkidu, his brother in arms. I learned that, based on our current archeological knowledge, it was the first story ever written, well before the *Iliad* and the *Odyssey*, and that the epic had, on several important points, most certainly inspired the Old Testament.

When we covered ancient Egypt, our professors told us about the influence of Nubia on its civilization and about the recurrent presence of Black Pharaohs. They showed us the famous sculpted portrait of Queen Tiye preserved at the Neues Museum in Berlin. Although the detail was usually absent from descriptions of the work, they explained that Queen Tiye, the wife of Amenhotep III and the mother of Akhenaten, played a significant role in politics and was very likely Black.

In contemporary art—the track I chose—Bernard Blistène, one of the most brilliant French museum curators, upended our meager certainties with his iconoclastic ideas. His lectures were full-blown performances, during which I lapped up everything he said. Thanks to him, I learned that an image doesn't exist in a vacuum but is instead a construct, that it is therefore never innocent, no more than our own way of looking at it is. His courses, however, stuck to a thoroughly traditional approach. He focused on the twentieth-century European and American avant-gardes in an ethnocentric dialogue that made the invention of modernity a strictly Western affair. All the artists we studied were white. It occurred to no one, not even to me, that there was something abnormal about this.

But then one day during one of his courses, Blistène brought up Basquiat. It was the first time I had heard the name. Jean-Michel Basquiat, the first Black star of contemporary Western art. Although he visited Abidjan in 1986, I knew nothing about him.

In a famous film interview I saw at the time, I was struck by his acute awareness of the ambiguity of his position as an artist and as a Black man in the world of white art, the skill with which he played with that ambiguity and, at the same time, the uneasiness he exuded.[2] This was especially striking when he described the anatomical fragments in his paintings as neoclassical studies inspired by Greco-Roman statuary. The art critic Marc Miller, who sincerely admired Basquiat's work, spoke of "imitation." Basquiat insisted that they were art-historical references. Put on the defensive, he worried about being viewed as a "monkey with a paint brush"—a trained monkey in whose work people have continued to emphasize the primitive. At a certain point, Miller asked him if the legend was true that he had been locked up in the gallerist Annina Nosei's basement to paint. Annoyed, Basquiat replied, "If I was a white guy, they'd just say artist in residence."

In his diary, Andy Warhol, a friend of Basquiat—they worked together on a series of paintings and Basquiat deeply admired him even though he regularly accused Warhol of exploitation—wrote the following terrible lines: "August 9, 1983. Paige stayed overnight with Jean Michel in his dirty smelly loft downtown. How I know it smells is because Chris was there and said [. . .] it was like a nigger's loft, that there were crumpled-up hundred-dollar bills in the corner and bad b.o. all over and you step on paintings."[3]

Basquiat died of an overdose on August 12, 1988, a few days before returning to Ivory Coast at the invitation of the Ivorian painter Ouattara Watts. He had planned on following a traditional detox treatment in a Senufo village in the north.[4]

Basquiat brought home my own situation to me. My desire for the absolute. The split between my Ivorian self and my French self. My difficulty being Black in France. My sense of inadequacy. As well as the anger that twenty-year-olds sometimes carry inside. I was so struck by the questions his peculiar status raised that I wrote a monologue about it in 1993, *Sexportrait of the Artist*, which the actor Alex Descas performed several years later.

# 15 The Adventure of *Revue Noire*

Along with contemporary art, I became more and more interested in film. My best friend was Lebanese. She was doing a bachelor's in film at the University of Paris and dreamed of going to La Fémis, France's top film school and a Grande École. Her boyfriend, whom she was seeing against her family's wishes, was Guianese and an aspiring actor. To earn money, he worked in a restaurant where he was relegated to dishwashing duties. His manager was concerned about his customers' reactions if he were made a server. Nowadays, you see Black servers even in swanky restaurants. Fortunately, some things have changed.

The actor-boyfriend was friends for a while with a young man of African descent, Éric, who wanted us to create a writing and acting group together. His plan didn't work out. But Paris has at least one terrific thing about it: you can see films from all over the world. The four of us were fixtures at all the local movie theaters.

New things were happening in French cinema. In 1988, Claire Denis directed the autobiographical *Chocolat* with Ivorian actor Isaach de Bankolé. In the film, she calls on her own childhood memories of Cameroon, where her father was a colonial administrator. Ambivalent race and class relationships, an underlying desire in the apparent friendship between the little French girl and the African servant—everything was there, depicted with precision and sensitivity. I watched it on TV one night with my parents during vacation and it shook me to the core. I could relate to both the little girl and the servant. For the first time, I had the feeling that a film was speaking directly to me about who I was. From then on, each new movie by Claire Denis was an event. It was thanks to her film

*No Fear, No Die* in 1990 that I discovered the actor Alex Descas, who plays one of the film's two protagonists, along with Isaach de Bankolé.

Isaach de Bankolé was already very well known. He had won the César Award for Most Promising Actor for the film *Black Mic Mac* in 1987, the first Black actor to win. Add to that his Ivorian origins and I immediately identified with him. I don't remember how, but I ran into him at a party, and later at an African restaurant, where he was having dinner with the supermodel Katoucha, Yves Saint Laurent's muse. I followed his career as if it affected me personally. I was appalled when I saw him in the films *Vanille Fraise (Strawberry Vanilla)* and *Les Keufs* (Lady Cops), comedies in which his skin color was constantly referred to, whether he was being called a savage, a *nègre*, suntanned, or *Black*—the term used in English in the film—all of it couched in humor, of course, and ultimately meant to denounce racism, although that racism remained ever-present in the film. This very superficial way of envisioning differences at least had the advantage of frankly displaying the stereotyped view people then had of Blacks in French society. Tired of the insubstantial characters and "Black roles" he was being offered, Isaach de Bankolé soon left France.

My new friends and I also closely followed Euzhan Palcy, the director of the beautiful 1983 film *Sugar Cane Alley*, which earned her the César for Best First Feature Film in 1984. She was the first and, to date, the only Black director to win such a prize for a feature film. When we saw the commercial flop of her film *Siméon*, which she herself described as "a West Indian musical fairytale," we took it hard. We assumed that her career would pay the price. Like Isaach de Bankolé, Euzhan Palcy moved to the United States. One sees her name less and less on the big screen. She is, however, the only French woman filmmaker ever to have directed a Hollywood film—with Marlon Brando no less.

In the meantime, thanks to the Young Francophone Writers Award, my novel *La Grande Dévoreuse* continued on a promising path and came out in an anthology of fellow award-winners. I also published a short story in the literary magazine *Le Moule à gaufres*.

But the small world of literature seemed extremely insular. I simply didn't know the codes that would allow me to break in. The idea of writing for the cinema slowly began to take root. I enrolled in a scriptwriting course, at the end of which I had a polished synopsis for an eventual screen adaptation of *La Grande Dévoreuse*. For me, of course, there was only one person for the project: Claire Denis.

Apart from his artistic ambitions, our friend Éric worked at France's electric company, EDF. Whenever he came across a film star's electric bill, he immediately copied the contact information. He was the one who gave me Claire Denis's address. I was lucky because her building didn't have an entry code, so I slid my synopsis into her mailbox. Two days later, I was sleeping when my phone rang. I heard a hoarse voice on the other end: "Your synopsis is great but what do you want from me?" She told me that she was working on her own projects but that my idea would definitely interest Isaach de Bankolé, who was looking for a film to direct. I obviously agreed to let her send him the synopsis. I don't know if de Bankolé looked at it; I never heard from him. However, when, after much perseverance, I finally met Claire Denis, she more or less told me that if I wanted to see my stories on screen, it would be up to me to direct them. I had never considered it.

Then, in 1993, while trying to meet everyone I could for a documentary on Abidjan's *loubards*—which is what people called gang members in the Ivorian capital, the first group to have invented a counterculture there—I suddenly found myself in possession of Simon Njami's telephone number.

Simon hadn't yet become the internationally renowned curator he is today. He had published two books whose titles didn't ring a bell to me, but which had earned him some recognition among those interested in the African diaspora. He was extremely cultivated, with a brilliant mind. When I called him, he told me, with that hint of pedantry that I'd soon discover was part of his persona, "It's a good idea, but a good idea isn't enough for a good project."

After reading my synopsis and other project materials, he suggested I write articles for *Planète jeunes*, a recently launched magazine for young French-speakers. I felt deeply honored. At just twenty-one years old, I'd be working as a journalist. At the end of my first year, during which he'd been evaluating me without my knowing it, he asked to speak with me. Affecting nonchalance, he offered me a position at *Revue Noire*.

*Revue Noire* had been created two years earlier by the architects Jean-Loup Pivin and Pascal Martin Saint-Léon, the journalist Bruno Tiliette, and Simon Njami. The incredibly luxurious magazine was intended to be a response to the exhibit "Magiciens de la Terre," which had caused quite a sensation at the Centre Pompidou in 1989, and which I remember having gone to see, without really understanding why the show was controversial. Whereas contemporary art history until then was seen as a dialogue between European and American avant-gardes, the exhibit endeavored to put artworks from throughout the world on an equal footing, including pieces created by people who didn't consider themselves artists.

The curator, Jean-Hubert Martin, had travelled the world with his team. In Africa, he deliberately bypassed established visual artists, considering them overly influenced by the "Paris school," too academic and, in short, too acculturated. He turned to self-taught creators and craftspeople, bringing these "magicians of the earth" together with Western artists. But when he selected the latter, he chose extremely well-known conceptual artists who also happened to be art-market celebrities. The editorial foursome of *Revue Noire* condemned the double standard. They deemed his approach ethnographic in nature and described the exhibit as skewed toward exoticism.

In contrast, the name of the game at *Revue Noire* was to show contemporary work from an Africa that was at once urban and firmly rooted in its time, imbued with its own traditions and with myriad external influences. The magazine also strove to document artists of the African diaspora throughout the world.

The day of my meeting with Jean-Loup Pivin, the magazine's director, I had a case of the jitters. To raise my confidence, I made sure I dressed well: a cashmere coat and a plaid skirt. It was raining. When I went to grab my umbrella, whose plaid pattern matched my skirt's, I figured that that was probably too much, but I didn't have another one and absolutely didn't want to ruin my hair.

In the drawing room of the magnificent Parisian house that served as the magazine's headquarters, I listened for over an hour to Jean-Loup bounce from one idea to the next as he intermingled various aesthetic and philosophical reflections. I did my best to concentrate so that I could answer his questions, but much of what he said went over my head. When he launched into a discussion of Roland Barthes's *A Lover's Discourse*, which I hadn't read, I was lost for good and simply nodded like a windup doll, while trying my best to seem intelligent. Jean-Loup later told me that he'd hired me because I was an incredible snob. I hope I wasn't. But on that day, as lost as I was, I clung to what I knew best: my French bourgeois manners, whose outward signs I no doubt unwittingly magnified.

It turned out, however, that that jibed with the outlook of the magazine, which was supposed to convey the opposite of the bleak image generally associated with Africa. The oversized format of its first issues, its glossy paper, the flawless quality of its prints, its stylish layouts, Simon Njami and Jean-Loup Pivin's disruptive public provocations—everything in *Revue Noire* defined itself as a rebuke issued by a proud and confident, and sometimes arrogant, Africa to a reductionist Western world whose knowledge of Africa was limited to *Art Nègre*, the latter viewed solely from the perspective of primitivism or ethnography. That's why the magazine was groundbreaking.

*Revue Noire* introduced, promoted, and publicized contemporary African artists and photographers throughout the world. It also became a place to meet, and even to create, when artists needed a place to do a photo shoot or film scenes for a video installation. Ever the gracious patrons, Jean-Loup Pivin and Pascal Martin Saint-Léon, the artistic director, held open-door editorial meetings that began with lunch and lasted late into the afternoon. Some artists slept at the magazine when they were passing through Paris. Rejecting the artworld's ethnoracial essentialism, everyone made forcefully clear: "We're not African artists. We're artists. Period." Which didn't prevent them, at openings and other social events, from taking full advantage of their dreadlocks, flamboyant style, and the cheerfulness people so readily associated with Africans to seduce white curators, gallerists, and buyers.

Although the magazine did impressive work on the visual arts, it didn't focus much on film. So I suggested to Jean-Loup and Simon that I write on African cinema, a subject I knew absolutely nothing about. The six years I spent at *Revue Noire*, until it closed its doors in 2000, would prove to be a tremendous education for me, the missing link to my years in Ivory Coast. I watched an incredible number of films. Through the work of sub-Saharan African directors, I came to understand how Africans experienced colonialism, their sense of dislocation, and how difficult it was to find a place for themselves between African tradition and Western modernity. Those were the themes that often framed their perspectives.

Generally considered the first film directed by Africans, *Afrique sur Seine* was a collective feature shot in 1955.[1] The short film, which explicitly takes Paris for the capital of Black Africa, presents a kind of picture-postcard of a metropolis in which immigrant workers and African students come together. Markedly more critical, the Ivorian Désiré Écaré depicts in two of his films (*Concerto for an Exile* and *Take Care, France*) the lost sense of meaning and belonging affecting African students living alone in Paris and portrays the transactional nature of relationships between Blacks and whites. In his 1966 film *Black Girl*, the first full-length feature directed by an African filmmaker, Ousmane Sembène draws inspiration from a local newspaper story in his unsparing account of a French couple's class- and race-based exploitation of their young Senegalese maid. A certain number of films also focus on the Senegalese Tirailleur. The latter returns home, basking in the glory of his French miliary service; he looks down on his fellow countrymen until he realizes that France wants nothing more to do with him. Another frequent theme in the films from the seventies and eighties: young Africans' difficulty reconciling their more individualistic ambitions with a culture based on the life of the community, a community in which the "we" is more important than the "I."

The magazine's wide-ranging themes piqued my interest in Zimbabwean cinema and exposed me to the freedom struggles in southern Africa. I also sought out rare films—rare, at least in Paris—like those from Ethiopia. I tried to draw connections with what was being done in France and England. I also discovered what went on behind the scenes, that is, the conditions in which these films were produced. The cinema of Francophone Africa, to stick to this region alone, was on economic life support. The cultural sector simply wasn't the priority in developing African countries. Except for certain isolated initiatives, such countries didn't invest in filmmaking on the grounds that they lacked the resources or had other priorities. They seem not to have understood that, on the international stage, a country's image is also formed through its culture, or at least through how it chooses to market aspects of its culture to support its economy: luxury goods and food for France, movies and, more broadly, entertainment for the United States, technology and manga for Japan, and nowadays K-pop for Korea. And for Africa?

Aside from wild animals, famines, tribal wars, and coups d'état—all obviously real but filmed and imposed on Africa by non-Africans and omnipresent on screens throughout the world to the exclusion of almost anything else—what had we put forward for others to see?

Until the early nineties, people said Ivory Coast was the Switzerland of Africa. Because the daily news on Ivorian radio and TV at the time opened with a quotation from Félix Houphouët-Boigny, not a week passed without hearing him repeat, "Peace is not just a word, it's a way of life." Money, prosperity, stability: this trinity, long proclaimed by our first president, filled Ivorians with pride and reassured foreign investors until Houphouët's death, when everything collapsed. But hadn't the true hallmark of Ivory Coast, or at least of Abidjan and certain of the country's other large cities, always been what came from society's grassroots, what I would call, to paraphrase Ivorians, the country's *vivancity*? A deep passion for celebration, festivals, performances, the arts and high fashion, humor and glamor, from which a genuine entertainment economy could have emerged, especially in the performing arts. But the Ministry of Tourism's posters preferred selling elephants, which, for my part, I have only ever seen in European zoos. And among the rare Ivorian filmmakers, there was really only Henri Duparc who ventured to capture this effervescence in one of his films, *Rue Princesse*. Maybe because he was the only director to produce his own films with his own money.

At the time, the films from Francophone Africa were essentially financed by the French Ministry for Cooperation, created in 1959 by de Gaulle to take over the work of the Ministry for Overseas France, itself called the Ministry of the Colonies before being renamed in 1946. The nomenclature changed along with French politics, but the relationship remained the same. Although the Ministry's funding resembled a kind of affirmative action to support up-and-coming film industries, it functioned on terms that very rapidly confined African cinema to a parallel track, to a kind of hothouse in which, after a quick bloom, it slowly died. Civil servants based in Paris decided what would and would not be produced in Africa. Among other criteria, they assessed the "Africanness" of the projects they received. That was in fact one of the preconditions for funding: the story had to take place on the African continent. As if African filmmakers were incapable of deciding for themselves how and where they looked at the world. These films, which rarely reached a mainstream audience, or sometimes any audience, traveled a closed circuit of festivals specializing in African cinema.

The system, which is said to have financed two hundred short or feature-length African films between 1960 and 1980,[2] nonetheless enjoyed some relative success in the late 1980s and mid-1990s thanks to the work of several major directors like Souleymane Cissé, Djibril Diop Mambéty, and Cheick Oumar Sissoko, who, despite the Ministry's money, still struggled to finance their films. Taking first place in the race for funding from the Ministry for Cooperation, however, was Idrissa Ouédraogo, who became widely renowned, starting with his International Federation of Film Critics Award in 1989 at Cannes. At *Revue Noire*, Ouédraogo was a turnoff. To our minds, his films personified the "calabash cinema" that we all loathed.

Now, the calabash is the fruit of the calabash tree and is traditionally used in African societies as a container. Thus, a "calabash film" glorifies a timeless Africa, an Africa of villages (at a time when nearly half of the continent lived in cities) miraculously protected from twentieth-century influences, where electricity seems an invention of the future, where, in the vast barren expanses, people walk for hours accompanied by a goat and the ethereal sounds of a kora or balafon. Now, that was exactly the opposite of what interested me. I was still only twenty-four years old. I wanted urban and transgressive, I wanted things that clashed and crashed. For the issue that the magazine devoted to Paris in March 1996, I hoped to discover French versions of Isaac Julien and John Akomfrah; a new Spike Lee; young women directors; and the equivalent of what Lamine Kouyaté, founder of the brand XULY.Bët, represented in the fashion industry, with his afro-aesthetic mixing punk and fetish. In short, I wanted to feature the cutting-edge of cool. I looked high and low. But to no avail. I finally unearthed three young guys who had just directed their first short films. Julien Séri, whose father was a mixed-race Ivorian, who didn't feel any particular connection with Africa, and who was already moving in the direction of advertising and action films. Amobé Mévégué, who in the end preferred journalism. And Jean-Claude Barny, who was patiently making a name for himself in film and television.

Jean-Claude was blessed with a friendship with Mathieu Kassovitz, whose blockbuster film *La Haine* had come out the year before. He and Idrissa Ouédraogo's nephew Adama Ouédraogo, one of the leads on the sitcom *Seconde B*, had created an association called Connus mais Connus, which ran acting classes and served as a casting agency for Black actors. It held very popular short-film screenings in the hip bars around the Bastille. I could tell that things were heating up for Jean-Claude. At the same time, it was hard for me to imagine that a young man who until then had made only a single short film, all in all a fairly conventional one, heralded the revival of French cinema. I changed my strategy.

Having failed to find the next generation of Black men and women directors, I sat down and wrote a script that drew on all the films shot by Africans in Paris since the 1950s. I pictured the directors with a young woman named Akissi, who happened to resemble me to a T—an obvious sign of my own desire to go into cinema. This journey through under-appreciated films, like those directed by Med Hondo and Sidney Sokhona in the seventies, allowed me to appreciate the evolution of Black people's presence in France, from the experience of uprootedness and social struggle to the tentative emergence of a new identity, an identity at once Black and French.

Although I watched a lot of films during my time at *Revue Noire*, I also listened to what people said about cinema in my everyday life. Indelibly etched in my memory were the especially condescending remarks made by a French civil servant, who declared that a very well-known African filmmaker would be nothing without his French cinematographer, "who does all the work." Until then, I wasn't sure that I wanted to take the competitive entrance exam for La Fémis. Studying literature at the Sorbonne suited me just fine. I thought, and I still think, that to be a screenwriter or director, one doesn't necessarily have to go to school. But after hearing this man's remarks, I promised myself that no one would ever be able to talk about me with such condescension. Euzhan Palcy had left for the United States and no other Black French director had taken up the torch. I assumed that I myself would be measured against African directors. France being a country of diplomas, I decided to go to the most prestigious film school the country had to offer. Or not go at all.

# 16 French "Integration"

La Fémis, also known as the École Nationale Supérieure des Métiers de l'Image et du Son,[1] is a Grande École that falls under the Ministry of Culture. Because of its small number of students—sixty per cohort in the core program—the entrance exam is even more competitive than at most other Grandes Écoles, such as Sciences Po, HEC, or Normale Sup. For the general entrance exam, the admission rate is about five percent. A few years before I decided to apply, my best friend had tried and failed. At the time, I'd become very invested in her success—probably too invested. For her "personal exploration" portfolio, the first step she would have to pass in order to continue the four-part exam process, I introduced her to a photographer who used pinhole cameras in his work with children from suburban housing projects. Since I was the only one in our little group with a computer, I typed up the whole portfolio. She was late in sending it off and the deadline was that night, so she, her boyfriend, and I jumped in a cab, praying that we would make it to the Louvre post office before midnight. After all the trouble we went through, my friend's failure at that stage felt like a tragedy. A friend whose one wish was to go into film now had to look for something else. It was a warning: my odds of getting into La Fémis were razor thin. Yet from the moment I made my decision, I never wavered.

Several months before the exam, I enrolled in a one-year program in theater at Censier, part of the University of Paris system, where I contrived the easiest schedule imaginable: very little theory and plenty of practice. When students declared a general strike that closed the university in November and December 1995, they did me a huge favor. Once the university reopened, I simply forgot to go back. Because it was obvious to me by then that if I didn't get into La Fémis, I would start looking for intern work on actual film shoots and learn how to make movies another way.

I passed the first two portions of the entrance exam, then the one specific to screenwriting. Only the oral portion remained. Driven by the vague desire to also be an actor (because why not?), I'd enrolled in private acting classes, which mustn't have been too shabby because most of us students continued on in artistic pursuits. When the examiners announced my name, I remembered my acting teacher's advice: Be present in the space, breathe with your stomach, look the person in the eye, carry your voice, everything calmly, no rushing. Despite my anxiety, I now had to step into the ring. Around it were the seven film professionals who would determine the fate of my application. A chair had been placed behind a desk for examinees. I found the arrangement too academic and too confining. I took the chair and set it down in front of the desk. I was now facing the examiners, unprotected. Marie-Geneviève Ripeau, who was the head of the screenwriting department at the time, later told me that she knew right then and there that she wanted me for the school. Her opinion wasn't universally shared, however, or perhaps the examiners had divided themselves up between good cops and bad, because very quickly they asked me why I wanted to study at a French film school given that I was African and that after La Fémis I would return to work in Africa. I answered as calmly as possible that I was French and that I would work wherever I liked. Ironically, the person questioning me about my roots was himself a foreigner. He was the head of the image department, Charles Van Damme, a Belgian cinematographer who had gained a certain renown working on films by French directors like Agnès Varda and Alain Resnais. He had won a César in 1987, before his dalliance with directing dimmed his star. Did that mean that it was acceptable for him to work in France, but not for me? Not only did my skin color make me a foreigner in his eyes, it also limited me to a single territory: Africa.

I passed the entrance exam. Georges was ever so happy. I had fulfilled one of his dreams by being admitted to a Grande École. It didn't matter that it was a film school. It was a *Grande École*. Along with my mother, he had spent years fighting my desire to work in film, but now suddenly he was repeating to anyone who would listen that his daughter was at La Fémis. I didn't mention the examiner's question about Africa. I didn't want to spoil his fun. In fact, I never had the courage to tell him about the difficulties I encountered because of my skin color, even when it was blatant discrimination, and even when he was indirectly involved.

The previous year, I had decided to move to the fifth arrondissement to be closer to Censier for my acting class. Searching for an apartment stressed me out. I knew that landlords were fussy when it came to references. As usual, Georges was evasive, giving me neither his tax returns nor his pay stubs, or anything else that might explain his income, which he never wanted me to know. His only advice was: When you find something you like, give me the agency's phone number. I'll call them and send them the papers they need.

I went alone to visit the apartments. I didn't really know how things worked. I figured that without a full application already prepared, I would have to present myself particularly well. At the first studio I visited, the landlord stared suspiciously at my Courrèges dress and low-heeled pumps. In her look I could see a thousand doubts about my being a student. Did she take me for a call girl? I revised my approach and went in jeans to my second visit, where a friendly building manager tried to unload an apartment on me I didn't like. I finally came across an ad for the ideal place, a small two-room duplex, facing the inner courtyard, a few steps from Rue Mouffetard. On the telephone, the woman from the agency was very courteous, quite high society. She took down my name and told me to meet her the next afternoon in front of the building. I showed up on time. When she saw me, she brusquely told me we didn't have an appointment. I repeated my name, which I thought she might have written down wrong. She refused to budge and even claimed we had never spoken on the phone. I kept at it, sure that I remembered things right, until she finally relented and let me see the apartment. The renters were still there, a very French couple in their thirties who immediately grasped what was going on. Embarrassed, they ended up showing me the place instead of the real estate agent, who was simply waiting for me to leave.

It was a charming apartment, exactly as I had hoped. I said that I was interested and that my father would be the one paying the rent. The woman asked me haughtily what he did. She was in her fifties. She was thickset. She spoke loudly. Her little mouth with its oxblood lipstick moved fast and jerkily. Everything about her was too emphatic, including her chichi intonation. She was putting me down, but I held my ground. I told her the truth: my father was on several boards of directors. She burst into an operatic laugh, lashing out at me with a scorn she no longer bothered to hide. "Board of directors!" she scoffed. Her laughter filled the room. Under the young couple's troubled gaze, I left the apartment humiliated.

For the whole rest of the afternoon, I brooded, tormented by a feeling of injustice mixed with rage. I had told the truth and I was treated like a liar because, in this woman's narrow mind, a young Black woman couldn't have a well-off father or live in Paris's fifth arrondissement. Of course, once she had made it past her initial rejection, she would have reacted differently if I had revealed to her that my father was white and that I was adopted. But why give her the pleasure?

The discrimination was patent. Despite my anger, however, a little voice in me whispered that I too bore some responsibility. I should have insisted more that my father give me the documents for a proper application, with proof of income and tax forms. I wasn't well dressed enough with my second-hand suede jacket, my long flounce skirt, and rawhide sandals. I didn't know how to play a real bourgeoise. In a way, the woman was right, I wasn't legitimate.

That's the whole problem with discrimination, its perverse effect: unlike what people often think, those who fall victim to it tend to minimize or even ignore it, when they aren't sticking themselves with the blame. We learn at school and elsewhere to take responsibility for our failures. We get a bad grade because we didn't do good work, not because our teacher doesn't like the way we look. In a certain way, it makes discrimination easier to accept. You can say to yourself, I'll do better next time and everything will work out. You're still in control of your life.

Recognizing that you're the victim of discrimination means confronting a whole series of destructive emotions. Beneath the anger lies sadness, beneath the sadness powerlessness, beneath the powerlessness the negation of your very being. Which is what discrimination is: the negation of who I am. Because, clearly, I won't be changing my skin color any time soon. My name was given to me by my family; it marks my place in my family tree. Whatever it might evoke, my name is precious. My gender? My age? What can I do? My weight? That would mean that there is only one valid norm for being socially acceptable.

People who discriminate against me take aim at the core of my identity, denying my right to exist. At least to exist as fully, and with the same status, as them. In doing so, they do me terrible harm.

With Georges, I kept silent about my inner turmoil and confined myself to telling him that the agency woman didn't believe me, and that the next time I really would need all the paperwork. It wasn't reticence on my part. I feared hurting him. Georges had such a high opinion of France I couldn't bring myself to tell him that the country he was so proud of didn't want me. It was enough that he wasn't my natural father. He hadn't passed down his physical features or genes. My surname was only half his; I planned on keeping my biological father's as well. I had stopped riding horses, our one shared passion, and he had taken it as a betrayal. I hadn't gone into any of the careers that he had dreamed that I would. Our views were almost completely opposite. What was left to reassure him and make him feel that, despite everything, he had passed along a bit of himself to me? His Frenchness? His certainty that France was a great and beautiful country that had unreservedly given me a home, just as he had given me a home when I came into his life at the age of two years old? I was already barely his daughter; I couldn't deprive him of this last little bit too.

The summer I was admitted to La Fémis, my cousin (the same one who would later be mistaken for a security guard) began at Sciences Po. That was another big reason for Georges to be proud. He didn't put it this way, but I sensed that for him the fact that we passed the Grande École entrance exams symbolized our integration into the French Republic. To use his own terminology, we did him honor. To honor us in turn, he took my cousin and me to dinner at Lucas

Carton, on the Place Vendôme, one of the most revered restaurants of French haute cuisine. At the time, in 1996, the chef Alain Senderens hadn't yet handed in his Michelin stars (the restaurant had three). I don't know if it was the rigid decorum, the heavy drapes, the double row of servers and maître d's welcoming us at the door, but I felt like I couldn't breathe. At the end of the first course, I passed out. Lying down in a private room upstairs for the remainder of the evening, I couldn't help but think that a part of me was rejecting my Republican integration. At least the version of it I had been offered.

# 17 Where Are You From?

When did I start to use my French nationality? I can't remember the exact moment. At around twenty years old, I imagine.

Before then, Georges must have thought all my visits to the prefecture to renew my student visa were becoming absurd. He took care of the administrative side. I may be mistaken, but I don't think that it was particularly complicated. The simple fact of my adoption hadn't erased my bloodline. Jean-Pierre, my biological father, was born French, in France, from a mother herself born French and a naturalized-French father. I was a full-blooded Frenchwoman, born abroad from at least one French parent. Which didn't prevent me from being Ivorian at the same time. France, like Ivory Coast, allowed dual citizenship.

The day I came home from the city hall with my new passport and ID, Georges called me, as excited as can be: "So, are you happy?" His question caught me off-guard. Happy? Happy about what? About being officially French? I couldn't see why I would be happy about something that was neither more nor less than an accident of birth. I had no more chosen to be French than to be Ivorian or female, just as I hadn't chosen my genes, which in large part determined my health, my emotions, and my IQ. It is one of the many factors that make up who I am, and with which I make myself who I am. I was already French, through bloodlines and the culture in which I grew up. I had a hard time understanding which additional benefits French papers were supposed to confer on me, since no one in France ever spontaneously considered me French.

Paradoxically, it was this recurrent, unprompted denial of my French nationality that would little by little make me value my French citizenship.

"Where are you from?" is no doubt the question the most frequently asked of Black people in France, the question that pops up the most naturally, so often, in fact, that it makes you wonder if it isn't the prerequisite to any conversation at all.

"Where are you from?" asks a friend of a friend at a party, asks the person sitting next to me at dinner, asks the colleague making small talk, asks someone I haven't met in my life. I'm on a beach in Portugal. A young Frenchwoman pounces on me: "Your kids are so beautiful! Where are you all from?" I want to tell her, "From France, like you!" But I know very well that that isn't what interests her. She is asking me where we are from the way she would inquire about the breed of a dog. What kind of crossbreeding could have produced the physical type she finds so exotic?

I attend a fitness class. The instructor, talking about his dream of one day retiring in Senegal, notices me and calls out, "Where are you from?" The question I would like to put to him is why he feels entitled to ask me about my background, because besides "hello" we haven't yet said a single word to each other.

2005. I was a member of the awards panel at the Amiens International Film Festival. Riots had broken out in the city's working-class neighborhoods, once again exposing the discontent of an outcast class of young people of non-European descent. A local politician held forth about these long-marginalized youths, making them out to be pariahs and adding fuel to their anger. He concluded his tirade, turned to me, and as naturally as can be, asked me where I was from.

One of my childhood friends to whom I confided feeling offended by the question's frequency couldn't understand my exasperation. She thought it was normal that people wanted to know about my background when they saw me. For her, it was simply a sign of interest and lacked any racial connotations. In that case, why didn't anyone ask her where she was from? Because she was white, therefore obviously from here? The question had never crossed her mind.

"Where are you from?" is one of the central points at which understanding between white people and Black people breaks down. The latter are fed up with a question that, they know all too well, they are being asked solely because they are Black. The former, in all good faith, just don't understand how this mark of curiosity could be racist.

The American psychologist Derald Wing Sue, drawing on the work of psychiatrist Chester Pierce, provides a definition of microaggressions, observing that after the gains of the civil rights movement, expressions of racism changed, becoming subtler and more ambiguous, and thus more difficult to identify. Racial microaggressions are commonplace words or behavior that, whether intentional or not, convey a hostile, degrading, or insulting message to the person or group concerned. Sue stresses that most of the time those who commit microaggressions don't even realize it.[1]

Since the eighties, when the antiracist organizations LICRA and SOS Racisme[2] convinced the French public that being racist was a bad thing, one would be hard pressed to find many people openly calling Black people monkeys or dirty *nègres* or Arab people ragheads, except among the ranks of the National Front,[3] other extreme right-wing parties, or in what in France is called the "fachosphère," the online community of fascist or fascist-leaning groups generally speaking. Microaggressions, on the other hand, are flourishing. In France, we often refer to cultural or everyday racism.

"Where are you from?" white people ask Black people, without realizing that the question itself entails a hierarchy. I'm from here, the person asking the question implies. I don't have to justify being French; my Frenchness is self-evident. It entitles me to inquire about your origins, you whose skin color tells me you came from somewhere else, you who could never be as French as I am, even if we share the same nationality. Everyone with French citizenship is French. But in the collective unconscious, a person with white skin is more French than anyone else. To ask about origins at the outset implicitly reestablishes a racial definition of national identity.

"Where are you from?" white people ask Black people, and the latter feel immediately thrown out of the national community. If Black people happen to forget the precarity of their situation, the question is there to remind them. Foreigners for life—that is how they are perceived, even when they are French by birth. Because any child of European immigrants will feel more legitimately French than a West Indian will, and that European child will be treated accordingly. Except, of course, if the child is Roma.

The same holds just as true among French politicians. Whatever one may think of their intrinsic qualities, when Rachida Dati and Rama Yade were named government ministers, all people talked about was their ethnicity, even in their own center-right political party. When Christiane Taubira was named Minister of Justice under the socialist President François Hollande, the right wing laid into her, the extreme right called her a monkey, and anti-same-sex marriage protesters threw bananas at her as she passed. In 2017, during the presidential elections, she decided against running in the Socialist Party primaries despite numerous behind-the-scenes calls for her to do so. According to media reports, her specific fear was that she couldn't provide a sufficient bulwark against the far right. I assume that Taubira knew that she was a divisive figure. Not only because of her political ideas or because she was a woman, but also because she was Black. Manuel Valls, a Spanish immigrant who naturalized when he was twenty years old, didn't have the same reservations. He didn't need them. The French weren't going to hurl racist insults at him. Nor would they throw themselves into the arms of the far-right Marine Le Pen to avoid electing a president of Spanish origin. If the French didn't want him, it was for strictly political, and perhaps also personality, reasons.

The same held true for the center-left French politician Arnaud Montebourg, who was open about having an Algerian grandfather. But Montebourg had a French surname. He wasn't Muslim. When young fascists attacked him one night in a Parisian street, it wasn't because of his ethnic background but because he was walking arm in arm with a Black woman, the journalist Audrey Pulvar. Arnaud Montebourg looked white. That was what counted. Once again, we return to a racial definition of French identity.

"Where are you from?" asks W., who is white, of B., who is Black, and the exchange that follows quickly becomes absurd. "From here," says B., who occasionally varies his answers: "From France" or "From [any birthplace located in France, besides its overseas departments and territories, which are considered the outback of

France].” Dissatisfied, W. persists, “But where are you really from? Where are your parents from?”

“From France,” B. replies with the same stubbornness, now determined not to indulge his interlocutor’s underlying query.

“What about your grandparents?” asks W., who has suddenly transformed into an immigration agent.

For my part, albeit with a certain dose of bad faith, I’m ready, if and when I have the energy, to climb to the most remote branches of my genealogical tree if I have to, to continue answering, “from here.” But then a tinge of guilt enters in. What if the person I’m talking to thinks I’m ashamed of my African roots?

W., recognizing the futility of his previous efforts, changes tack and rephrases the question—does he really think his interlocutor misunderstood what he was driving at? Now he asks, “Where are you from originally?” If he still isn’t satisfied, we already know the rest: “Where are your parents from originally?” “And your grandparents?” “What about your great-grandparents?”

When, at last, worn down, I answer, “French and Ivorian,” W. lets out a great sigh of relief: “Ivorian!” His suddenly selective hearing fails to register the word “French.” And for good reason, since he has finally managed to elicit what he was looking for from the start: someplace other than France to connect my Black skin to.

Occasionally, W. is wily. Instead of asking me where I’m from originally, he wants to know where I was born. “In Ivory Coast,” I say. W. frowns, “I thought you were born in France.” Implicitly: “Given your job, the way you behave, your knowledge of our culture, the fact that you speak French without an accent, honestly, I didn’t take you for an immigrant.” The hypocrisy of his reaction is mind-blowing. If W. figured that I was French from the beginning, why did he ask about my birthplace?

This insistence on connecting Blacks to someplace other than France doesn’t arise solely in interpersonal relationships. It is omnipresent in the French public sphere, whether expressed by journalists or politicians, or even sociologists. “Visible minorities,” “diverse people,” “children of immigrants,” “people from immigrant backgrounds,” “second-generation immigrants”—even when they’re third or fourth generation or, for West Indians, the generations go back even further. Any euphemism works as long as it avoids stating explicitly the ethnoracial background of non-white French people. There is this fear that naming race—again, I'm using the sociological meaning of the term—would risk exploding the French universalist model and thus plunge us into the depths of communitarianism. The model, while liberal on paper, proves utterly hypocritical in practice. Nine times out of ten, when people who don't know me refer to me, they mention my skin color. "You saw that tall Black woman . . .": *Tu as vu la grande Black là* . . . Note that they don't say "Noire." In France, in French, people are loath to use the word *Noir* for fear of appearing racist; they prefer the euphemism *Black*. Personally, each time I hear someone call me this, I feel like I've become a marketing brand, a catchphrase. I suspect that to those who use it, *Black* sounds more easygoing, more chill. Yet there is nothing bad or dirty about saying *Noir*. Far be it from me to impersonate the Franco-Spanish Manuel Valls: I'm not about to refer to *les blancs* as "les whites" in French.[4]

The same awkwardness exists when naming Arab-Berber people, who, through a troubling semantic shift, have now all become Muslims, as if a religion could replace an actual physical birthplace. The situation is still worse for Asian people. The result is nonetheless obvious: no one knows how to refer to French people of extra-European descent. So, they turn to convoluted expressions that allude to skin color (visible minority, diverse people). Immigration is used as a benchmark (second generation, from an immigrant background, etc., when and if one avoids, through a terminological slippery slope, the blanket term "immigrants"). Which returns us to the ever-repeated question: "Where are you from?" Instead of concentrating on our Frenchness, the focus here is on a history of immigration that makes us perpetual foreigners. A history that for many of us simply isn't ours.

Or, alternatively, the emphasis is placed on where people live. To refer to a large number of non-white working-class people living in suburban housing projects, people speak of "young people from the neighborhoods," or merely of "*les banlieues*"—shorthand, in both cases, for "problem" areas. The euphemisms are just another way to name us.

This absence of nomenclature, this void in the French language, which might otherwise allow us to apprehend and, more importantly, to speak accurately about French ethnoracial backgrounds, sometimes leads to epic gaffes. For example, the child abduction alert sent out by the Ministry of Justice on October 18, 2016, in which we learned that the authorities were looking for the child's father, a suspect "de race noire," of Black race, wearing glasses, etc. After an immediate public outcry, the alert was changed, mentioning, in a convoluted formulation, a "suspect whose skin color is black."

Amused by the blunder, which spoke volumes about the racial unconscious of the person behind the initial alert, I went back to consult others. The differences in the descriptions were edifying. Most of the time, when the suspect was, I imagined, white, his race or ethnicity wasn't mentioned. When the details were available, his size, hair and eye color, and approximate age were plainly stated. On occasion, the alerts noted that the person was European or Mediterranean. Certain alerts mentioned the "couleur noire" of the potential kidnapper or kidnapped child. There were even times when that was the only description. Other alerts didn't specify skin color, no doubt assuming that the photo accompanying the alert would suffice. Still others spoke of suspects "de type africain," suspects "of African type." *What we conceive with ease, with ease we can express*, says Boileau, the seventeenth-century French poet. Obviously, the people writing these alerts needed an official terminology to make their work easier. The same goes for the rest of the French population, who still has such a hard time calling a Black man *un Noir*.

# 18 Coming Out of the Race Closet

At La Fémis, no one mentioned my racial background. On the contrary, everyone seemed to do their best not to see that I was the only Black student who had successfully passed the entrance exam. The political correctness quickly began to wear on me. Still, I was used to being the only Black person in school. That was the case at my primary school in Paris and at my high school in Bordeaux. At the École du Louvre, there were two of us, a Haitian and me. At the Sorbonne, in a lecture hall of several hundred other first- and second-year French literature students, there were three of us, three girls. So, the situation was nothing new. But at La Fémis, at a school where I was supposed to explore who I was artistically, I felt frustrated by not being able to fully exist as a Black person at the same time. I was just beginning to give up on the illusion of French universalism, just starting to understand that it was constructed on white norms that simply weren't presented as such. I had zero desire to fall back into a process of assimilation. Although I still couldn't quite put it into words, I was looking for a way to articulate the apparently contradictory but ultimately complementary demands that the historian Pap Ndiaye speaks so eloquently about in his discussion of French Black people: "We want to be invisible in terms of our social life such that the injustices and abuses that affect us as Black people are reduced. But we want to be visible in terms of our Black cultural identities and unique and precious contribution to French society and culture."[1]

In my first year at La Fémis, all of our professors—all of them film professionals—were white, of European descent. During our film analysis classes, we examined cinema from around the world.

Not once did we stop off in Africa. For a unit on violence in film, Claire Denis came to show us her film *I Can't Sleep*, based on the life of the serial killer Thierry Paulin. Two years earlier, for my first article in *Revue Noire*, I had asked her if she was afraid of reinforcing certain stereotypes by depicting a Black character on screen who represented absolute evil, Thierry Paulin being of West Indian origin. Claire Denis sensibly answered that protecting minorities through political correctness aggravates the problem. "I prefer to operate in a no man's land," she said. "That's the only place where reflection is possible."[2]

At La Fémis, we had lengthy discussions about the way to film, or not to film, the violence of murder. But no one seemed to notice another form of violence nonetheless very present in Denis's film: the violence of exile, of immigration, and of difference from the norm.

Without a space to be myself, I seized the first opportunity I had to break away. The school had developed a program, called Fiction 16, that allowed us, regardless of our future specialization, to learn about all the different jobs necessary on a film shoot. Three sets were constructed in the school's studios. We each chose one of the sets for a 5-minute screenplay that we would write, direct, and edit. During the shoots, we took turns handling the lighting, sound, and grip duties, supervised by specialists in the field. The school, of course, provided everything, including the 16 mm film.

In the late 1990s, digital hadn't yet replaced analog. Shooting film instead of video was the Holy Grail of every apprentice filmmaker. But anyone who has ever tried to shoot a short film with one's own money knows how expensive film stock is. Having all the necessary equipment available for free and the crew to go with it was an incredible luxury. I look back on our little group—my best friend, her boyfriend, and their friends—and on our dreams of breaking into an industry that seemed inaccessible to us, and I can't help but think that something wasn't right. On the one hand, the school lavished us with all the resources we needed to make a film. On the other hand, to rein in people's egos and reassure students terrified at the prospect of directing, they kept telling us that the whole thing was merely an exercise whose ultimate aim was . . . a shelf in the school's archives. All that work just to sit in a storage closet? What a waste! So I decided to make my own film.

I don't know why exactly but at the time I was interested in human sacrifice, the kind practiced in the secret societies of African witch doctors. From what I understood, by ritualistically appropriating a body or certain bodily organs, they sought to capture a human being's vital principle. I adapted the idea in a experimental short story in which a sculptor and his muse hire a woman ostensibly to serve as a model but actually as part of an erotic ritual, itself the prelude to a sacrifice. The sculptor and his partner were Black. Their victim was white. The Black woman performed the sacrifice. Black. White. The two opposite and complementary halves of the same circle. The film was called *The Genie of Abou*.

By stealing the soul of a woman who is his negative, Abou, the male protagonist, attempts to become omnipotent. The quest for omnipotence, for the plenitude that in theory only a god possesses, is inherently diabolical. In my story, I wanted to suggest that the relationship between Blacks and whites was not the bed of (thornless) roses La Fémis was trying to sell me, but rather cut through with fantasy, desire, hate, and fear. All the things that Lars Von Trier, with his usual perversity, would brilliantly depict in *Manderlay*, his film about slavery.

For the role of Gaëlle, the white model, I wanted a very full-figured actress. I had loved the Virgin Megastore ads with Anne Zamberlan as an over-sized goddess of culture. I dreamed of having her in my film. Thanks to Fred Houessinon, the actor who played the sculptor Abou, I was able to meet her. She told me with the utmost sincerity that she wasn't comfortable enough with her body to act nude in front of a camera. She directed me to a colleague from Allegro Fortissimo, the association she had founded to fight discrimination against people with obesity. Her colleague, Églantine, had never acted. She arrived at La Fémis's terrace, where we had arranged to meet, carrying a suitcase full of photos. We had barely said two words when she took out a large, framed snapshot of herself completely naked facing the camera. I got the message. Églantine had zero problem with nudity. She spoke with a little girl's voice despite being at least forty-five. She had pink skin and blond hair. Églantine was a piece of candy.

But I still had a technical problem. How would I handle lighting Black and white actors without the former disappearing in the shadows of my set?

The general public doesn't usually notice it, but in many films Black actors are less well-lit than white actors. When you see them in half-light or night scenes, their features are partially swallowed up; viewers have a hard time making out their facial expressions. Cinematographers will tell you that lighting Black people is difficult. Which is both an admission of defeat and a force of habit. Everyone knows that black absorbs light and white reflects it. You either need more light for a Black actor or cameras that don't overdo the contrasts, which isn't generally a problem with today's smartphones. Things get complicated when lighting Black and white characters in the same shot. The former require more light, the latter less. When a balance between the two can't be reached, who, in your opinion, gets sacrificed?

I found this particularly striking in Mike Figgis's film *One Night Stand*, where in the actors' love scenes Nastassja Kinski looked magnificent, but I struggled to make out what Wesley Snipes's face was doing. Which was a shame for a film depicting a love story between a Black man and a white woman at a time when showing that in a movie in the United States was still considered risky.

Since I had access to an acclaimed cinematographer, I put the problem to him. There was no problem, he assured me. Most people simply didn't know that instead of adjusting your lighting to the white actors, you adjust it to the Black actors. And if your white actors are overlit, if you don't want them looking like cream cheese, you darken them with makeup.

I couldn't thank him enough for the precious piece of advice. In short, everything was simple. All you needed to do was flip the script and accept the fact that the norm would be Black rather than white for once. The same lesson applies, I suspect, for a slew of other areas of life. In my opinion, it perfectly encapsulates what integration should be: not a minority's one-way efforts to fit into a predefined mold, as is drilled into us every day in France, but a series of two-way adjustments in which the majority has to adapt as well.

Bolstered by this new perspective, I began shooting. When the big studio plunged into darkness and the lights came on, I experienced a moment of grace. Like a childhood dream come true, what I had imagined in my head took shape before my eyes. In the space of a few seconds, everything was perfect . . . I was overcome with emotion. It was at that moment I knew I wanted to become a director.

Several weeks later, my rushes came back. I was about to start editing when the school's Director of Studies called me to her office. She informed me that I wouldn't be able to edit my film. After viewing the rushes, Céclie Decugis, the venerable editor of Godard's *Breathless* and the professor assigned to supervise my work, had decided that what I had shot was racist and unacceptably violent. Since I didn't take things lying down, the school concluded that I would go before a committee, specially created for the occasion, that would make the final decision. Several students very obligingly came to testify against me. I could see why they might be annoyed by my determination to make my short film even if it meant breaking the rules—rules they themselves had followed. I would never have imagined they would go whispering to the administration that I had made an anti-white film. Because that is what I was accused of: shooting a film with a pro-eugenics message. Eugenics was a strong word; it came up several times. On what basis was I being accused? I was told that Frédéric Houessinon and Peggy Ngo Yanga, the two Black actors, were young, good-looking, and had flawless physiques. For the white character, on the other hand, I had chosen a fat woman with a deformed body. They claimed that the cast reflected my desire to affirm the superiority of the Black race over the white race. I was taken aback by the argument's stupidity. Furthermore, why were they talking to me about race in the biological sense?

As heavyset as she may have been, I had always found Églantine beautiful. It was narrow-minded of people to automatically associate corpulence with ugliness. They conceded that, yes, of course, an overweight woman could be beautiful, but that the body of the actress I had chosen was damaged. This time, I understood. Not once had I noticed that Églantine's breasts didn't point up to the sky. And mind you, this was a woman making the observation, someone who clearly nurtured a normative view of what a woman's body should be in order to appear on screen. I looked at my judges. Had they all suddenly developed amnesia? Had they never seen a Fellini film? Unless—and this was the most likely possibility—they didn't credit me with being enough of a cinephile. That afternoon, I was a mean Black woman looking to kill some white people. Which was another thing they called me out for.

Based on my rushes, my professors had concluded that I had treated my sole white character like an object and denied her her humanity. I reminded them that Gaëlle wasn't passive, that she was the one who tells Abou to continue making love to her when he hesitates. I reminded them of her words: "Come on! Keep going!" The committee members looked at each other. If Gaëlle verbally expressed her pleasure and her desire for him to continue, that was because she had agency over what was happening to her. The tide had turned. Someone noted that when she dies at the end, Abou seems genuinely grieved. They recognized a moral dimension to my film. In the end, they allowed me to edit it.

But what kind of morality are we talking about? For me, there was never any doubt: for my censors, it was a great relief when they finally came to the conclusion that, although a couple of Black people kill a white woman, it's the Black people who come out the losers in the end. If all the characters had been white, there wouldn't even have been a discussion. The most they would have said was that my story was a bit violent. So, yes, morality was saved, the kind that told you that you couldn't portray white people with impunity if you aren't white yourself. It didn't matter that my own interpretation had nothing to do with theirs, that what interested me was exploring the tension between the dominant and the dominated, knowing that those who dominate only exist because the dominated exist, and that without the latter, the former are nothing. The dynamics between the two raises the question of real power, even when the terms are reversed, as was the case in my short film, which more bluntly approached the mechanics of their relationship. That is precisely what James Baldwin is talking about in the television interview in Raoul Peck's superb documentary: "I am not a nigger, I am a man. But if you think I'm a nigger, it means you need him. [. . .] [T]hen you've got to find out why."[3]

That was how I came out of the race closet, how, for the first time, I stated loud and clear that I was Black, that it wasn't easy for me to live in a world of whites, and that, yes, at a visceral level, I could feel anger and wanted to express it.

Later, after having seen the film edited, Cécile Decugis apologized for having caused unwarranted trouble for my project. The irony was that my DIY short film, which should only have been an exercise for school, was noticed by a film journalist and sent to the Créteil International Women's Film Festival. After bitter negotiations—because until then La Fémis had never allowed first-year students to show their work in public—the school agreed to let me create a projectable print of *The Genie of Abou*. Then there was a version with English subtitles. Then it was selected for some thirty festivals around the world. Even academics weighed in. And one day, I received a call from the journalist and TV personality Michel Field's assistant, asking me to join the philosopher Michel Serres and the actress Brigitte Lahaie on his primetime show to discuss France's "new sexuality." How had they known about my film? Why had they invited someone so completely unknown? I didn't have the chance to ask. At the last minute, I decided not to go on *La Marche du Siècle*. To the great disappointment of my family in Gaillac, who had seen my name in the TV weeklies and had already invited friends and family to watch. But that's another story.

# 19 Good Hair

After directing *The Genie of Abou*, I shaved my head like the actress in my film. Was it a symbolic gesture? In fact, and more simply, because of straightenings, ill-timed colorings, and blow drying, my hair was wrecked. A girlfriend had told me to shave it all off and grow it back. When I came out of the salon hairless, I felt an extraordinary sense of freedom. I felt the breeze blowing on my head, every variation in temperature, as if I were at one with the elements. Suddenly, this forgotten part of my body was alive.

Having a shaved head was much less frequent in 1997 than it is today. People stared at me in the street. Girls started to hit on me in the metro, assuming I was a lesbian. Some asked me if I had had chemotherapy. Several Africans offered their condolences, since shaving one's head is generally perceived as a sign of mourning. The baker called me "sir." In the end, that may have been what I was looking for: a different way of asserting my femininity.

I've always been very feminine. I started wearing makeup and heels at a young age. I liked beautiful dresses, fuchsia pink, and costume jewelry. I sat with my knees pressed firmly together, made sure that I didn't speak too loud and always had impeccable manners, all the things that young girls are taught so that they stay in their place. My laugh, on the other hand—no one was ever able to reign it in. The determination I needed to complete *The Genie of Abou* allowed me to tap into another, more assertive part of myself, what others might call my masculine side. Exposing my bare face, going without the embellishment that hair offers a woman, was a way to affirm my newfound strength. I would remain feminine, I would still be a woman, but on my own terms. With one not insignificant benefit that I hadn't expected: men found me more appealing. My nape, laid bare and vulnerable, as if already undressed, unsettled them.

Cutting my hair, which was artificially straight because of the products I used, made me question the treatments I had been putting myself through since early adolescence to hide my naturally kinky hair. All women have a complicated relationship with their hair, regardless of their race or ethnicity. Asian women deplore their straight hair. Arab women think theirs is too curly. White women, depending on the fashion of the moment, find their hair too straight or too curly, too fine or too thick. Not to be outdone, men recoil in horror at the first sign of a bald spot. But no one, whatever their gender, hates their hair as much as Black women. To the point where the word "crépu"—"kinky" in English—is actually avoided in conversation. We prefer euphemisms, saying that we have very curly or difficult hair. Difficult to do. Difficult to like. Difficult to accept.

From our earliest childhood, anxious eyes survey our heads, trying to discern in our first curls what texture our hair will ultimately have. The initial glimmers of hope are generally disappointed: Black or mixed-race children are born with lighter skin and straighter hair than they later end up with. Mothers gloating over their newborn's dainty ringlets have to face a new reality when the child turns one: the curls have tightened, the Cs have become Zs, their child won't be saved, she will have the same kinky hair as her ancestors and her ancestors' ancestors.

Why this loathing of kinky hair? In photos from the early twentieth century, African women had extraordinarily elaborate hairstyles, specific to each ethnic group, that showed off the unique nature of their hair. Fifty years later, as colonization came to end, they were all wearing wigs.

The same was true for West Indian women. When I was a teenager, all the stars of zouk, with the exception of the singer Jocelyne Béroard, had long, straight or curly manes of hair. I concluded that, due to creolization, West Indian women naturally had light complexions and mixed-race hair—the two often going hand in hand. I was very surprised on my first visit to Guadeloupe to see so many people with African features and straightened (that is, originally kinky) hair. Like African women, West Indian women in early-twentieth-century photographs still have their natural hair, beautifully arranged. Even when they lived in France, West Indian women attended public dances wearing traditional madras dresses and headscarves. What happened in the meantime? The same thing that happened in the United States and Brazil. Upon contact with whites, Black women began to dislike their hair.

In Africa, women as well as men spent a lot of time on their hair. It represented an important moment of sociability and intergenerational cultural transmission. But slavery destroyed that shared know-how. Africans were imprisoned, subjected to the intense pace of plantation work, and deprived of their hair tools and natural products and of the necessary time to use them such that they could no longer take proper care of their hair, which inevitably deteriorated. (Anyone who has kinky hair knows how quickly it gets tangled and damaged if you don't take care of it daily.) Women became accustomed to covering their hair with tightly knotted pieces of cloth, in other words, they got used to hiding it. Aesthetic norms were transformed. As soon as they landed in the New World and were put up for auction, Africans were subjected to the judgment of whites, who inspected their skin, teeth, and hair to determine their commercial value.

> This meticulous examination of hair and bodies, which months of neglect had damaged, communicated to prisoners more clearly than words ever could that they were different. White people's reactions during these humiliating inspections conveyed to Africans the contempt for and rejection of Black skin and hair already visible in the slave traders' eyes.[1]

It makes me think of all the pejorative references to sheep's wool that people still make today—except, of course, when they prefer the more up-to-date version of comparing kinky hair to steel wool or a toilet brush.

On the plantations, it seems, female slave masters gave their used combs and brushes to their slaves. Gone was the African wide-tooth comb; the European fine-tooth became the standard by which to judge one's hair quality. "Good" hair passed through the comb's narrow teeth—in other words, it was "good" because it was most like European hair. As the sociologist Juliette Sméralda writes, once "torn from the environment that gave African aesthetics its full meaning, Blacks were prevented from transmitting their sense of beauty, their sense of self-worth, and their self-esteem through a process of shared recognition."[2] Sméralda even speaks of a collective trauma related to kinky hair.

In the United States, the end of slavery was followed by the exodus of several million Black people to the large industrial cities of the North. They moved from a rural way of life to an urban and almost exclusively white environment. During that time, the use of the straightening iron began to spread. Straightening one's hair meant both affirming an urban sophistication and integrating more easily into the world of whites. Former slaves, whether American, Caribbean, or Brazilian, understood that the closer one's physical features were to those of whites, the better one's social status. Slaves with light brown skin got out of hard work in the fields and were more readily employed as servants. They benefited from somewhat less harsh living conditions, even if their proximity with whites sometimes became sexual promiscuity, since masters appreciated having slaves as concubines, when they didn't simply rape them. Hence was born a mixed-race caste that long preferred endogenous marriages to preserve its color privilege. Blacks themselves established a socioracial scale going from the darkest to the lightest, from the least desirable to the most coveted. For evidence of this, one need only look at the incredible inventiveness of Creole when designating the level of melanin in people, including these two expressions I find truly awful: "lapo sové" or "lapo chapé"—literally, people who have "escaped from their skin," whose "skin is saved," because they were born with light skin.

Along the same lines, in Jamaica, a young woman with fairly dark skin told me that in her family people suggested she "put a little milk in her coffee," in other words, marry a light-skinned man so that she would have children whose skin color would be more acceptably brown.

If you didn't have light skin or didn't want to get cancer from lathering yourself in whitening cream, you could always straighten your hair. Little did it matter if the iron burned whole swaths of hair and scalp in the process, the results were worth it. The stakes were clear as day: people increased their chances of survival by finding a way out of segregation in whatever way they could, whether segregation existed merely in practice or was codified in the country's laws, as was the case in the United States.

Although the complex tied to kinky hair especially affects women, in the early twentieth century, American men weren't spared. Just look at the pictures of Black jazz musicians of the time: they all have neat wavy slicked-back hair. For their "conks," they applied a homemade mix of lye, potatoes, and eggs, which burned dreadfully. In his autobiography, Malcolm X, who was still Malcolm Little at the time, describes his first conk:

> The congolene[3] just felt warm when Shorty started combing it in. But then my head caught fire.
>
> I gritted my teeth and tried to pull the sides of the kitchen table together. The comb felt as if it was raking my skin off.
>
> My eyes watered, my nose was running. I couldn't stand it any longer; I bolted to the washbasin. I was cursing Shorty with every name I could think of [. . .].[4]

But Malcolm was rewarded for his suffering when he saw the results in the mirror: "my head was this thick, smooth sheen of shining red hair—real red—as straight as any white man's.

"How ridiculous I was! Stupid enough to stand there simply lost in admiration of my hair now looking 'white,' reflected in the mirror in Shorty's room. I vowed that I'd never again be without a conk, and I never was for many years."[5]

In 1954, George E. Johnson, once a poor boy from Mississippi, improved the process by creating a chemical relaxer for men. In 1957, he launched a version for women. Cold straightening, instead of with an iron, was officially born. Johnson became a millionaire, the first Black entrepreneur to have a company listed on the American Stock Exchange. Brands multiplied. Product lines exploded. Millions of Black men, women, and children throughout the world were inundated with the new products. Like their do-it-yourself predecessors, industrial straighteners contained lye, which is particularly caustic on the hair and scalp. Not to mention the awful smell. Chris Rock's hilarious film *Good Hair*[6] shows how much Black women will suffer through to avoid kinky hair. A chemist in his documentary is genuinely surprised that people put lye on their heads. He shows its effects on a piece of meat and on soda cans dipped in a solution of sodium hydroxide (the scientific name for lye). The cans simply dissolve.

Later in the twentieth century, hair relaxers without lye came out. They were supposed to be gentler, without the burning. For my part, I've never felt the difference. Hair straightening is an ordeal. After coating your scalp and ears with Vaseline or any other ultra greasy cream allegedly meant to protect them, the hairstylist applies the chemical relaxer to first the roots and ends of your hair. Then the nightmare begins. After a few minutes, if your scalp is in the least sensitive, you feel the burning sensation described by Malcolm X. You want to cry. You fight the impulse to dunk your head in the sink. Suddenly, the hairstylist is a coach, urging you to keep going. C'mon, five more minutes, ten more minutes, you're going to make it! Otherwise, it won't work!

"It won't work." Your hair will still be kinky! The word blazes in red in your brain. You think of the money you're spending, of your irrepressible desire to finally have the straight hair of Rihanna's latest style, of the inches in length you'll gain. Your mind is quickly made up. You clench your teeth and watch the seconds tick by. When the burning sensation is finally too much, you beg for mercy, trying to ignore the disappointed look of the stylist, who really thought you were stronger than that. The sensation of water on your flaming head is at once a relief and a torture. But the vision of your straight hair, a third longer than it had been before, makes you forget everything, until, several days later, the scabs that form where your scalp was burned remind you of your recklessness. But two months later, you're at it again. "I'm on the creamy crack," says one of the young women interviewed by Chris Rock. "I'm addicted to relaxer."

Nonetheless, even when your hair is relaxed, you still aren't in the clear. Although chemical relaxers have been sold as a major advance, an irreversible process that allows Black women to attain, once and for all, the straight hair of Western women, the advertising,

I can assure you, is false. Relaxed hair will never look like white women's hair. It doesn't give your hair that rising and falling motion that we've all admired in the movies, on TV, or in nightclubs, the moment when a white girl strides onto the dance floor and waves her hair around, tossing it to the right, the left, the right, the left, up, and down. You'll never see a Black girl dance like that with her hair. Kinky hair grows horizontally, not vertically. It forms a compact mass that can't be thrown around. When straightened, it hangs there stupidly, straight and flat, with no bounce, and needs daily blow-drying to bring it back to life.

After twenty minutes in front of the mirror shaping your hair, you aren't going to waste the effort playing cute on the dance floor. You dance with your hips, with your behind, with your breasts if you have to, but you leave your hair where it is. You don't dive headfirst into the pool. You dip your pinky toe with a dignified air and declare the water too cold to swim in. Or you doggy paddle, your neck above the waterline, head raised, to minimize the damage. You *know* that water is disastrous for your hair and that if it comes in contact with water, you can say goodbye to the straight and the smooth, your clumpy hair will return with a vengeance, shrunk by an inch or more until your next blow-dry. When it rains, you take cover. You never go out without your umbrella or, like me, you always have a scarf in your bag to put over your head just in case, *en cas de cas*, as Ivorians say. If, like me, you like wearing black, people who pass you in the street think that your scarf is a veil. Their wary looks give you a glimpse of how ostracized women who actually wear a veil feel. On the other hand, you attract the insinuating smiles of many French Arab men. Anything for your straightened hair. You obviously refuse motorcycle rides and, more broadly, any activity requiring you to wear a helmet. There too, you *know*. A helmet will destroy your hair. And when you take the helmet off, you'll never be able to casually shake out your hair to give it back its bounce and volume. Your hair will stay plastered to your head. And if you've sweat even a little bit, your frizzy friends will be there to greet you. In other words, you behave yourself, as prim as a Sunday-school teacher, forgoing some or all of your freedom. Then, two months later, when you start to see your "real" hair growing back, obsessed by the vision of straightness, you return to the salon. After so many treatments, your hair breaks at its roots and ends. Your scalp gets flaky. You're losing your hair. But you keep at it. If needed, you hide your hair with a wig or a weave—a technique in which pieces of artificial or real hair (sold, in this case, by Indian or Brazilian women on the other side of the world) are sewn directly onto a person's braids. It makes no difference that your own hair is slowly dying; you never liked it anyway.

No one made me straighten my hair. Not consciously, anyway. Obviously, I always saw Danièle with straight hair and, whether in Paris or Abidjan, she only went to European hair salons. She always took good care of my hair, using the right products she special ordered, and without ever referring to them in a negative way. Although no one made fun of my hair at school, camp was hell. Left in the untrained hands of my white camp counselors, who always gave up anyway, my hair was transformed into an embarrassing knot-laden mess. Then there was my first cousin: between her hair and mine, there was no comparison. She had the long sinuous hair of a Tahitian that fell in bluish-black waves all the way down her back. She got so fed up with people talking to her about her hair that she kept it in tight buns day and night to conceal its splendor. I was appalled by the wasted opportunity. If nature had endowed me with hair like hers, I would have flaunted it shamelessly. Instead, I had to make do wearing the same pigtails, ponytails, or braids day after day—there was no question of leaving my afro as it was. On the cusp of adolescence, I was so tired of these little-girl styles that I started wishing with all my might for a miracle that would make me seem cool. As luck would have it, Michael Jackson came into my life and my wish was granted.

The release of *Thriller* was a worldwide explosion whose shockwaves reached Ivory Coast in 1983. Michael Jackson's oily ringlets, which he had already worn on his first album, *Off the Wall*, popularized the Jheri curl. In France, it was called *le curly*. For me, it was either *le curly* or death. Danièle preferred I get a *curly*, which involved a highly corrosive chemical process that loosened curly hair before assailing it with perm rods. To maintain the wet-curl effect, the hair had to be completely saturated with ultra-greasy activator. Watch the satire of the Jheri curl in *Coming to America*,[7] specifically the scenes with the "Prince of Soul Glo" and the famous sight gag in which three members of the same family get up from a couch, leaving three oily head prints behind them. You'll understand just how ridiculous the style was.

The hairstylist who did my Jheri curl mustn't have been a specialist, because when I look at pictures of me from the time, I have a big afro ball on my head from which only a few vague oil-dripping curls appear. Nothing like Michael Jackson's cascading ringlets. But I was happy—and required to constantly wipe my neck to prevent the activator from dripping on my clothes. Without knowing it, I was sucked in. Danièle, too. Until then, she had always been opposed to my having my hair straightened but she accepted that I have it detangled—in other words, that I have a relaxing treatment that didn't actually straighten my hair but softened its texture. One day, the same less-than-talented hairstylist got the treatment time wrong and I left the salon with straight hair. I was beyond happy. Now I could put in rollers and give myself the same "leonine" hairstyle immortalized by the singers Kim Wilde and Bonnie Tyler and the actresses on *Dallas* and *Dynasty*. It was a rite of passage. I was entering the big leagues. At last, my hair matched what I saw in the French press, movies, TV shows, and music videos. I was finally part of the norm. I had "good hair." And, I should add, the good luck that it was strong and abundant.

Even straightened, my hair always kept its volume. In a superbly ironic twist, Parisian girls stopped me in the street to ask me where I went for my weave. The pain had clearly been worth it! But these encounters were revealing. Black women are so convinced that they have horrible hair that when they see a girl who isn't mixed race with hair they find attractive, they assume that it can't be hers.

Most young Black girls and women who straighten their hair do it for less frivolous reasons than mine. They want to avoid their classmates' teasing. They feel ugly. Their mothers, deprived of the tools and knowledge of previous generations, simply give up when confronted with their daughters' tangled mop of hair. Black girls and women want to be better accepted, better loved, including by Black men. They've internalized the idea that they have to straighten their hair in order to reassure their potential employer and land the job they want, because in the world of whites, Black hair is unwelcome.

It was with good reason that American civil rights activists and followers of the Black Power movement started wearing afros in the sixties and seventies. It was a symbol that announced their rejection of white oppression. They took up James Brown's slogan "Say it loud—I'm Black and I'm proud," by showing that ideals of African beauty also had aesthetic value. But above all, by wearing afros, they let it be known, without even needing to express it verbally, that from then on they would be acting according to their own rules and not those of white America. Their hair quite literally stood up to white power.

In the Nigerian author Chimamanda Ngozi Adichie's novel *Americanah*, the narrator remarks during Barack Obama's first presidential campaign in 2008, "Imagine if Michelle Obama got tired of all the heat and decided to go natural and appeared on TV with lots of woolly hair, or tight spirally curls. [. . .] She would totally rock but poor Obama would certainly lose the independent vote, even the undecided Democrat vote."[8] Yes, if Michelle Obama had shown her afro hair, Barack Obama wouldn't have been elected or reelected. She would perhaps have been compared to Angela Davis, whom the FBI long considered a terrorist. She would have been perceived as dangerous, anti-system, vindictive, and her husband would have been too, through a kind of hair contagion. From the outset of Barack Obama's campaign, the conservative media had already been pegging her as an "angry Black woman," a very fashionable American stereotype that labels Black women as outspoken, bossy, and full of resentment. In 2008, the political columnist Cal Thomas complained on Fox News about the possibility of having an angry Black woman as First Lady. Implicitly: a woman who deep down wants revenge against whites. Now, to get elected, Obama had to reassure the white majority. His wife's straight hair helped. It also revealed that the brilliant female attorney had internalized the dominant norm from an early age—it was only in childhood photos that we saw her with natural hair. Or later, by accident, in pictures of her on vacation after her husband left office.

Kinky hair raises another difficulty: finding a suitable professional in France who knows how to take care of it. The cliché of the undocumented African doing hair in a dingy salon in Paris's predominantly immigrant neighborhoods may delight fans of the exotic, but not Black consumers who prefer to have their hair done in better conditions. But in Paris a clear line separates Blacks from whites when it comes to hair. I discovered it at my own expense when I was still living in the fifth arrondissement. I was in a hurry and didn't have the energy to take the metro to the other side of town. So I walked into the salon of a well-known franchise for a quick wash and dry. Despite my relaxed (read: straight) hair, they answered curtly that they couldn't do it. Luckily, I ended up finding a little salon in the eleventh arrondissement run by a Togolese mother and daughter whose motto was: "We do anyone's hair as long as you've got hair to do."

One summer, to get some practice with the camera (I was still a student at La Fémis), I decided to do a documentary about the Togolese daughter, Marceline. This was shortly after the World Cup in 1998. France, they told us, was now *black-blanc-beur*, Black, white, and Arab, in other words, multiracial. The soccer stars Zinedine Zidane, Marcel Desailly, and Lilian Thuram had become the icons of successful integration into French society. I wanted to explore the reality of integration through the everyday life of this small family salon, a destination for neighborhood locals whatever their skin color or hair type, just as the sign said. Marceline, who had earned a professional hairdressing certificate, told me that in France the program didn't include training with Afro-textured hair. I shot this short documentary in 1999. In 2007, afro hair was still absent from the curriculum. After pressure from a former L'Oréal executive who took an interest in the issue, it should, according to certain articles in the press, be included soon. Overlooking kinky hair is not only bad business—Black women spend a lot of money having their hair done—it also deprives stylists who work with hair of this type of truly professional training. And leads to the curious segregation of white and Black stylists, with the former doing white customers' hair in salons effectively reserved for whites and the latter handling the hair of their fellow Blacks.

For me, the situation was indicative of the mindset of a country that continues to think according to a single ethnoracial norm and leaves non-whites marginalized. Given that professional training programs are established by the French Ministry of Education in consultation with its professional commissions, one might have thought that, in the republican spirit of inclusion, those programs would have reflected the diversity of the population and considered the needs of French overseas departments and territories. That wasn't the case.[9] A field as seemingly frivolous as hair demonstrated the limits of French universalism, which is universal in name only—unless one believes that whiteness is indeed universal.

After spending around twelve years with a shaved head, I finally wanted to let my hair grow out. Adamantly opposed to straightening, which for me had become a symbol of cultural alienation, but still secretly dreaming of long, opulently curly hair, I opted for a mid-length afro. I had no idea how to care for kinky hair. When I was little, Danièle took care of it for me. I stumbled onto the internet forum *Boucles et Coton* (Curls and Cotton), which no longer exists but had its moment of underground glory in the aughts.

Girls with exquisite pseudonyms employed esoteric terms like "big chop," "no poo," 4a, 4b, and 4c. They recorded with maniacal care the number of days since they had cut their relaxed hair, exchanged recipes for organic products to hydrate it, and posted pictures of the latest afros they were trying out. I didn't know it, but I was witnessing the beginnings of the *Nappy* movement in France, *nappy* being both the English translation, albeit historically derogatory, of the French word "crépu," and a portmanteau of the English words "natural and happy."

Imported from the United States and spreading to Africa, the natural hair movement encourages Black women to return to their natural hair and includes icons like Solange Knowles (Beyoncé's sister), Lupita Nyong'o, and Erykah Badu. In France, one of the founding acts of the movement was the creation in Paris in 2004 of a natural-hair salon exclusively for Black women, Boucles d'Ébène, Ebony Curls, by two sisters of West Indian descent, who themselves had gone through the torment of straightening. Boucles d'Ébène was an immediate success and has become a genuine cultural center, where one is as likely to talk hair as literature, and where self-esteem is put front and center. As Juliette Sméralda observes,[10] wearing one's natural hair has become something that people notice, a fashion statement, whereas it ought to be the norm for Black men and women.

Although the natural hair movement no longer conveys the same direct political activism as the afro did in the sixties, it nonetheless retains a certain militant charge. White people rightly have ambivalent reactions to kinky hair. In France, some find kinky hair funny. Others find its texture so unique that they plunge their hands into it without bothering to ask permission. Others are immediately put off by hair so different from theirs. But they are all forced to react, and some get upset. Because what this Black man and woman with natural hair is telling them is that they are no longer playing the game, no longer following the tacit rules defined by the white majority. Forget assimilation. Never-ending compromises. Backs bent. From now on, you are going to have to deal with who we are, as we are, without the mask we wear to try to make us more acceptable to you. We've stopped giving you the power to define who we are.

The norm is resilient, of course. And it doesn't need much to stay that way. The majority of Black women and men have internalized the idea that straight hair is a "symbol of status and prestige," whereas kinky hair, in the same way as Black skin, is part of a "devalued social identity."[11]

Who would take pride in having a devalued identity?

Have you ever seen female members of an Air France cabin crew with kinky hair or even braids? How about French TV news anchors? Things may have changed in certain areas, since in 2017 we had a Miss France for the first time—a woman from French Guiana—who on certain official occasions sported a beautiful kinky afro. But in the world of business, what possibility do Black women executives have of wearing their natural hair without breaking corporate codes?

With the exception of certain artists, antiracist activists, and the rare Misses and fashion models, the only Black women in the French public sphere we see with non-straightened hair are politicians on the left: Christiane Taubira and the former deputy and minister George Pau-Langevin. Neither made a secret of the activism motivating their return to their roots. Christiane Taubira explained that when she first ran for deputy in Guiana, her opponents would ask voters, "You're not really going to elect someone with braids?!"[12] She was elected. She even became a government minister. But it was only when she was in Guiana that, both literally and figuratively, she let her hair down.

Accustomed to spending five minutes a day on my hair when my head was shaved, I have to admit that I quickly had enough of devoting several hours a week to taking care of it. I find that the demand for perfection placed on women and the time they spend responding to that demand— the waxes, manicures, styling, and makeup—not to mention the fortune they spend to enrich the beauty industry, is a great way to keep them busy on something other than the pursuit of their own ambitions. In the meantime, men advance. Rather than trimming their cuticles, they tend to their careers.

One evening, for my birthday dinner, I wasn't sure how to do my hair. So, I ran to the nearest store, bought myself clippers, and shaved it off again—the same hair that I had just spent several years growing back. Then, after my children were born, I wanted to straighten it. Then I wanted a mix of shaved and straightened. Then a combination of kinky hair on the side and relaxed on top. Then braids. My own fickleness led me to reconsider what had been my staunch belief that straightening was a sign of alienation. I'm more open now to getting my hair straightened because I do so intentionally, fully aware that it damages my hair, and that sooner or later I'll have to shave it off and return to my true nature. I straighten my hair less and less often, however, because the process is really too toxic.

In theory, my children won't have the same worries. My daughter has long, fine, curly hair no different from many white girls'. One day, my French Moroccan tailor, surprised as he looked back and forth at my head and my daughter's, asked rhetorically, "How did she get such wonderful hair?!" His heartfelt remark struck me as funny. It didn't flatter me, but he was saying aloud what the looks in the street expressed silently. Another time, we were in a restaurant: a white woman with tight curly black hair stared at my daughter's chestnut brown locks, repeating to her partner in a wounded tone, "Can you imagine, my hair is curlier than hers!" Her inferiority complex pierced through the armor in those few words. It wasn't unreasonable to think that, because of her hair, this woman, perhaps of Italian, Portuguese, or Spanish descent, had suffered the rejection usually reserved for "dirty immigrants." Or maybe it was that a partially Black child was challenging her fragile whiteness by being, in this respect, whiter than her.

I've come to the conclusion that it's decidedly complicated for women to feel pretty, and that there is absolutely no need to add new demands to the many already placed on us. I simply hope that women who straighten their hair will do so more out of a sense of playfulness—to experiment with their appearance from time to time, the way people sometimes change the way they dress—rather than as a rejection of their "Black" side.

# 20 Alphonse's Dilemmas

Let's return to my grandfather. Was he acculturated? Definitely. Assimilated? The Toulouse prefecture said as much in his application for citizenship. How did he handle belonging both to France and to Ivory Coast, to the people of the colonizers and to the people of the colonized? I simply don't know.

Given his background, I suspect that the speed and brutality with which the new colonial order established itself, the bloody repression with which even the slightest resistance in Ivory Coast was met, left him, like so many others, stupefied. A collective shock to which he managed to successfully adapt but from which he was never completely free. People are often surprised that even after its independence, Ivory Coast remained a willing vassal state of France. But Houphouët, like Alphonse, like a large portion of the young Ivorian political elite at the time, couldn't imagine a future outside the French fold. France had convinced them of its power and their fragility. The rare times Houphouët really tried to break away, when, for example, he created the Democratic Party of Ivory Coast (PDCI), allying himself with the French Communist Party, or later, in the late eighties, when he withheld the country's cocoa supply—Ivory Coast being the world's leading producer—in an attempt to raise prices on the world market, he was so severely brought to heel that he quickly fell back in line.

My grandfather thought anti-colonialists were unrealistic. Convinced of France's dominance and of the need to work within their relationship for a long time to come, he favored gradual self-government. He nonetheless had a very critical, disillusioned view of colonialism. In a dialogue in my grandmother's manuscript, she records him saying:

"Imagine someone from the bourgeoisie in 1900. He thinks he rules the world, he believes in progress. For him, Africa is the complete opposite. He sees a continent fraught with war and superstition and plagued by poor, unexploited land."

"The jungle, you mean!"

"In the name of reason and Christianity, at the dawn of this new century, these people must be provided with the wisdom of Civilization and the fruits of Western technology."

"Sure, I understand. People waved the flag of charity to hide their enormous profits."

"Black troops were considered military assets."

"So that explains the colonial monopolies and plenty of other kinds of exploitation, right?'

"Can I continue? The start of the colonial period varied from place to place, with French rule established between 1880 and 1900. In 1920, the trade economy began—the cultivation of timber, palm oil, and rubber. In the 1920s, cities were created. And the farming of cocoa and coffee and other new crops led to new social classes."

"Your father didn't become part of a new social class until 1920?"

"Of course not. Don't be silly. Chiefdoms had always existed. But since natives were asked to pay taxes, they had to be given the means to do so, hence the need to either build plantations or go to work on European ones [. . .]."

"And the missionaries, what did they do?"

"They destroyed our fetishes and baptized the little pagans, like me. For the greater glory of God."

Was he being ironic or did he really believe the missionaries' propaganda? Going by my grandmother's manuscript, Alphonse had enthusiastically converted to Catholicism.

Given the care with which African societies of the time chose a child's name, the name's many symbolic meanings, and the importance of its place in the family line, I'd gotten it into my head that the change from Boni to Alphonse was a blow to my grandfather—a form of dispossession. I'd also imagined that his religious conversion was no more than a formality, an opportunistic means to an end, and that it was only later, during the solitude of his middle-school years in Angoulême, that genuine faith came to him. But according to Rose-Marie, none of that was true.

Due to a convergence of factors, when the young Boni arrived at Bingerville's upper primary school in southern Ivory Coast in the twenties, he hadn't yet been baptized. Despite this, he was proud to show off his catechism certificate, the proof of his knowledge of the Old and New Testaments. The schoolmaster sent him to the missionary in charge of the students' religious education, Father Darius Duhil, who belonged to the Society of African Missions. "No sooner had they met," writes Rose-Marie, "than a spirit of friendship developed between the boy and the priest. He was enrolled in singing class." Father Duhil had created a choir in Bingerville. He had also laid the foundations for a Catholic clergy in the country. After his definitive return to France for health reasons, he made his house in Paris an "annex of Ivory Coast," where he "happily provided a place to stay to young Ivorians newly arrived and disoriented in France, offering them guidance and overseeing their studies." My grandmother describes him as a young priest who gave himself "passionately" to Africa and its children. "In his colleagues' eyes, he passed for having bold ideas, assuming there is something bold about his wanting to turn the children in his care into an elite." A week later, the priest decided to baptize my grandfather, although not without first subjecting him and the other unbaptized boys to a brief test of their knowledge.

> The exam day came. The students were gathered into Bingerville's little church, which to them looked like a cathedral.
>
> "Boni, stand up. What is a sacrament?"
>
> "A sacrament is a perceptible sign."
>
> "And a perceptible sign is?"
>
> "One perceived by all the senses."
>
> "And a sense is?"
>
> "A census counts all the people so we know the population."
>
> The priest burst out laughing, followed by the students, even those who hadn't understood. Had Boni been able to blush, he

> would have turned crimson. He was convinced that he had said something so foolish that it was all over: his baptism would be put off to the following year. The verdict wasn't long in coming. Father Duhil read down the list of those who had passed. Boni's heart pounded wildly; then he heard his name. The priest turned to him and said, "You'll study the questions a little better next time, won't you? Now, what name have you chosen for your baptism?" Without hesitating, Boni answered "Alphonse." The following Sunday, Boni Ehouman became Alphonse Boni and received his baptism.

Because of the clever rhetoric that made Catholicism inseparable from education—that is, from the promise of emancipation—it seems my grandfather had no qualms about casting off a part of his African identity. It was with enthusiasm, perhaps even fervor, that he threw himself into his new religion.

Similarly, when he arrived in France in 1924, there wasn't an ounce of resistance in him, as if the country whose soil he was setting foot on for the first time wasn't the same country that had humiliated his family back home in Ivory Coast. In Alphonse, the Jesuits were getting a fresh piece of clay, a young man eager to learn everything about this new world that impressed him so much.

My grandfather always told me that he had found a second family among the Jesuit fathers at the Collège Saint-Paul. From the day he arrived at middle school in Angoulême, they took him in hand, devising an intensive yearlong program to address his deficiencies in French, the subject in which he had the most gaps to fill. Brilliant, hardworking, and a quick learner, Alphonse completed secondary school in five years instead of six. But to fully master French, in addition to Latin and ancient Greek, both of which he spoke as fluently as if they were living languages by the time he finished school, he had to unlearn his own language. Was he required to? Did it happen naturally? After all, from the age of fifteen to twenty-nine, he lived cut off from anything having to do with his original culture. Despite his desire to return to Ivory Coast, he avoided imposing further sacrifices on his father, who already paid for everything he needed at school, and never once asked him for a trip home, not even for a summer visit. He didn't spend time with Ivorians, because there were none to be found. For fourteen long years, he didn't speak his native language. The limited contact he had with his parents was through letters and telegrams that he wrote in French and that an interpreter in Ivory Coast translated, before responding to him in French in turn. Even with his own family, he no longer had access to the spontaneous language of his childhood.

What do we lose of ourselves if we lose our language?

Alphonse, my mother told me, still understood Baoulé but didn't speak it. Was he afraid that the words would come out wrong? Had he, after years of schooling in France, buried his native language so deeply in himself that he could no longer bring it back? The middle-aged man I knew, already well past middle age, spoke little, and even less about himself. I put it down to his reserve and a peculiar kind of modesty. But when at fifteen, in a foreign country, you no longer have anyone to open your heart to the way you did in childhood, don't you eventually, quite literally, lose your tongue, don't you eventually just keep quiet?

He passed down nothing of his Agni-Baoulé language or culture to his children or grandchildren. Only with his wife did he share a few fragments about this most personal part of himself. In reading her words, I can just catch a glimpse of the little boy as he heads to the field with his father after a breakfast of grilled bananas his mother made.

Something else filled the void left by language: Catholicism. Because the Jesuits did more than instruct my grandfather's mind; during the five years he spent with them, they also molded his spirit. Under Father Duhil's tutelage, he had been baptized and received his first communion. Among the Jesuits, he became deeply religious. He almost entered the seminary. Perhaps the promise he had made his family to become an attorney steered him back to the law. But he always remained very closely tied to the clergy, whether the Jesuits in Angoulême, Father Duhil, who came to Gaillac to perform his and Rose-Marie's wedding, or, in Abidjan, Cardinal Yago, the first Ivorian cardinal. His Christian faith undoubtedly informed his approach to and his conception of his profession, whatever the concessions, or moral compromises, he later made to further Houphouët's political power.

What is Good? What is Evil? What is our place between the two? Danièle recalled the profound moral dilemma into which Alphonse was thrown by a decision he had to make when working as a prosecutor in Congo-Brazzaville. Should he or shouldn't he seek the death penalty? After a long, internal struggle, he sought the death penalty.

I remember him in his office at the Supreme Court in Abidjan. The space, imbued with austere solemnity, was always plunged in darkness because of the tall silk-cotton trees that lined the building and blocked the sun. When one entered, a hideous painting by Bernard Buffet loomed on the right-hand wall. It had been purchased by the Ivorian government and represented an unidentifiable French cathedral painted in a dispiriting range of blacks and grays. The left-hand wall was taken up with floor-to-ceiling shelves of bright-red law books, with the Civil and Penal Codes given pride of place. Alphonse sat behind a long dark wooden desk directly between the two walls, midway between the Church and the Law, a metaphor for his life.

And yet my grandmother, who was herself very devout, describes him at the time of their marriage as "quite superstitious by nature. Every human being is, but even more so when one's childhood is immersed in legends that then become quite extraordinary beliefs, when one grows up in reverential fear of household gods who either protect you or banish you from the house." I have to think, then, that the traces of animism never totally disappeared, even though he steadfastly condemned the practice.

What kind of inner balancing act did that mean for him? As I've tried to answer these questions, I only have bits and pieces to go on.

Alphonse loved France deeply; that's a fact. He felt good there, especially in Toulouse, where he'd spent some very happy years at school, and in Gaillac, where the clan-like way of life of Rose-Marie's family suited him perfectly.

In a speech he gave on April 25, 1971, as chair of the annual meeting of alumni of the Collège Saint-Paul, my grandfather reflected on his time there:

> Nowadays, people talk a lot about cooperation, but isn't the most admirable form of cooperation—before there was a name

> for it—the cooperation of your institution, which provided the young African I once was, on an equal footing with his French classmates, the knowledge and instruction that made me their equal and their friend.[1]

That is perhaps what he appreciated in France: a racial order that was less segregated than what existed in the colonies. It allowed him to free himself from his status as a native. But genuine cooperation has to cut both ways. Alphonse doesn't mention here what his French friends might have learned or gained from him, the Ivorian.

He was nonetheless proud of his origins. He may have smiled when his university friends called him Salsify, but not once did he try to make them forget his African roots. He asserted them straightforwardly, confidently, and unwaveringly.

Thus, for example, one summer day in 1935. He had just received the news that he had been hired as an assistant in the public prosecutor's office in Toulouse. He was happy. His salary would finally allow him to be less reliant on his father's money orders, which came . . . when they came, depending on the family's cocoa crops. To celebrate, and since it was still afternoon, his friends dragged him to an open-air dance hall.

> Under the shade trees, couples and groups of young people sipped on icy drinks while the most daring of them braved the heat and threw themselves into a wild Charleston on the dance floor.
>
> Alphonse joined in, transported by a rhythm that made his blood flow faster in his veins. He excelled at the new dance with its frenzied tempo; it made him nostalgic for Africa, for the Africa of moonlit nights when the tom-toms called the villagers out to dance.
>
> Alphonse hadn't forgotten those sweat-streaming bodies, bodies swept up in the dance's beats twirling on the verge of hysteria. A few notes and his extraordinarily vivid memories came flooding back. Dance is how one expresses oneself in Africa: joy, loss, it conveys everything, and that's what Alphonse thought of as the sweat trickled down his face.

His dance partner—my grandmother wasn't there—got annoyed with him for not paying her enough attention. He told her that the Charleston's rhythms had transported him back to Africa. He apologized, ordered two "ice cold peppermints," and exclaimed, "It sure does get hot in your country!"

He had had French citizenship for a year. He had French papers. But he didn't say "my country" when talking about France. He never did. His homeland, his country, his nationality, would always be Ivory Coast. A classmate standing nearby thought it was pretty rich of him, the African, to complain about the heat. Alphonse, unphased, doubled down, "In my country, the weather is actually quite pleasant this time of year." In fact, it was the rainy season in Ivory Coast. My grandmother noted that according to popular belief, the rainy season always ended on July 14, just in time for the veterans' parade.

In 1944, all of France's colonies except Indochina united behind their governors in support of General de Gaulle's Free France. With de Gaulle in attendance, the administrators of the country's African colonies met in Brazzaville. They feared that France, weakened by the war, would lose its empire. As they prepared for liberation, they wondered what they could do to block both the development of the anti-colonial movements emerging in the colonies and the "greed of other colonial powers."[2] The hypocrisy is impressive. On the one hand, Free France must rid French territory of the German invader; on the other, it obviously must continue its occupation of African territories and keep their populations under the French yoke. Might the freedom of some be more legitimate than the freedom of others?

The same ambiguity existed at the time of the French Revolution in 1789. The Declaration of the Rights of Man and the Citizen asserted that "men are born and remain free and equal in rights," but it failed to accord that same freedom to slaves, who would have to wait until 1794 for slavery to be abolished, before Napoleon reestablished it in 1802.

Like other colonized peoples at the end of the Second World War, Ivorians had reached the limit of what they were willing to tolerate. Deprived of their civil rights, they had already been subjected to forced labor, to porterage (because of the country's lack of freight trains), to poll taxes, and to the draft and war effort. They had already been robbed of the best farmland, which had gone to French plantations. They then had to watch as Vichy France legitimized the colonizers' racism.

"There was no need to draft racist legislation as had been done in European France for the Jews. The Code de l'Indigénat was already in place. But there is no doubt that for the colonists, the racism back home represented a resounding endorsement of their own racist practices."[3] Economic discrimination was added to segregation. France not only paid higher prices for agricultural products from European farmers, it granted them a subsidy for the maintenance of their plantations of 1,000 francs per hectare (2.41 acres) that it refused to African farmers.

The Brazzaville Conference abolished the Code de l'Indigénat but not forced labor. It did, however, include African people in the postwar politics of the colonies by creating a national Constituent Assembly to which they could elect representatives as part of a second electoral constituency. The first constituency was reserved for French citizens. The elections were announced in August 1945 and set for October 21, 1945. There was suddenly a whirlwind of activity in Ivory Coast. Some thought that Houphouët-Boigny, who had created the African Agricultural Union and won certain improvements for African farmers, would be a shoo-in. He wasn't. Many Ivorians believed that for someone to sit in the National Assembly in Paris, that person needed to be an "intellectual," someone with a university education. All Houphouët had to show for himself was his auxiliary doctor's degree from Dakar.

In all, there were three Ivorians who fit the bill. First, there was my grandfather. Second, Kouamé Binzème, who after numerous twists of fate, managed to finish his law degree in 1941—like my grandfather, at the university in Toulouse—and worked as an intern at the appeals court in Paris.[4] Third, there was Alcide Kacou, an engineer from a Parisian Grande École. Alphonse's reputation was not inconsiderable. The first Ivorian to earn a doctorate in law, the first Ivorian to become a magistrate—a deputy judge in Togo, then an assistant prosecutor in Bamako—and, not least, the first Ivorian to marry a Frenchwoman.

> In short, his résumé was quite a bit more impressive than Houphouët's. He also enjoyed the prestige of being married to a white woman, an extreme rarity in the 1940s. His marital status, which was both exceptional and invaluable at the time, made him popular even in areas where he wasn't known."[5]

His popularity nonetheless had its limits: nationalist feeling didn't yet exist, and candidates were chosen by prospective voters based on ethnicity and, therefore, region. The Baoulés spurned Houphouët, despite his having their same ethnicity, and opted for my grandfather and Kouamé Binzème. Since Alphonse was partially Agni, he also garnered the support of that powerful ethnic group. When Houphouët finally declared his candidacy, French colonists, who already despised him—and for good reason, since his African Agricultural Union threatened their interests—drummed up a host of alternative candidates in an effort to dilute his support. No less the manipulator, Houphouët tried to convince Alphonse, a French citizen, to run in the first constituency in order to stack the deck against the colonial administrators. Alphonse declined and began his campaign. During speeches at the handful of campaign events he held, he declared,

> I know that European interests are opposed to native interests. I have refused to be a candidate in the European constituency in order to devote myself to defending my Black brethren. Given the difficulty of the task at hand, you must choose a representative who is well acquainted with legislative matters.[6]

It seems that my grandfather's extensive knowledge of the constitution didn't move the crowds. When he saw that his campaign wasn't gaining traction, he withdrew in favor of Kouamé Binzème.

Later, however, Houphouët offered a different version of events, claiming that he had presented my grandfather's candidacy for endorsement by the leadership of the African Agricultural Union but that "they refused Boni because he was married to a European."[7] Instead, they backed Kouamé Binzème, a man whose supporters proved so utterly unprepared when voting began that he soon wondered how he had gotten mixed up in an election in the first place.

According to still other sources, Houphouët-Boigny, my grandfather, and Kouamé Binzème were forced into a run-off for the African Agricultural Union's endorsement. During the night of September 22, 1945, Kouamé Binzème came out on top. Houphouët-Boigny broke away and, with the support of an "election committee," ran without the support of the union that he himself had founded.

In the end, there would be no fewer than fourteen candidates voted on by the second constituency. According to one version of what followed, Alphonse ran in the election's first round but didn't win enough votes to advance to the second round, which was carried by Houphouët, who thus became one of Ivory Coast's two deputies and, for the first time, boarded the boat to France. My grandfather very briefly returned to Bamako, then left for Dschang, Cameroon, where he was named justice of the peace.

Until then, Alphonse, had only ever known success. Stung by his defeat, he never set his sights on elected office again. When he later returned to politics in 1950, it was only because François Mitterrand, his former middle-school friend, called on his expertise. The escalating struggle between colonists and nationalist supporters of independence had pushed Ivory Coast to the brink of war. Mitterrand needed someone who knew the terrain.

Six months after his election on April 11, 1946, Houphouët brought the abolition of forced labor to a successful vote in the French Parliament. He became a hero throughout Francophone Africa. The Ivory Coast colonists were infuriated by the end of a system of exploitation that had worked so well for them and now feared the collapse of the country's plantation economy. Furthermore, Houphouët's political party, the PDCI, joined the party of pan-African liberation, the African Democratic Rally (RDA), within which it represented the largest contingent. The RDA itself was aligned with the parliamentary wing of the French Communist Party. Hence the specter grew of a communist party taking possession of Africa on Moscow's behalf. Considered too accommodating by the colonial lobby, Governor André-Jean-Gaston Latrille was replaced in 1948 by Laurent Péchoux, who expanded operations aimed at destabilizing Houphouët and the PDCI-RDA. On February 5, 1949, during protests in Abidjan, he had thirty-two members of the PDCI-RDA arrested and sent to jail in Grand-Bassam, among them eight party leaders. On December 24, after several months of resistance that included a boycott of French imports, the party's women marched on Grand-Bassam to demand the release of their husbands and brothers. Their brave act left an indelible impression and continues to be celebrated today.

The year 1950 was no less turbulent. Expressions of opposition—some of them mere fabrications cooked up by the colonial administration itself—were brutally suppressed by the army. In January 1950 in Dimbokro, the canton administrator ordered his forces to fire on protestors. Thirteen were killed and their bodies thrown into a common grave. The RDA was prohibited from meeting. Houphouët barely escaped arrest and contemplated going underground before abandoning the idea for fear of provoking an insurrection.

It was in this tumultuous context that on July 12, 1950, François Mitterrand was named Minister for Overseas France. He was only thirty-two years old. A year earlier, he had traveled to Equatorial Africa for the first time. During his visit, he was marked by the injustice of the colonial system, the institutionalized plunder of natural resources, and the ongoing humiliation of the colonized peoples. Yet he remained opposed to independence. He thought that the French empire should be preserved through reforms that granted greater autonomy to the colonies but maintained France's sovereign authority. "I had a kind of fear," he wrote, "of seeing France's empire collapse if she proved unable to quickly come to grips with the new era.

> But I envisaged independence only at the end of a long process. It seemed to me that in the short term Black Africa would otherwise split apart, that it had neither the structures nor the political leaders necessary to form and govern nation states, and that its territories, whose borders had been drawn in embassies with a ruler and a compass, had no ethnic or geographic reality.[8]

For the moment, his most pressing task was to prevent the clashes between the PDCI-RDA and Ivory Coast colonists from escalating into open war. Negotiations were carried out with RDA leaders through intermediaries. My grandfather, who had joined Mitterrand's staff, was one of those intermediaries.[9] A secret agreement was reached between Houphouët-Boigny and the young Minister for Overseas France. On October 18, 1950, the PDCI-RDA officially broke with the Communist Party and joined Mitterrand and René Pleven's political party, the UDSR (Democratic and Socialist Union of the Resistance). RDA activities were again authorized. A year later, Mitterrand visited Ivory Coast to inaugurate the new port in Abidjan accompanied by a large delegation that included Alphonse and African deputies from the RDA. Félix Houphouët-Boigny attended as well. The colonists were outraged by this official political rehabilitation of the PDCI-RDA and its leader, especially given the pomp and ceremony. It appears they gave Mitterrand a particularly icy reception.

Whether to his family, parents-in-law, or friends, my grandfather always said that he wanted to return to Ivory Coast to live. Still, when the opportunity arose, he at first refused.

In 1958, de Gaulle, recalled to power because of the crisis of the Algerian War, offered self-governance to African colonies within a "community" governed by France. The Ivory Coast Territorial Assembly voted in favor. Alphonse had returned to his career as a magistrate and was then living in a suburb of Paris. The French Community, as it was called, seemed a dubious proposition to him. He wasn't wrong; it would last less than two years. He preferred to take the post of public prosecutor in Congo-Brazzaville, and therefore didn't participate in Ivory Coast's first autonomous government. Nor did Houphouët, who remained a minister in Paris.

In 1959, as a second Ivorian government was being formed, one in which Houphouët-Boigny would this time serve as prime minister, Alphonse wasn't sure what to do. He gathered his wife and children together. Just as family members had assembled thirty-five years earlier to consider whether to send him to France, he now asked his family council if they were ready to live in a country they had only ever visited. Rose-Marie and their children thought it would be quite selfish of them to prevent him from returning to Ivory Coast. They said yes.

On June 12, 1959, Alphonse left the French civil service and became Ivory Coast's Minister of Justice. He was fifty years old. After thirty-five years of exile, he was finally going home. This time, for good. A year later, Ivory Coast chose to become independent.

My grandfather was part of the group of experts who wrote the Ivorian Constitution. He had the honor of presenting it to the Ivory Coast Parliament on October 31, 1960, before the first presidential elections were held. He had had an excellent career up to that point. Now he was someone important. After Minister of Justice, he became president of the Supreme Court, an office he held until he died. Still, his appointment to the court took place under murky circumstances, to say the least.

Fearing an alleged coup and eager to rid himself of his political rivals, in 1963 Houphouët-Boigny accused a portion of the Ivorian political class of two plots, both of which served as a pretext for far-reaching purges. After the first "plot," the president of the Supreme Court, Ernest Boka, chose to resign rather than head the State Security Court tasked with trying the conspirators. He was replaced by Jean-Baptiste Mockey, one of my grandfather's close friends. Following the second plot, however, Mockey was among the accused. As for Boka, he was arrested and died from a mysterious "suicide" in his jail cell. That was when Alphonse was appointed president of the Supreme Court. The Security Court, of which he was also president, sentenced six defendants to the death penalty, including his friend Mockey. In the end, there would be no executions, however, as the sentences were commuted several years later. Houphouët himself would ultimately acknowledge that there had been no plots.[10]

Had my grandfather joined in this mockery of justice simply to save his skin? His job? His family? Had he acted out of political conviction or opportunism? How could the same man who had been so riddled with doubt when he sought the death penalty as a French prosecutor condemn six innocent men to death? Did he know that the sentences wouldn't be carried out?

Everyone has gray areas. Alphonse, it seems, capitulated to the autocratic power of the Ivory Coast President. The incident is all the more difficult to understand because Jean-Baptiste Mockey had been his close friend since the early forties, when Alphonse was working in Bamako, then capital of French Sudan, present-day Mali. Alphonse's daughter, Marie-Françoise, had come down with life-threatening meningitis. The doctors said there was no hope for her. Rose-Marie, who venerated the Virgin Mary and never parted with her vials of holy water from Lourdes, sprinkled it on her daughter and prayed her rosary hoping for a miracle. Jean-Baptiste Mockey, an auxiliary pharmacist at the time, was also posted in Mali. He hadn't gotten involved in politics yet. He took my grandfather aside and told him that Western medicine had limits that African medicine might not share. Alphonse had nothing to lose. He gave his friend a free hand on one condition: he couldn't tell Rose-Marie. Mockey discreetly gave Marie-Françoise a traditional remedy of his own concoction. They took her for dead. A few hours later, she regained consciousness. Rose-Marie, convinced that the water from Lourdes had worked its longed-for miracle (this is the woman who called my grandfather superstitious!), promised her daughter to the Virgin Mary. Until she reached adulthood, Marie-Françoise was allowed to wear only blue and white. Jean-Baptiste Mockey became her godfather. In a cruel twist of fate in 1981, after escaping the death penalty Alphonse had handed down in 1963, he was killed right in front of us in a car accident on his way, like my grandfather, my mother, and me, to an official government ceremony.

The Security Court's deliberations took place behind closed doors. During his lifetime, Alphonse always refused to talk about them. Their only trace was the report locked in his office safe at the Supreme Court. When he died, my mother immediately tried to get her hands on it to learn what had really happened. She found the safe empty. The office of the President of the Republic had gotten there first.

After this traumatic episode, which established Houphouët-Boigny's supreme authority until his death, the country's political life, like Alphonse's career, settled down. Over the years, Alphonse solidified the Ivorian legal system with numerous articles of law, ensured their constitutionality, and oversaw the highest judicial bodies of the state. When in 1975, the UN turned to the International Court of Justice for an advisory opinion on the conflict in Western Sahara, the King of Morocco, Hassan II, took offense that there was no African judge on the Hague court to consider a dispute whose origins lay in European colonialism. He was granted an ad hoc judge and appointed my grandfather. The reports of the International Court of Justice mention that Spain voiced no objection.

Known for his shrewd understanding of the law, Alphonse joined the prestigious World Jurist Association—at the time, the World Peace Through Law Center—whose aim was and continues to be to strengthen the rule of law throughout the world in order to alleviate armed conflict. Always a fervent Catholic, he was made a knight of the Order of Malta.

At my grandfather's side, Rose-Marie became the third most prominent woman in the country. She can be seen in official photos, the only white person next to Thérèse Houphouët-Boigny and Monette Yacé, the wife of the National Assembly president. She greeted foreign heads of state and traveled the world on my grandfather's official trips. I doubt she ever imagined having such a life when, looking out of her family's butcher shop, she dreamed of leaving Gaillac.

Her nieces and nephews recognized how exceptional Rose-Marie was in the Galou family. She owed her fate—so very different from theirs—and her dazzling rise up the social ladder to a Black man. My grandfather, the former colonized native of the French Republic, had made my grandmother a member of the bourgeoisie. He was the big shot of the family.

I grew up surrounded by these extremely well-educated, cosmopolitan upper-middle-class African people, who lived between Africa, Europe, and North America and, nowadays, the Middle East, and who mastered several foreign languages and different cultures.

In France, forty percent of the descendants of Guinean and Central African immigrants hold a post-secondary degree. That's more than France's majority population (thirty-four percent). Twenty-five percent of descendants of immigrants from Sahelian Africa have a post-secondary degree, and that figure climbs to thirty-one percent for women. As for the children of parents from overseas departments, they hold diplomas at exactly the same rate as the majority population: thirty-three percent have completed their post-secondary education.[11] But that isn't the image we have of Blacks in France. I realized this when I started working. A Black person with an education or who earns a good living still takes people by surprise.

# 21 Fault Lines

After leaving La Fémis in 2000, my very first job as a screenwriter involved leading writing workshops for middle- and high-school students participating in screenwriting competitions. The workshops took place over two days in different schools in and around Poitiers. To help with travel, the festival that hired me assigned me a volunteer to take care of logistics and drive me from place to place. A very young, nice, and capable white man.

My first workshop was held in a vocational high school, with students working toward a baccalauréat specific to the electrical trades. There were only boys in the class, already dispirited by the prospect of listening to someone talk about narrative for three hours. Their white teacher, who had had the bright idea of signing them up for the competition, was either a bit late or had gone looking for something in another classroom. When he entered, he headed straight for my volunteer assistant, warmly shook his hand, and said in a loud enthusiastic voice, "So, you're our Paris screenwriter!" "No, I'm the driver," said the young man, slightly amused. He pointed at me: "She's the screenwriter." The French teacher looked at me in astonishment then burst out laughing, exclaiming to the class, as if the whole thing had been a great joke, "In other countries, it would've been the other way around!" I told him that I couldn't imagine which countries he was talking about. Which was true. But I understood that for this French teacher, the drivers were Black and the teachers white. Screenwriters were men, and Black women were . . . And Black women? Did they even exist for him except as inferiors?

When I finally began my workshop, I was seething with barely suppressed anger. Most of the students were of Maghrebi, African, or West Indian origin. Why did this man sign them up for the competition if he had such a limited view of their abilities?

I had brought several short films to show as examples. One of them, by a director friend, Owell Brown, seemed to me particularly appropriate: *Lunettes noires* (Dark Glasses) with Hubert Koundé. When the boys saw him, they started nudging each other. "See that? It's Hubert!" The memory of Kassovitz's *La Haine* was still very much alive and they all recognized one of that film's lead actors. From then on, they were all ears. Screenwriting suddenly stopped being something bookish and became a tool for talking about life in general and—why not?—about their own lives. The teacher was the only one who didn't understand the message I was trying to convey by sharing the story of a young man who is killed because he is Black, because he drives a nice car, and because he is taken for a thief instead of the car's owner. Obviously.

As if the initiation to my new job hadn't been tough enough, the next day I found myself at a middle school where there raged the most dogged "whereareyoufromist" I had ever encountered. The teacher who met me when I arrived insisted that we have lunch together in the faculty dining hall. I shuddered when I saw the menu: beef stew, during an outbreak of mad cow disease. I was making a mental list of excuses not to eat that wouldn't offend my host when one of the teachers stood up from his table, planted himself in front of me and, once the customary greetings were out of the way, looked at me head to toe, then blurted out, "African?" Dumbstruck, I didn't respond. He took a moment to think, inspected me again, and declared, "No. Probably West Indian." I had become a Black specimen. Did he want me to undress so he could examine my buttocks and genitals, the way they did to Saartjie Baartman, the "Hottentot Venus"? Given my silence, he finally asked me where I was from. "From France," I said. Naturally, that wasn't good enough for him. He wanted me to tell him where my parents were from, too. I shot back curtly that I couldn't see what gave him the right to ask me. Had I asked him where he and his family were from? He looked at me with surprise. Apparently, he hadn't considered the possibility that someone might react this way.

When we left the dining hall, the teacher who had invited me to lunch, now quite embarrassed, came to his defense. She reassured me that he hadn't meant any harm. "He really loves Africa," she said. "He goes every year with an association to build wells for local villages."

I didn't respond. What good was there in wasting one's time with people in thrall to their own stupidity? Those who used the poverty of the Global South to ease people's consciences in the Global North were no friends of mine. I knew from experience that the people who supposedly loved Africa were often the worst of paternalists and the most fervent of essentialists. The same people who were surprised when I ate steak tartare—because "Africans" prefer their meat very well done—told me that I didn't have an accent when I spoke French and ultimately found me arrogant because I failed to show them the lapdog gratitude they expected of Blacks in whom they had so charitably shown interest. I couldn't care less if someone loved Africa or African people. I wanted nothing to do with a love that negated me as a person. The only thing I asked for was respect. And that was something I should have the same right to as anyone else in France, without having to explain where I was from.

Often, I was asked what I did—a perfectly normal question. When I explained that as a screenwriter I had cowritten several television series, I invariably got two types of reaction. There were those, the majority, who thought it was fantastic, because screenwriting is considered glamorous, when in reality you spend your days in your socks in front of a computer. Then there were those who asked, "A screenwriter for African TV?" Because they simply couldn't imagine that the thoroughly French programs they watched after work could have been written by a Black woman. Or did they regard French television as too prestigious and difficult for people with my skin color?

For various reasons, which have to do with the structure of media professions in France, there are in fact extremely few Black screenwriters working in film and TV. But how could these people know that? No one knows the names or faces of screenwriters, an unsung profession if ever there was one. Imagining them as uniformly white was sheer bias, even if that bias, alas, hardly differed from the truth.

Among the twenty-two forms of discrimination prohibited by French law, those based on ethnicity and race are the most frequently encountered. Their effects are the most pernicious in the workplace. The outright rejection of job candidates, the lack of opportunities for career advancement, stereotypes, prejudice.

Whereas discrimination against women and people with disabilities is precisely measured and subject to quantifiable objectives by lawmakers, with financial penalties for businesses that fail to meet those objectives, nothing exists to promote the inclusion of ethnoracial minorities. In France, we prefer to rely on the employer's good will. We refuse to establish so-called ethnic statistics on the grounds that they are prohibited by law. They aren't. What French law prohibits is the computerized storage of personal data, for it rightly considers that race and ethnicity are too sensitive to be stored with one's name attached to them. No one wants to see another Vichy. But that doesn't exclude the mere gathering of statistics, which, unlike police files, are anonymous. Yet the ambiguity between statistics and the collection of personal data keeps coming back, and few people know that statistics bearing on race and ethnicity are allowed "for reasons of public interest upon authorization of the commission by a decree of the Council of State."[1] Still fewer are those willing to go through the process of seeking authorization, which, in any case, isn't always granted. The researchers at the National Institute for Demographic Studies who carried out the baseline study *Trajectories and Origins*[2] were initially prohibited from including questions about skin color in their questionnaire. They had planned to ask, "When someone meets you, what color(s) do you think that person sees?" "What color would you say you are?" But France's Constitutional Council determined that these questions ran contrary to Article 1 of the Constitution. So it threw them out. On the other hand, the same questions were authorized for a study on job discrimination carried out jointly by the French administrative body Defender of Rights and the International Labour Organization. In it, we learned that women perceived as Black, Arab, or Asian aged eighteen to forty-four are far more likely to experience discrimination in the workplace and on the job market. They have the double disadvantage of being women and non-white.[3]

Despite this, quota policies that might lead to the inclusion of discriminated workers are banned. The reason? It would be unfair to the other employees, degrading to those who benefit, and would silo both groups in their own racial and ethnic identities. But when the law tells companies with more than twenty employees that at least six percent of their workforce must be people with disabilities, or when it requires that the boards of directors of publicly traded companies must be forty percent women, what else is it doing but imposing quotas?

In these specific cases—women, people with disabilities—"positive discrimination," as it is called in France, or affirmative action in the United States, is accepted by French legislators and public opinion alike. It is even considered—and this is a good thing—essential for establishing real equality. So why is it refused when it comes to ethnoracial diversity?

Is it because the very lack of precise statistical data, which would tell us the actual proportion of racial minorities in each professional field and their corresponding job ranks, means that we simply don't have a good grasp on this kind of discrimination? Indeed it does. But in that case, why is there such resistance to ethnoracial statistics?

People talk about the risks of collecting personal data, but, I repeat, statistics are anonymous. People invoke the sacrosanct principle of color-blind universalism. Anyone whose skin color isn't white knows that this principle is an illusion; a beautiful ideal, of course, and one we all must aspire to, but an illusion nonetheless. Is it because the overwhelming majority of the deputies and senators who vote on our laws are white that they pretend to still believe in it? Probably, but that can't be the only reason. In order for there to be such a consensus on this principle, it must have some usefulness. The real question is: Who benefits from French universalism? The majority of French people, one is tempted to say. The white majority of French people, to be specific. Which is still seventy-five percent of the population.

In a supposed meritocracy, who wants to admit that, starting from equivalent economic backgrounds, white French people begin life with a significant leg up over their non-white counterparts? We prefer to focus on class inequalities, which have historically been at the root of the country's social struggles. With that said, if unemployment is two-and-a-half times higher in underprivileged neighborhoods, it's not only because working-class people live there, but because that's where the majority of the immigrant and non-white population live.

Personally, I have never been discriminated against in my TV and film work—not directly, anyway. In fact, when I first started, the opposite was the case. I seemed to provoke a certain frisson in those around me.

Given the dearth of Black female—let alone Black male—directors in the early aughts and the fact that you could count the number of Black screenwriters on two hands, my presence piqued interest. As I had anticipated, the Fémis brand opened doors, and I immediately found plenty of work. First as a script reader with the film subsidiaries of three television channels. Then during a screenwriters' festival, I pitched the feature-length script I had written for my degree at La Fémis. An up-and-coming producer bought it and several agents proposed their services. On a different front, *Afrique Magazine*—part of the *Jeune Afrique* publishing group—which had just interviewed me about the release of my novel *La Grande Dévoreuse*, offered me a monthly column. The French filmmaker and theater director Patrice Chéreu, whom I was dying to meet, left me a message on my answering machine asking me to call him. In addition, I'd been helping young French and African directors write their films; they were thrilled to finally be working with a screenwriter who had an insider's understanding of the cultural aspects of their projects. And, finally, as I've mentioned, I don't really know how it happened, but Michel Field invited me to come on his prime-time talk show. Yet I was profoundly unhappy.

Georges had died the year before, in early 1999. Nine months later, my biological father, Jean-Pierre, died. When his illness struck, he was sent from Abidjan to Paris for hospitalization. Because he was a career diplomat, the Ivory Coast government covered the costs. The social worker at the Ivorian embassy in France oversaw his care. That social worker was none other than Léonie, my biological mother. She and Jean-Pierre hadn't seen each other since their separation shortly after my birth.

Several months earlier, I had begun to feel the need to know more about my birth mother. The last time I had seen her I was eight years old. At her request, I had spent an entire day alone with her, without Danièle or Georges. It was very difficult for me at that age to understand why I had four parents, all of whom claimed me as their daughter. I came home from my day with her so thoroughly upset that I told Danièle I didn't want to see her again. Danièle was all too happy to oblige.

Nineteen years had passed since then. I was twenty-seven years old and felt a kind of void in myself. I constantly wondered what my birth mother looked like and if I looked like her. What in me had come from her? When a Black woman in the street looked at me insistently, I wondered if by chance that woman was her. It was time for me to know. I called my biological father. I had assumed that she was in Ivory Coast, and that finding her would be a long and complicated process. Jean-Pierre replied, "Call the embassy. She works there." All those years, she had been living in Paris, right next door.

I asked her to meet me in a café not far from the Place Saint-Michel. She arrived in tears, thin and fragile, her hair tied in a small, tight bun, dressed all in black like a Sicilian widow. She put her hands on my face and said, "My daughter." A steady stream of tears rolled down her cheeks.

I discovered that I had an eighteen-year-old brother and an eleven-year-old little sister. We slowly began to get to know each other. One afternoon I went to visit Jean-Pierre at the hospital. I had been there for only a few minutes when she entered the room. We both froze in place, stunned. At which point, Jean-Pierre, emaciated by his illness but still handsome, struck his bedsheet several times with his thin arm and, speaking with an intensity that gave his voice an almost angry tone, said, "I am happy!"

It was the first time since my baptism that the three of us were together. It was also the last.

After Georges's funeral in February 1999, I returned to Abidjan in December for Jean-Pierre's. Several weeks later, I was staying alone in Ivory Coast when the first coup in the country's history broke out. This accumulation of bad news pushed me over the edge; short of dying myself, I let my life slip away.

No more work. No plans for a film. No place to live. No money. Nothing. In the space of two years, bit by bit I sabotaged every opportunity that had come my way. When nothing remained, I left Paris for Marseille, where I didn't know a soul. In the end, I was saved by a movie.

Before I abandoned my first feature-length project, my producer had urged me to write a short film that would capture my vision as a female director more fully than *The Genie of Abou*. I wrote a script of around thirty minutes about a young mixed-race woman who attends her mother's funeral in Abidjan. Feeling like a stranger in her own family, she sets off into the city night to find herself. The film was called *For the Night* and received a sizeable pre-production grant for short films from France's National Center of Cinema and the Moving Image (CNC).

But in September 2002, a bloody "rebel"-led coup attempt hurled Ivory Coast into what was a virtual civil war that would ultimately last nine years and resulted in the de facto partition of the country between the Muslim North and the Christian and animist South. Shortly after the coup began, General Robert Guéï, who had overseen the political transition after the country's first coup in 1999, was assassinated under murky circumstances along with his entire family. The "death squads" of President Laurent Gbagbo and his wife also went after a political rival who had earned the animosity of a bevy of political adversaries since the death of Houphouët-Boigny in 1993. That rival? Alassane Ouattara, Ivory Coast's future president.

As fate would have it, Ouattara and his wife, herself white and French, had purchased and were living in my grandparents' former home in Abidjan. They narrowly escaped the death squads thanks to the property's proximity to the German ambassador's residence. At the very last moment, they climbed over the adjoining wall and into German territory. The house, which my grandmother had spent so much time and care constructing, was set ablaze.

Danièle would end up siding with Gbagbo's camp, which was significant, not least because in 2011, when Gbagbo claimed to have won the presidential election and refused to cede power to Ouattara, this time it was Ouattara's supporters who pillaged my grandfather's house in his hometown of Tiassalé. While they were at it, they desecrated the graves of my grandparents, biological father, adoptive father, and one of my cousins.

Given the climate of insecurity following the second coup in 2002, it was going to be tricky to shoot a film set at night in the streets of Abidjan and the dicey suburb of Yopougon. In any case, I no longer had a producer. Alerted, perhaps, by a sixth sense that I was about to leave for Marseille, Morad Kertobi, the head of the CNC Short Films Department in Paris, asked me to meet him at his office to discuss my film. With great kindness, he encouraged me to adapt the story to take place somewhere other than Ivory Coast. He repeated that he thought my script was excellent and that I absolutely had to shoot it. I assured him I would. As I was leaving, he gave a sigh of relief and confessed that he had been very worried I would give it up. Several weeks later, he called with the contact information of a young producer in Marseille.

When you hit rock bottom, sometimes all it takes is the attention of a kind soul to make you want to climb back up. Without knowing it, Morad Kertobi had been my guardian angel. I suspect that he has done the same thing for many other young directors, especially when I see the dynamism of the Short Films Department, which he continues to lead, and its initiatives to open filmmaking to people from underrepresented groups. Through "Talents en court," for example, a program run jointly with Jamel Debbouze, audiences have had the opportunity to discover otherwise unknown talents, among whom the French-Senegalese director Maïmouna Doucouré, whose film *Maman(s)* won the César Award for Best Short Film in 2017.

I made *For the Night* in Marseille between 2003 and 2004. The day I finished editing, I knew I needed to dedicate it to my father. I realized then that in the process of making my film I had come to terms with his death. It won several awards. Charles Van Damme, the same cinematographer who had asked me why I wanted to attend La Fémis given that I would be going back to Africa to work, told me categorically that a Black character in such a bourgeois setting wasn't plausible. I screened my film at numerous festivals throughout the world, including at African film festivals, where offended moviegoers informed me that I hadn't actually made an African film. I told them they were absolutely right, I had made a French film. *For the Night* attracted the attention of the actor Danny Glover, a Hollywood star and committed political activist, who offered me the chance to develop a new feature-length project for the production company he had just created. I had already been playing with a very liberal adaptation of Valérie Tong Cuong's novel *Où je suis* (Where I Am). We shifted the plot to the United States. I went to live in Miami for a few months; I hammered away at it for several years. But in the end, I didn't make the film. I may never make it. That's how things go. Life sometimes makes us rethink our dreams, but that doesn't mean we've failed.

# 22 French TV: Keeping Out the Color

I have always stopped myself from thinking that being Black is a liability. I have tried to put my disappointments to good use. But in hindsight, it's clear that doing so hasn't helped. The film industry is this amazing world in which there are no racists but in which, strangely, everyone is white. In which women are overrepresented in positions like hairstylist, makeup artist, costume designer, and script supervisor, while men monopolize positions with the most power, the most money, and the most prestige. Eighty percent of movies released in theaters are directed by men.[1] Fewer than a third of those films are written by women.[2]

Earning the trust of producers or financers is simply more difficult when you're a woman director. There is this widespread belief that filmmaking is a manly venture, that women don't have the technical expertise or the necessary authority to command respect on a film set and ensure that the huge sums of money at stake will be put to good use. And that's leaving aside day-to-day male chauvinism.

I remember a well-known producer to whom I explained my plan to make a movie about the violence surrounding the world of Ultimate Fighting. He looked at me pityingly and said, "I just don't understand why you women want to make films about these kinds of things." What I don't understand is why genre films should be the reserve of men. Nor why, on every one of my film shoots, at some point or another I had to remind the technicians, friendly enough under normal circumstances, that I was the one in charge, not them. As if the adrenaline of a film shoot had suddenly given them enormous testicles.

Although we have exact statistics on gender inequality in the French film industry, the same statistics don't exist when it comes to the level of inclusion of ethnoracial minorities. However—and this is the upside with so-called visible minorities—when non-whites are on screen, you see them, and when they aren't, you see that too. Take a minute to look at the audience at the César Awards ceremonies on TV. How many Black, Arab, or Asian people do you see?

Their absence is so glaring that, even without statistics, you can't help but notice that the profession is monochrome. The presence of a Black male or female director in television or movie credits is so rare that when, by some miracle, they are there, they're hard to miss. And I say Black because I am talking about French directors, not about the handful of French-speaking African directors who still manage to find the financing necessary to get their films made.

For a sign that things have in fact begun to change, in 2017, two young Black directors, Alice Diop and Maïmouna Doucouré, were both awarded Césars for Best Short Film.[3] It had been thirty-three years since any Black filmmaker, man or woman, had won.

In 2009, the actor Lucien Jean-Baptiste was the talk of the town. More than one and a half million moviegoers saw his first feature-length film, *Meet the Elisabethz*. A record for a film directed by a Black man, with a protagonist played by a Black man, about a Black family, albeit in the exotic setting (at least for the general French public) of a ski vacation. The film is certainly worth more than this synopsis because of its touching portrayal of an irresponsible father who slowly regains the trust of his family. But it's easy to imagine certain French people cutting right to the chase: Hold on, Blacks skiing?! Now that's funny! This I've got to see!

In 2011, Thomas Ngijol and Fabrice Éboué, made famous by the French cable channel Canal Plus's show *Jamel Comedy Club*, directed their first film, *Case départ* (Back to Square One), a half-baked comedy about slavery. They hit it big: more than 1.7 million moviegoers in France. Then Fabrice Éboué directed the very funny *Crocodile du Botswanga* (Botswanga Crocodile), which more than a million people went to see. In 2017, Lucien Jean-Baptiste made a comeback with *He Even Has Your Eyes*, a spirited comedy in which a young Black bobo couple adopts a white baby.

These directors' successes represented a significant breakthrough. Producers, distributors, and theater operators could no longer say that a film with Black people would never attract an audience. Their films, however, had one point in common: they were all comedies. As if white moviegoers were incapable of relating to Black characters except through laughter, which only perpetuated a very old tradition.

Indeed, the first successful Black performer in France was the clown Chocolat in the late nineteenth century. A self-taught freed slave from Cuba whose real name was Rafael, Chocolat rose to fame by skillfully getting kicked in the ass by the white clown Georges Foottit. Audiences loved it and kept coming back for more. Chocolat's celebrity lasted twenty years. But the day he turned his ambitions to "a space reserved for the elite—the theater—he was told: 'Stay in your place.'"[4]

In a dizzying coincidence, Omar Sy, another self-taught actor, and the side-splitting TV buffoon made popular by a booming laugh and his comic duo with Fred Testot on a long-running French TV news satire show, played Chocolat in Roschdy Zem's film *All Out* in 2016.

Four years before, Sy had received the César Award for Best Actor. French media were in awe. For the first time in the history of the Césars, the precious statue went to a Black actor. I was even happier for Sy because I didn't agree with those critics of *The Intouchables* who, echoing the searing review in the American bible of cinema *Variety*, had found the film inherently racist.

Jay Weissberg, *Variety*'s film critic, didn't mince words. He found that Omar Sy's character was treated like

> a performing monkey (with all the racist associations of such a term), teaching the stuck-up white folk how to get "down" by replacing Vivaldi with "Boogie Wonderland" and showing off his moves on the dance floor. It's painful to see Sy, a joyfully charismatic performer, in a role barely removed from the jolly house slave of yore, entertaining the master while embodying all the usual stereotypes about class and race.[5]

Yes, Omar Sy plays a poor man working for a rich white guy whom he helps find joy in life—a cliché that has long stuck to Black people's skin. And yes, in one of the film's hallmark scenes, he dances, and he dances very well. But do we have to stop showing Black men dancing because too many people automatically associate Black men with dancing? It's true that Driss's character is a good Black man, a kind poor person, who doesn't question the privileges of rich white people. That alone could make him a walking stereotype. But he is substantial enough as a character to exist as a full human being. Since I don't expect a mainstream comedy to be subversive—on the contrary, one of the functions of this kind of film is to reassure audiences by validating the established social order—I liked *The Intouchables*. But besides Omar Sy's personal success, I didn't see much reason to be thrilled by the César. While everyone in France was congratulating themselves, I couldn't help but think of Isaach de Bankolé, winner of the 1987 César for Most Promising Actor.

1987. 2012. It took no less than twenty-five years for the promise identified in a young Black actor to be fulfilled by another Black actor.

Twenty-five years. Meanwhile, Isaach de Bankolé left France for the United States, where he has had a fairly modest career, whereas he had the talent and charisma to be a star in France. As for the Best Actress Award, to date, no Black actress has won. Not because, as people sometimes still claim, there are no Black actors—they're there, hundreds of them, dying to finally be given the chance to act—but because performers are nominated in the category only when they have played a leading role that is substantial, intense, and/or appealing enough for their talent to be recognized.

Do you see many movies with a Black woman in the leading role? No. The reason, once again, is simple. People write stories, create characters, based on what they know, based on what moves them emotionally (most often close to home), or deeply resonates with them. The profession is white. Naturally, it opts for stories whose heroes fit the mold.

I remember a long conversation we students had with Tran Anh Hung at La Fémis. I had loved *The Scent of Green Papaya*, the Vietnamese-born French director's first film. When he met with us, he was struggling to find financing for his third film and attributed his difficulties to his need to include the Vietnamese side of himself in his films. Do you know many bankable Asian actors in France? There are none. Because there are no roles for them in French movies, so almost zero opportunities for them to succeed, to find an audience, or to become famous. Why? No doubt because Asians in France continue to be considered a very marginal part of the French population.

To go back to Tran Anh Hung, I was struck by the word he used: "need." He needed to film Asian faces, needed to see a certain skin and hair texture on screen. It wasn't an intellectual argument but the expression of an artistic and existential necessity. He needed to get back to the aesthetic emotions that sustained him as an artist. And those emotions, at least at that moment in his life, were Asian.

How many directors, when they aren't themselves Black, feel the need to film Black characters?

In 2001, I submitted my first feature-length script to Émergence, a prestigious multiweek workshop created by Élisabeth Depardieu during which a handful of young directors had the opportunity to shoot one or two scenes of their future film with some of the biggest actors in French cinema. The recognition that came with being chosen as well as the possibility of finishing with something close to a pilot considerably improved the likelihood of finding financing for a first film. After making it through the first round of the admissions process, I had an interview with the selection committee, chaired by one of the most important producers in the industry. My script was fairly incendiary, mixing dark family secrets, homosexuality, sadomasochism, and class and race relations. Still, Catherine Breillat had gotten her provocative film *Romance* made; Virginie Despentes and Coralie Trinh-Thi had secured the release of *Baise-moi* despite its being banned initially; and Patrice Chéreau had just made *Intimacy* with actors engaging in unsimulated sex on screen. The time was ripe. At least that was what I thought. During the entire hour of my interview, the actress Catherine Frot, evidently shocked by my script, sat in disapproving silence. From time to time, she looked at me scoldingly, but not once did she unclench her lips. Supported by other committee members who had actually liked my script, I was in the middle of defending my project when the committee chair murmured, "Even so, upper-class Africans is a curious choice . . ."

I knew then and there that I wouldn't be chosen. For a man like this producer, so accustomed to living among the upper class, it was impossible to identify with upper-class Black characters. They didn't fit the mold. Perhaps it didn't occur to him that I had written the story because that was my own social class. Laying the groundwork for a decision he had already made, he mentioned my producer, who had a solid reputation, and the fact that I had just directed a short art film for a museum in Spain. He wasn't the one who didn't want me for Émergence; I was the one who didn't need the program. Essentially, he was insinuating that I was doing too well already for them to want to help me. Doing too well for a Black woman?

Did he even realize that he was punishing me for not living up to his own stereotypes?

In his book *Les Noirs dans le cinéma français*, Régis Dubois identifies three kinds of stereotypical Black characters in France: the Uncle Tom and its female version, the nanny; the overgrown child; and the African savage "and its modern avatar, the *banlieue* thug."[6] In my experience and in the experience of many Black director friends, I can confirm how hard it is to try to make films with Black characters who diverge from these types.

That's one of the main forms of violence in this ostensibly non-racist industry, an industry that decides for you what stories you can and cannot tell about yourself. The minute you choose to film something that veers from the stereotypes and puts Black characters center stage, or, alternatively, the minute you resolve to get to the very root of those stereotypes from your own point of view, it becomes very difficult to get a project off the ground. Is it a coincidence that there are practically no French films about slavery or colonization and that their treatment on French television is so rare? I see the situation as symptomatic of a country that continues to black out an integral part of its history.

None of this would matter if movies and television didn't play such an important role in our lives. They're part of a constant feedback loop, both reflecting and shaping our collective imagination and the image we have of ourselves and the society in which we live.

The world of French cinema demonstrates how, despite the lofty speeches and occasional awards, ethnoracial minorities remain sidelined from the creative process of constructing France's "national narrative." Because French film and television leave no room for expressing genuine cultural diversity, they reinforce the image of a monochrome and monocultural society. It's no doubt a reassuring image for some people, but it frustrates many others. Exclusion does nothing to foster the mutual respect and tolerance people are constantly harping on about. It's also a huge waste of talent.

There were some changes, however, after the riots in the suburbs of Paris and other French cities in 2005. Lasting for weeks, they forced the country to face up to the fact that a portion of its population was Black—not foreign and immigrant, as in the past, but Black and French. At the time, the CNC, an arm of the French Ministry of Culture, implemented a program called Images of Diversity to promote representations of difference in French cinema. However, to apply for funds, applicants needed to have previously been granted funding from the CNC. Furthermore, the amounts awarded were too small to do anything more than supplement other financing. While useful in that respect, the new funding simply wasn't a decisive factor in starting production, which meant that one still had to go looking for money to cover one's budget. Just as opening French cinema to more ethnic diversity shouldn't be limited to spotlighting a handful of directors and actors, so the entire profession, including the technical trades and financing, needs more diversity.

As for French television, it focused its efforts on putting more ethnic minorities on screen. It made greater strides in this area than the film industry, no doubt because France's television regulatory authority, the CSA,[7] kept a closer eye on its progress. Nothing would have changed, however, without the activism in the late nineties of the organization Collectif Égalité, whose work culminated in an event that left a deep impression on me.

It was February 2000, at the 25th César Awards. Before an audience of celebrities and César officialdom, Franco-Cameroonian writer Calixthe Beyala and Guadeloupean director Luc Saint-Eloy burst onto the stage and delivered a truly exhilarating speech. "Just imagine," they said,

> imagine, in this country, TV programs that only broadcast images of Black people. Imagine, in this country, in every movie theater, screens that only showed stories about Blacks, for Blacks, and excluded every other skin color. Imagine, in this country, advertisements on television, at the movies, on the walls of every major city, that extolled the virtues of products made for Blacks to eat, to drink, to wash with, and to entertain themselves with; products to wear, to sleep in, and to educate their children with, in other words, for Blacks to have a life. For Blacks simply to have a life—every minute of every day, of every week, of every year, since the birth of radio, television, and the movies. Now you, fellow French people, imagine that you're missing from all this, that you're invisible—just imagine . . . But no need to worry, the role of invisible people, that's *our* role. Except that it's not a fiction. It's our bitter reality in a world of white people that excludes an entire part of the population whose only mistake is being Black or Yellow."

To which Alain Chabat, the evening's emcee, rightly added, "There aren't many Arabs, either."

The CSA didn't agree to Égalité's demand to set quotas for French television, although several months after the Césars it published a study that factored in the skin color of people appearing on television. The purpose was to tally the number of those perceived as non-white, regardless of the program, and to determine whether they were shown in a discriminatory way. The study revealed that ethnoracial minorities by and large served as extras and very rarely played leading roles. On news programs, very few non-white experts appeared. Black people were more present than Arab or Asian people thanks to American TV programs. They were most often seen on shows having to do with (surprise, surprise) music or sports.[8]

The French government expanded the CSA's duties to include efforts to advance social cohesion and fight discrimination. Agreements were reached with private TV channels to increase the representation of minorities in programming. As of 2017, however, there was still a long way to go. If one includes French overseas departments and territories, about twenty-five percent of the French population is non-white. Yet non-whites comprise no more than sixteen percent of people appearing on French television.[9]

I started working in television somewhat by accident. A Franco-Cameroonian director friend, a fan of the soap opera *Plus belle la vie* (A More Beautiful Life), was serving on a commission with one of the show's woman producers. He had complained about the portrayal of Black characters on the show. The producer told him that the problem was that she had no Black writers on any of her writing teams. He gave her my name.

Since the process of selecting writers for the series was extremely rigorous and went beyond the producers' purview, the series showrunner oversaw the different interviews, tests, and probationary periods I had to go through to determine whether I would have a future on the show. This was in 2007. As it turned out, I was the first Black screenwriter on *Plus belle la vie*. Since then, despite some breaks of varying lengths, certain of them lasting years, I've continued to write for the series, the most watched daily show in France. As of 2017, and notwithstanding the high turnover, I'm still the only Black female writer on the writing team. I say the only Black female because I'm a woman, but to my knowledge no Black male writer has ever worked on the show.

The situation isn't specific to *Plus belle la vie*. Regardless of the other series I have written for or my many other projects in TV or film, I have always been the only Black writer. That hasn't created any particular difficulties for me, whether in getting hired or in supervising other writers. On the other hand, no one, neither my fellow screenwriters nor the producers, has ever seemed puzzled by this blatant lack of diversity over such a long period of time.

As I've said, people may not be racist in the TV and movie industries, but they do seem to find nothing unusual about sticking to their own kind, about keeping things between whites. I tend to associate the phenomenon with what some have called racism by omission.

If, as the CSA noted in its report, French TV is white, that's because the profession is white.

The movies and shows we see on television emerge from the imagination of writers who submit them to producers, who in turn present them to networks. Directors only enter in much later. Unless the subject matter dictates otherwise, and despite the supposedly dominant position of under-fifty-year-old housewives (whose skin color no one knows anyway), the overwhelming majority of TV protagonists are white men. When someone comes up with a non-white protagonist for a series or movie, networks tremble in fear. Take, for example, the following anecdote. The long-running ratings-topping TV series *Cherif* was initially supposed to be called *Kader Cherif*, after the show's police detective main character. But network executives at France 2 found the title too "segmenting," that is, they thought it cut out a segment of the show's potential audience. They went with *Cherif*, which, because it sounds like *sheriff* in English, may have evoked cowboys and Indians.

"Segmenting." A fatal word for networks that want their programs to attract as wide an audience as possible. But what basis is there for thinking that the French public can't relate to non-white leads? Has anyone conducted an opinion poll? Have Black, Arab, or Asian viewers signed a petition insisting that they not, under any circumstances, be represented on French shows?

One day, a TV producer with whom I worked explained to me in a very serious tone that it really was hard for people to identify with Black people. I bit my lip to keep myself from laughing. I was Black and my favorite actress was Marilyn Monroe. In Ivory Coast, life stops during broadcasts of Brazilian telenovelas, programs overrun with light-skinned, European-looking actors. In working-class neighborhoods, children pretend they're Bruce Lee or Jackie Chan. In shops, pirated DVDs of Bollywood films are hugely successful.

As long as film and television have existed, millions of viewers throughout the world have identified with characters and actors who don't look like them. If I had had to wait for a Black protagonist before going to the movies or turning on my TV, I would only have seen a handful of films, and I would have stopped paying my cable bill long ago.

We connect with a story because it moves us and reminds us of our common humanity. Emotions are universal; they have no color. But white audiences were apparently so used to seeing only themselves on screen that they had forgotten such basic facts. That, in any case, was the conclusion the TV execs had come to.

Among my various activities over the years, I worked on the short-lived soap *Seconde chance* from 2008 to 2009. The network, TF1, had bet big on the show, which had a substantial budget—close to thirty million euros—and large production and writing teams. When I arrived, the show's writers had already been at work for several months.

One morning, the showrunner entered the writing room with something urgent on his mind. We had to create a Black character. TF1's new director of fiction programming, who had just watched the series' first episodes, couldn't understand how, out of some thirty characters, none of them was Black. Yet several dozen writers had been churning out pages for months, their scripts had been given the green light by the show's producers and the network, and shooting was well underway. No one had noticed anything amiss. What changed? The network's new director of fiction programming was Canadian, gay, and Black. Accustomed to a different notion of diversity, he found it inconceivable that a supposedly mainstream series would fail to reflect French society. With that, we frantically got down to work. The showrunner, a shrewd man, was especially anxious that we avoid a stereotyped character. After numerous false starts, we finally decided on a geek, a shy and awkward, unwittingly sweet character, the finance director of the ad agency where the story was set, who gradually comes out of his shell and falls in love. In a little wink to my own background, I asked that we call him Koffi Diakhité, combining a first name from Ivory Coast's Christian South with a last name from its Muslim North. This was at a time when political tensions between the two communities were at their height, when people were accusing Muslim Ivorians of not being true Ivorians. The character was a great success and helped the actor David Baiot, in his first substantial role on screen, kick-start his television career.

It then became clear that we had to create a Black female character. That's how Stéfi Celma, today known for her work on the series *Call My Agent!* got her start on TV.

Without a high-level decision-maker sensitive to the issue of minority representation, these leading roles would simply not have existed. To exemplify the diversity of French society, the show would have settled for a single non-white character, a French North African, as the writing teams (all white, it's worth noting) had initially envisioned. Hence the importance, if one is really looking to put more diversity on French television, of diversifying hiring practices as well.

Several months later, we decided to bring our geek character's family to life. Because good plots feed off of conflict, we dreamed up a father whose personality was the exact opposite of his son's, an apathetic jazz musician who, uninvited, moves in with his CFO son. Needless to say, he outstays his welcome. As was typical in this kind of series, the writers split into two teams. My team wrote the plots, the other the dialogues. Soon, the episode our team came up with was sent to a dialogue writer. When I read what he'd written, I fell out of my chair.

Because the character was African, he had him speak pidgin, going so far as to take out, in writing, every one of his Rs. It was like a mash-up of one of the comic Michel Leeb's Africans and Baba, the thick-lipped Black pirate of the Asterix comics, who speaks with every R elided. The episode simply couldn't run with such insane dialogues. I alerted the showrunner who, this time around, was very upset.

The writer explained that he was trying to be funny. It was a clumsy attempt at humor. The showrunner reassured me that the writer wasn't—no, really, not even the slightest bit—racist, that there was nothing intentional about it. Maybe not. But it was enough for him to have the words "African," "musician," and "comedy" lumped together in his head for the old racist associations to reemerge.

I've had other similar experiences several times. One of the most memorable had to do with a well-known TV writer with whom someone had suggested I work on one of my own projects. He had just written a film that featured two major French movie stars.

His film hadn't yet finished when I asked to read the script. Good thing I asked. I appreciated the expert writing until I came across a mind-boggling scene.

The heroine, affluent and uptight, goes to a carwash operated by a crew of women bombshells, along the lines of the videos and reality-TV shows where half-naked suds-covered girls wash cars and pose lewdly to the great delight, I imagine, of male viewers. I'll note that the heroine goes to the carwash at night. The water jets start to unload, spraying her windshield and shrinking her field of vision. In this slightly unsettling scene, she notices a "human form." Suddenly afraid, she locks her doors. But a "living mass of bodies" jumps onto her hood, whereupon she lets out a "cry of terror." Then the water stops, the heroine's field of vision returns to normal, and she sees, I quote, "a bikini-clad Black, with huge breasts and an enormous ass, coming toward her, armed with a foam-dripping sponge." "La Black"—that's what she was called—begins washing the windshield with her breasts. Even when she actually had lines, this girl wasn't referred to by her name or function like the other characters, however secondary. She was "la Black," a bestial, primitive, oversexed creature, who frightened the fragile white heroine.

Still more fascinating, the script had been read by several dozen people. Producers, financers, distributors, broadcasters, agents, actors, tech people, friends. Although the scene brought together all the most simplistic and degrading racist fantasies, no one had found anything wrong with it. Which also meant that a Black actress, or, in any case, a Black woman, whoever she was, had agreed to play the role. It was only in editing, I was told, that the woman director, no doubt because she'd registered the truth of the scene, decided to cut it.

In my film project, the protagonists were Black. Edified by what I had just read, I told my producer that I wouldn't be working with the screenwriter she had recommended. Her response? But he isn't racist, his partner is a Black man!

As if that by itself were enough to redeem him of anything. Whole generations of white masters and colonizers have fantasized about, slept with, raped, and sometimes loved their Black slaves and subjects without it somehow erasing their racism. Desire, as we all know, is a winding road.

Realizing that I wouldn't be moved, my producer, an intelligent woman, who, out of friendship, had stopped using the English word *Black* in French and conscientiously started using the French word *Noir*, suggested that my antiracist commitments were driving me to focus on the bad in everything. I could see the moment coming when I would be called intolerant, when I'd become that "angry Black woman," always complaining about everything.

The showrunner and producer were both more eager to defend the writers, insisting the latter weren't racist, than to try to understand the racism at work in their writing. And what if the two of them were out-and-out racists? Why not simply concede the fact and respond accordingly? If, on the other hand, they had, without realizing the repercussions, given voice to their unconscious, again, why not just acknowledge it and explain to the writers how their scripts echoed racial stereotypes which, of course, all of us in France were already steeped in but were now unacceptable?

Instead of responding rationally, both the producer and the showrunner reacted emotionally and immediately went on the defensive. As if they felt that they themselves were being attacked.

The American academic Robin DiAngelo, a white woman, as she herself conscientiously points out, calls the characteristic discomfort whites feel when confronted with conversations about racism "white fragility." Accustomed to defining themselves as individuals and not as part of a racial group, whites have a hard time, according to her, recognizing the systemic nature of racism. They turn racism into a personal problem and reduce it to a moral issue: racism is bad. Good people aren't racist. Being racist is, therefore, the worst of all insults; it means you're a bad person. To maintain their self-regard, to stave off the negative emotions the issue raises, to preserve what DiAngelo calls their "racial innocence,"[10] white people erect defense mechanisms, like those I mentioned above, that prevent them from questioning themselves or changing their ways of thinking about the issue.

The few meetings in which I have brought up aspects of a script I found questionable from a racial point of view, or asked people to stop writing the English word *Black* every time they wanted to refer, in French, to characters who were *Noirs*, I have very distinctly felt the atmosphere change. As if the air had suddenly been sucked out of the room, as if a pall had been cast over everyone. Utter silence and nervous looks were people's response. In one fell swoop, I had broken my colleagues' illusion of universalism, the façade of "it's okay, we're all the same," which is easy to believe when you're white, because you have had no—or very little—experience of racism, but which you know when you are Black is an illusion meant to reassure white people.

These discussions were uncomfortable for me, too. I always had knots in my stomach before speaking up. One option was to say nothing and preserve the semblance of unity, the reassuring drone, of the group, but at the risk of betraying my convictions. The other option was to say something necessary but unsettling that I knew would shatter the prevailing harmony, make everyone else uncomfortable, and isolate me from the group.

For the sake of honesty, I generally chose the second option. Did it do any good? I'm not so sure. I don't know how many times I have explained to white people that the euphemistic use of the English word *Black* was demeaning in French. After seeming to understand, they went back to using it five minutes later. A force of habit.

In her discussion of white fragility, DiAngelo explains that most white people live in environments where they only spend time with other white people, without being the least bit bothered by this lack of diversity. Although she focuses on the United States, her analysis applies to France as well. "Our society," she laments, "does not teach us to see this as a loss. Pause for a moment and consider the magnitude of this message: We lose nothing of value by having no cross-racial relationships."

Within this very white French context, screenwriters and producers tried to respond to the need for greater diversity on French television, especially in fiction programming, that President Jacques Chirac underscored at the time of the 2005 riots and that the CSA itself repeated later on.

As part of an effort to counter negative stereotypes about ethnic and racial minorities, long confined to playing drug dealers, illegal immigrants, prostitutes, or nurses, Blacks—as well as some Arabs, although rarely Asians—more regularly appeared in roles with more edifying job responsibilities. The police chief on the show *Deux flics sur les docks* (Two Cops on the Docks), for example, was played by Ivory-Coast born Mata Gabin. In *Louis(e)*, Eriq Ebouaney played the head physician at the hospital where the series' protagonist works. The actress Félicité Wouassi was the Prime Minister's PR officer on the show *Paris*. And so on. But the perverse effect of what I would call work-roles is that they are precisely that, job types. They put some color on the screen, of course, but they don't elicit empathy. Who identifies with a job? For viewers to form an attachment with a character, for them to enter the character's inner life even the slightest bit, emotion is needed, the stakes have to be personal.

Certain television series went further, assigning a Black partner to a white protagonist. Much less frequently, they gambled on a Black lead. Such was the case, to take just two examples, in *Les Tricheurs* (Cheaters), starring Pascal Légitimus and Sara Martins, and *Un flic* (A Cop), with Alex Descas.

In *Un flic*, however, one detail confused me, despite the undeniable quality of the show and Descas's acting. Why was the character given the typically Alsatian name Schneider? *Why not?* you might say. Except that, physically, Alex Descas doesn't look mixed race. So it was hard to imagine him with a fictional father from Alsace. Was the character adopted as a child? The show never said.

Somewhat more recently, in the police series *Duel au soleil* (Duel in the Sun), the character played by the Cameroon-born actor Yann Gael was called Sébastien Le Tallec. He was presented as a young Black Breton. Of course, nothing prevented him from being born or raised in Brittany, and therefore culturally Breton. That's the case for the actor himself. But the choice of family name implies a Breton family connection. Since Gael doesn't look any more mixed race than Descas, were viewers to conclude that a wave of adoptions had overwhelmed the Black protagonists of French television? Or had the producers simply been so smitten with the idea of having a Black Breton character that they hadn't bothered to think the logic through?

Some production companies also began holding open casting calls, that is, calls that didn't specify the ethnicity or race of the character they were casting for, which was certainly laudable. However, because they often didn't modify the character's name, even when the background inferred by the name contradicted the actor's physical appearance, they would then declare: You see how progressive we are? The role was clearly written for a white person, and the actor could have been white, but we picked a Black (or an Arab) person instead. What their attitude was telling us was that Black or Arab actors who got parts were so assimilated that they could have been white. The sociologist Éric Macé calls this a "denial of ethnicity."[11] Sure, we would love to put non-whites on the air as long as they speak, think, and act as if they were white.

Now, let's recall the historian Pap Ndiaye's observation mentioned in an earlier chapter. Black people want to be invisible in terms of their social life, in other words, they don't want to be discriminated against because they are Black, but they want to be visible culturally.

From time to time, television movies get made that offer a new perspective. *Fais danser la poussière*, known in English as *Dancing Forever*, inspired by the autobiographical novel of the same name, tells the moving story of a young mixed-race girl raised in a white family who dreams of becoming a dancer. In realizing her dream, she finds a wholeness—an identity—that her parents' short-lived mixed-race couple was unable to give her. For once, we enter the inner life of a Black heroine.

In a more historical vein, *Rose et le soldat* (Rose and the Soldier), based on a little-known episode of French history, depicts the rise of the "Dissidence" movement in the West Indies during the Second World War. From four thousand to five thousand men and women refused to toe the line of the Vichy Regime, left Guadeloupe and Martinique for nearby British islands, then joined the Free French forces.[12] Unfortunately, they were excluded from the National Council of the Resistance in 1945 and their heroism soon faded from memory. *Tropiques amers* (Bitter Tropics), the first French TV series about slavery, came out in 2007. Like *Rose et le soldat*, it was directed by Jean-Claude Barny, who had been working on the unique project since we first met at *Revue Noire* twenty years earlier. Despite *Tropique amers*'s successful ratings, the network turned down a second season.

These examples remain the exceptions. French television may love family comedies, but as I write these words, there are still no series that invite viewers into the daily life of a Black family—or a family of any other ethnoracial minority. On television, as elsewhere, we continue to exist on the margins.[13]

# 23 The White Norm

When you're Black, living in France is a strange adventure that requires you to contort yourself in a thousand different ways every day. The image that immediately comes to mind is of having to put on a pair of shoes that are simply too small for you. You scrunch and wriggle your toes, you suffer through a thousand little—or big—discomforts to try to make them fit. In the end, you have a single alternative: either give up on shoes that were made for someone else and that stop you from moving forward, or put up with the pain and pretend not to feel it, even if it means you're no longer free to walk the way you'd liked.

Our parents, our grandparents, and their forebears tended to choose the second option, either because they didn't have a choice or because they already considered themselves lucky to even have a choice. Nowadays, French Blacks refuse to make themselves small in their own country. Which is why they face so many barriers.

Finding a place is no easy thing in a society that wasn't made for you. Even when you think you have found a place, little things—less trivial than they initially appear—remind you that you haven't. But how could things be any different give that, for centuries, France considered itself a country of the white race, asking nothing from its immigrant populations but their complete assimilation?

French society has been changing, as have its demographics. Blacks comprise six percent of the European French population,[1] to which should be added all those living in French overseas territories and departments. That's not nothing. Except that, like Cinderella's wicked stepsisters, we have to struggle to fit into someone else's shoes. At least the fairytale had a moral: the stepsisters were wicked so didn't deserve to marry the prince. Do Black people?

Two years ago, I had my glass-slipper experience with a Photomaton, one of the photobooths you find all over Paris. My passport had expired so I went to the local office of the Paris prefecture to have it renewed. For my pictures, I made sure to go to a Photomaton, which guaranteed they would be the official size and format. No such luck. My picture was refused. I came out much too dark. I figured that my neighborhood Photomaton must have been on the older side, that its lens or printer must have been grimy. Anyway, I had no reason to worry.

The local prefecture office had a photobooth, so I repeated the process, although I did grumble to myself about having to pay a second time. The headshots were refused again. My skin came out too dark, much darker than my actual skin color, and the person at the prefecture couldn't sufficiently discern my features. I asked how it was that a government-certified photobooth issued pictures that weren't up to government standards. All the Photomatons had signs on them saying, "Photos compliant with all official documents" and affixed, in case one still had any doubts, with the French flag and the symbol of the French Republic.

The chief, a West Indian man, heard my question from his nearby office. He walked over and, with a resigned look, admitted, "It always does that with us Blacks. The pictures are never accepted." All right, so what was the solution? Whiten my skin? Give up my passport? He suggested that I go to a professional photographer. Needless to say, the price for that service wasn't the same. Ultimately, I had to have my ID pictures taken three times and pay that much more before they were finally accepted.

Now, Photomaton is a private company. But it was certified by the Ministry of the Interior for its booths, which supposedly met the ISO standard established in 2005 and reviewed every five years, and that included a whole slew of criteria, including lighting and color. Did that mean that at the Ministry of the Interior, like at Photomaton itself, no one had accounted for—or even thought of—the fact that certain French citizens have dark skin and that that would require them to adjust the booths' settings? Wouldn't it have been more honest to specify from the start, "Photos compliant with all official documents if you are white or have light skin"?

That, in a nutshell, is the glaring hypocrisy of French universalism. It claims to encompass us all, making no mention of ethnic background or race, when in fact it is merely the extrapolation of features specific to one ethnoracial group applied to everyone else.

In order to fit this model when you are neither white nor "pure" French, you would have to erase everything that makes you unique. You can change your name, your religion, your hair texture or eye color, the way you speak, your accent, your cultural references, and even your gender if you want to. But if there is one thing that you can't get rid of, it's Black skin. That may be the reason why we are perceived as irremediably other. Even artificially depigmented, bleached skin won't be the skin of a white person, it will always proclaim its Blackness, just like a tiger will always proclaim its tigritude. And yet, in everyday life, we are asked to behave as if we could simply dissolve into white society.

I hate shopping. Yet strolling the aisles of supermarkets and department stores offers a mine of information. Simply looking for a pair of nylons can prove more enlightening than reading a book of sociology. This is how, as a teenager, I discovered that "nude" was the word universally used to refer to the pink-beige color specific to the majority of white skin tones. Strangely, the potential universality of my brown nudity had never been taken into account.

On the other hand, according to a very well-known French nylon brand, I was a member of the animal kingdom and specifically—how original!—a "gazelle."[2] In any case, that was the name of the only available hue that more or less corresponded to my skin color. It was also the darkest. Pleased with myself for having found nylons that matched my skin, I had left things at that when, one day, seeing a Black actress at a celebrity event wearing nylons that were clearly too light for her, I started wondering how all these women with complexions darker than gazelle fur managed. Did they stop wearing nylons in winter? Did they track down specialty brands? Did they just wear black? One revelation led to another until I realized in a kind of epiphany that, if certain nylons made my legs look fat, it wasn't because they were shiny, as I had often thought, but because they were too light for my skin color. Then, two years ago, the same French brand launched a line of nylons for Black and mixed-race skin colors. I have yet to see them at the major stores.

Confined to black or gazelle, I learned to look away as I passed aisles overflowing with nylons that promised their wearers a sun-kissed tint or a deep bronze tan. After repeatedly hearing saleswomen talk about my "color" to avoid saying "Black" as I tried on clothes, I nourished the fleeting hope that "color"—in the newspeak of the French clothing industry—might mean brown. I was quickly disabused. Then again, I expanded my vocabulary when I discovered that "shade" and "skin tone" were synonymous with "nude," and that "bronze" meant going from pink-beige to golden-beige.

I also gained precious time by not stopping to browse the aisles of lingerie actually labelled *nude* in English, with their allegedly neutral tones that clashed on me like neon.

Similarly, when I was twenty years old, buying a foundation or lipstick was an ordeal that left me completely drained and vaguely humiliated. The desolate smiles of the saleswomen telling me one after the other that they probably didn't have a color that would work for me finally made me feel like I was the one who wasn't right for their products. Although Sonia Rolland, the first African-born Miss France, is mixed-race with skin much lighter than mine, she too has recalled how in the 2000s the quest for a suitable foundation played out like a treasure hunt. Whenever she discovered one that worked with her complexion, she immediately stocked up. The situation was even more ludicrous because the same major French cosmetic companies that only offered variations on pink and beige in France sold colors extending into the darkest of dark browns in the United States. A white actor friend saved my self-esteem by introducing me to a brand available only to professionals that offered absolutely every hue.

Nowadays, I no longer have to track down specialized or American brands to find a foundation that won't make me look like a block of gray stone or a lipstick that won't turn me into a clown. No doubt due to competition from brands like MAC (bought out by L'Oréal, incidentally) or Bobbi Brown, French companies have expanded the color ranges they now sell in France.[3] The proof, if proof were needed: Lupita Nyong'o, a dark-skinned Black actress with kinky hair and Kenyan parents, became one of the faces of Lancôme in 2014, which would have been unthinkable only a few years earlier in the world of women's beauty, where the only Black women you saw were mixed race.[4]

Research by "ethnic" marketing agencies had undoubtedly revealed that Afrodescendant consumers were buying five times more makeup and related products than other groups and up to six times more products for hair.[5]

Along with the introduction of these new lines, I also discovered that I had "ethnic" beauty, and that, like the "world cuisine" aisles in supermarkets, where they throw together tacos, Chinese soups, curry paste, udon noodles, and jars of harissa, I was entitled to my own little corner specializing in women's magazines and their online offshoots. There I learned that my skin didn't have the same characteristics as white skin, that it was drier, more prone to hyperpigmentation, and yet more resistant to aging—in short, the basics that any Black or mixed-race woman already knows by heart, to the point that I wondered who these articles were really for, if they weren't published solely to give their editors a clear conscience.[6]

Black . . . Sometimes I sense that it's the only thing that people see, to the detriment of everything else about me. Yet when I look at myself in the mirror, that isn't what interests me but whether or not I have shadows under my eyes, a good complexion, if I need to put on makeup, and what products I should use to get the desired result. For this, I either turn to media meant for an Afrodescendant readership or head to Black influencers. One day, while perusing one of the most well-known of these blogs, *Black Beauty Bag*, I made a mini-discovery that gave me food for thought. The devil is in the details, but so is the truth.

In one of her blogposts, Fatou N'diaye warned against the dry shampoos sold at large retailers. Made for Western hair, which quickly becomes oily, these shampoos absorb a large amount of sebum, which, unlike white women, Black women tend to lack.[7] I immediately thought of the double pack of dry shampoo I had bought thinking I had found a good deal. The saleswoman had been very attentive. She recommended the brown dry shampoo rather than the white of another brand to prevent visible residue from building up in my dark hair. But clearly she had missed this key piece of information N'diaye mentioned in her blogpost. As had I. Then I thought about all the things I did believing that they were good for me without knowing whether they really were. About the sunburns I got because, according to the general consensus, Black skin didn't need sunscreen. The result? I didn't have the instinct to put any on. About the doctors who explained to me that if I had backaches, it was because my back was arched, as if all the world's Black people suffered from lower back pain. About my consternation when trying to find glasses that sat on my nose rather than my cheeks, until a Black optician explained what should have been obvious but hadn't even crossed my mind, because even if I knew better, I sometimes forgot that what is supposedly universal is in reality only universal for whites: the glasses sold in stores weren't designed to sit on noses with wide and low bridges—they weren't designed for Africans.

Even with the best intentions in the world, it's hard to construct a coherent identity for oneself as a Black person. The framework we have for perceiving ourselves was created for others and only includes us by accident, when our features just happen to be taken into account. In these circumstances, loving oneself as one is becomes a challenge.

The same is also true for children. I understood that I was Black the day someone assigned me to being only that. Most adults whom I have heard talk about this pivotal moment in their lives consider it a negative experience. Another child refusing to play with them, an unkind remark at school or in the street, an offensive nickname, the rising awareness that, despite the magical force of their thinking, their skin color won't get any lighter as they grow up. Black skin can be a burden from one's earliest childhood.

Now I too am a mother. When my children were born—with their fine, straight hair and skin as white and pink as mine was brown, even if, of course, like all Black or mixed-race children, barring certain exceptions, their skin grew darker and their hair curlier as the weeks went by—I was quickly forced to think about how and what I should tell them. Should I explain to them that they would be perceived as Black or should I wait for their questions? How should I speak to them about racism, about racial inequality? At what age should I do it without saddling them with needless anxiety? After all, their history wasn't the same as mine. Their experience of these issues would undoubtedly be different. Prepare them, yes; weigh them down, no.

After some reflection, I decided to take the initiative by explaining to them myself why they were brown, as they put it, before someone else did it in a way that might be disparaging. They must have been three years old and were already surprised that most of the people they came across were white and they weren't. I deliberately presented myself as completely neutral and approached the topic very simply; in my tone and phrasing, I tried to ensure it remained a non-issue for them, both to avoid influencing them and because a little voice in me hoped that their generation would be more open, that they wouldn't have to endure the same racism and discrimination as ours did. Don't all parents hope that their children will be spared the hardships that they went through themselves?

"We all have something in our bodies called melanin," I explained. "When people have a lot of it, they are dark brown. When people have a medium amount, they are light brown, like you. When people have a small amount, they're white. When it's sunny outside, melanin is released and people tan, meaning they become a little darker than usual." They wanted to know why there were a lot of white people but not a lot of brown people around. I offered a similarly simple answer: "France is a country in Europe. Before, almost everyone in Europe was white. That's why today, even if there are people of every color in France, there are more white people." They seemed satisfied with my explanation.

A children's book about cowboys and Indians mentioning (with the requisite drawing) that former slaves had become cowboys led us to the issue of slavery. Again, I simplified things a great deal. I told them how Europeans had killed nearly all the Indians in order to take their land, but because there were so few Europeans, they went to Africa to capture men, women, and children, whom they forced to work all the time with no pay in America. My son, wide-eyed, replied, "We Europeans were really mean!" I found his response heartening. I appreciated that, since he knew he was French, he naturally identified with the Europeans without connecting where he lived with a skin color, a skin color he was already well aware of.

When he was in his first year of preschool, his teacher invited me to take a look at the drawings hanging on the classroom wall. "I laughed so hard," she said. A row of twenty-five clown heads in every color of the rainbow. Only one was colored brown: my son's. I couldn't see what was so funny. On the other hand, I was happy that as young as he was, he already had a very clear awareness of himself. Even today, the people he draws are brown with heads topped with little tight curls, just like him. But there are already times when he finds whites better looking, no doubt because he sees more of them in the images he encounters and has unconsciously internalized that they represent the norm. I have occasionally had to show him pictures of Black stars and remind him of the names of all the Black and mixed-race people he likes before he agrees that brown people are very beautiful too. As for my daughter, even though she likes her brown dolls, she instinctively prefers her white ones.

Providing a positive image of Africa to children growing up in France is no easy task, either. One only needs to look at the way the continent is represented in children's books: the bush, wild animals, naked children, poverty, and so on. I gave up on buying my kids a children's atlas when I paged through several of them and noticed that the illustrations of African countries only included animals, whereas the illustrations of other continents, if there were any, pictured monuments and cultural symbols as well.

Africa isn't an open-air zoo. Yet that's the image French children are given. When mine started asking me if there were cars and furniture in Africa and if everyone walked around shirtless, I knew it was time to do something. So, I started bringing back children's books from Ivory Coast. At least now they see brown children in "normal" family situations with whom they can identify.

With the help of a provincial bookseller who understood my concerns, I also found a very cute story about Mariétou, a little girl who wants an Olympic champion bathing suit.[8] When I looked for more of the author's books, I was disappointed to find that the publisher made them part of its collection called "Les Ethniques" (Ethnics). Once again, there had to be a pigeonhole to keep things separate and confined. But what really encouraged my children to reconsider how they thought about Africa was *Akissi*, the children's graphic novel by Marguerite Abouet, the author of *Aya of Yop City*. The life of a little brown girl in Abidjan wasn't too far removed from their life in France, even if the time period and cultural references weren't the same. Funny, quick-witted, and resourceful, the book's heroine gets into all sorts of trouble and cracks my kids up. I regularly send Marguerite text messages to let her know how much my kids love *Akissi*. I should also tell her how relieved I am, because finding children's books with Black characters in France is like running an obstacle course. The same is obviously true for toys. Although Mattel has a whole line of Black Barbies, you have to go from store to store in France just to find one or at best two that are actually kept on the shelves.

To compensate for this absence of representation, I take my children to exhibits of Afrodescendant artists as often as I can. They accompany me to workshops run by artist friends who explain their work to them. I make sure to tell them that the Black person they just said hello to makes movies, that that other Black person writes books, which I make sure they see. It doesn't matter if they can't read the books. I want it to be normal for them to think that the beautiful and intelligent things that they see around them may have been made by Black people.

Is that enough? I doubt it. Children aren't stupid. Even if they don't say it, they can see perfectly well that in the universe created for them—games, books, cartoons—few children look like them, that the brown people are rarely the heroes, and that, as a general rule, the protagonists, more complex and more virtuous than the other characters, are white. Just as gender stereotypes are ubiquitous in the world of children's toys, clothes, and socialization, a default image of Blacks is given to children. Blacks are the people they don't see, the absentees from children's mythologies. While I'm very glad that Disney princesses are now more diverse, they're all girls. What Black male heroes are there for little boys?[9]

# 24 Run, Black Man, Run!

In 1952, Frantz Fanon observed, "The black man wants to be white. The white man slaves to reach a human level."[1] For my part, I would say that today Black people are preoccupied with being both human and Black, whereas whites still bear no more than the burden of their own individuality.

I would so love to stop thinking of myself as Black, to concern myself, like whites, solely with realizing my unique being. Of course, I don't wake up every morning reminding myself that I'm Black. Not everyone I talk to is obsessed with my skin color. Otherwise, I wouldn't be able to live. But all too many things force me back to it: newspaper articles, a Facebook post, a new victim of police violence, the extreme-right politician Éric Zemmour's latest nonsense, a politician's supposed gaffe, a compliment in the street: "That red dress goes so great with your skin." A seemingly harmless remark slipped in when I was least expecting it, when I had let my guard down, when I was thinking that I was merely myself, Isabelle, and that the person in front of me and I were just two people having a conversation.

"How are you doing?" an acquaintance asks me during a meeting.

"Okay. A bit tired."

"Stop it! You Africans have all sorts of energy!"

At the endocrinologist's office: "Hi, doctor. I was hoping you'd check to see if I have a hypothyroid problem. I get so tired. I just can't explain it."

"Hm. You're West Indian, right? I've noticed West Indians are pretty listless."

Yet these are merely psychological blows. I don't have to fear for my physical safety. I live in a good neighborhood, where the police are courteous with locals, where they call me "Madame" and use the formal "vous," where they are ready and willing to protect me, where they don't say "Bamboula," which Luc Poignant, the police-union spokesman, apparently finds appropriate to say on TV, but rather a person "of African type."

One Saturday night, after parking in a street in the center of Paris, I waved down some policemen, scampering in my heels. I wanted to be sure that with the new parking regulations I could park in a spot marked for delivery trucks. The Black friend I was with burst out laughing: "I bet it's not often cops see a sista running up to them with a question like that!"

The teenagers Zyed and Bouna had run in the opposite direction when the cops arrived. Even though they had done nothing wrong, they were so scared of being arrested that they scaled a thirteen-foot wall to hide in an electrical substation. The consequences, as everyone in France knows, were fatal.

At the end of his furlough, Amine Bentounsi didn't return to the detention center on the outskirts of Paris where he was being held. He was a thus fugitive. When the police showed up to arrest him, he ran. A policeman panicked, fired four shots, one of which struck him in the back and killed him.

Adama Traoré ran to avoid a police checkpoint. He didn't have his ID on him. When the police caught him, three officers forced him to the ground and held him facedown. Adama complained that he couldn't breathe. He died of asphyxiation.

Neighborhood police were doing random ID checks. Théo Luhaka, who had no reason to worry about himself, intervened in an escalating encounter between an officer and another young man. The police restrained Théo. Théo resisted. They slapped him and hit him several times with truncheons. One officer took out his baton and penetrated it four inches into Théo's anus.

They were all from the suburbs, from the *banlieue*.

How many others like them are killed or injured every year?

A young man between the ages of eighteen and twenty-four identified as Black or Arab is twenty times more likely to be stopped by the police than the rest of the French population. But the police, we are told, don't employ ethnic or racial profiling, and François Hollande, when he became president in 2012, abandoned the idea of requiring police officers to provide a statement of the grounds for identity checks.

Myself, I'm a woman and a mother; I mind my manners. The police treat me with respect. They don't make inappropriate remarks. They hand me a tissue when I shed a tear as I file my police report at the station. I like to cry; it's a relief to not always be strong. They tell me, "Don't worry, Madame, we'll find him. We don't like guys attacking women." It doesn't matter if the sex offender who tried to assault me was white and I'm Black, everything is as it always should be. I'm not *une Black*, *une Bamboula*, or whatever else, but myself, Isabelle, a woman who, according to the police, has the right to walk down the street at night without becoming someone's sexual prey.

I was returning home. The last metro had stopped one station before mine, leaving me with a twenty-minute walk. I was alone in the street. As I walked past a brightly lit shopping mall, I noticed a shadow on the sidewalk trailing me close behind. A man with his penis pulled out started trying to rub himself against me. I told him to stop; he continued following me. For a second, I thought I had lost him. Then he reappeared, his pants down. There was still no one around. I had to think fast, before I was too scared to act. Either I would be a victim and risk getting raped or I would do my best to turn the tables. I took out my cell phone; he turned his back. I shouted: Since you're showing me your ass, I'm going to take pictures of it. I snapped away, telling him to turn around so I could get a better shot of his face. Finally, he started to walk away, insulting me as he went. I immediately called the police. I wasn't home yet. At any moment, he might come back. I was still on the line with the dispatcher when an unmarked police car pulled up. The two officers invited me to get in to help them search for the man. Since my attacker was wearing a hooded sweatshirt, they obviously headed for the nearest housing projects.

At each hoodie, every one of which was worn by a young Black or Arab man, we slowed down. How satisfying it was to tell them, in a reversal of the usual clichés, "No, that's not him. The man was white." The cop in the passenger seat turned to me, "You mean the individual looks European?" He spoke into his police radio: "A Maghrebi-type male. An African-type male. We're continuing our pursuit." In the backseat, I looked out the window, taking in my little tour of the city, nice and warm in my red hooded jacket.

I sometimes find the cops amusing. For example, one of them, just starting out on the job and clearly befuddled by the mysteries of spelling, had to consult a dictionary every three words as he typed up my statement. Seeing him no less bewildered by the dictionary, at a loss to find the right entry words, I offered to spell the words out for him. It would speed things along.

I was still giving my statement when one of the undercover cops returned. He showed me a picture of my assailant on his cell phone. I commended him for being so quick and efficient. You would have thought I was his boss. Probably a quirk I picked up from being escorted with my grandfather by deferential Ivorian police.

Like everyone else, I prefer the cops in movies. But the real ones don't frighten me. What would it be like if they stopped me for no reason several times a year? Or several times a month? I'd be a little less of a smart-ass, that's for sure. And I'd undoubtedly know the visceral fear that Ta-Nehisi Coates describes so well in *Between the World and Me*. The ancestral fear instilled in Black bodies subjected to attack dogs, the lash, and the whip. Yes, massa. Yes, boss. Yes, sir. Lower your eyes, bow your head, even when you feel like screaming. Acquiesce. Don't move. Make a servile show of your eagerness to hand over your ID. Of course, officer. Save your skin.

Amsterdam Airport Schiphol, November 2016. I was flying home from a film festival where I had shown my documentary. As I was going through the metal detector, the alarm went off. I looked at the monitor. Something near my neck. Sure enough, I had put hairpins in to keep my braids back. The girl who was now going to inspect me suddenly drove her hands into my hair. I was shocked by the level of intrusiveness; security agents generally showed some respect. I didn't say anything. She patted me down; the usual process. Then, with no warning, she started tugging at my bra and underwear through my clothes. She wanted to make sure I wasn't hiding anything. What about my physical space? It was too much. I screamed at her in English to stop touching me. She shot back that she hadn't finished the body search. I refused to let her put her hands on me again. I was trembling with rage. She called her supervisor over who told me that this was the procedure, that if I didn't want to be frisked, I could follow the two of them to their office and they would search me there. I could only imagine how that would play out: I'd be completely undressed and subject to a full body search. I swallowed my pride. I gave in. The girl patted me down again, starting from scratch. She clearly got a kick out of pulling on my underwear in front of the other passengers.

I can't imagine how I would react if I had to undergo these arbitrary stop-and-frisks on a regular basis in France. I have zero doubt that one day or another, the mix of rage and impotence that overcame me that afternoon in Amsterdam would finally explode.

# 25 The Guerlain Affair

When the riots erupted in 2005, I was in Miami. Americans told me that it looked like things were really bad in France. I called my cousin in Paris. "What's going on? Is it a Black revolt?" He assured me that it was only a few troublemakers. He was upset. He couldn't identify with French young people's anger. The media, according to him, conflated everything, putting all Blacks in the same basket. He wasn't from a housing project. He wasn't a delinquent.

I didn't argue; I'm very fond of my cousin. But I rejected the idea that there were good Blacks on one side and bad Blacks on the other. The oppression that stemmed from our being Black was something we all experienced to differing degrees and in different ways. I could have been born or grown up in a *banlieue* and endured not only racism but social and geographic exclusion. I have never forgotten that I'm the daughter of a woman who was denied the right to raise me because she was considered too poor. Yet after I was born, she went to school. She has a job. Her other children have good careers. What we aren't given, it's up to us to take.

I didn't participate in the tumult of 2005 or in the many debates that followed. Too wrapped up in my American adventure, I don't think I completely grasped the importance of what had happened. The riots nonetheless represented a major turning point. For the first time, a president of the French Republic officially acknowledged the existence of racial discrimination and the need to combat it.

Broadcast live from the Élysée Palace, President Jacques Chirac's speech was watched by almost twenty million French people.[1] His tone was solemn, his words forceful.

> [. . .] Following the law and values of the Republic necessarily requires a sense of justice, fraternity, and generosity. That is why we belong to a national community. It is in how we speak to each other, how we look at each other, it is in our hearts and in our actions that we show the respect that every one of us deserves. And I want to say to the children of troubled neighborhoods, regardless of their origin, that they are all the sons and daughters of the Republic.
>
> We won't be able to build anything lasting without respect. We won't be able to build anything lasting if we allow racism, intolerance, abuse, and contempt to grow, whatever their causes may be.
>
> We won't be able to build anything lasting without fighting the poison that discrimination represents in our society.
>
> We won't be able to build anything lasting if we fail to acknowledge each other and if we fail to accept the diversity of French society. This diversity is part of our history. It is a blessing and a strength.

Chirac then ran through a series of measures he planned to take. He called on French communes to comply with a law requiring them to ensure that twenty percent of housing stock be public; he created the now-defunct Haute autorité de lutte contre les discriminations et pour l'égalité, an equal opportunity and anti-discrimination commission; he called on French political parties, corporations, and labor unions to better reflect France's diversity; he mentioned establishing a more equitable school system, etc.

Even now, years later, his speech leaves a bad taste in my mouth. Because things have barely changed in any substantial way.

Still, like everyone else, I noticed the greater visibility of Black people in French public space in the years that followed. In 2006, on the prompting of then-Interior Minister Nicolas Sarkozy, the Black journalist Harry Roselmack became anchor Patrick Poivre d'Arvor's replacement on TF1's nightly news program "20 Heures." Sarkozy would later be the first French President to appoint two non-white women to ministerial positions that only whites had held until then, although non-white appointees had previously served in the

Ministry for Overseas France and as State Secretary for Integration (under Mitterrand) and Deputy Secretary for Equal Opportunities (under Chirac).

The addition of Rama Yade and Rachida Dati to Sarkozy's government caused quite a sensation. But at the same time, as if to prove to the right wing that their appointments were mere window dressing, Sarkozy created the Ministry of Immigration, Integration, National Identity, and Codevelopment. He insulted Africans and their diaspora during his notorious speech in Dakar, where he explained in front of an audience of Senegalese officials and students—in a university, of all places—that "the African has not fully entered history." In 2009, he launched a debate about national identity. During a speech in Grenoble in 2010, he delivered a violent attack against immigration and Roma, and said that he wanted to expand the grounds for stripping French citizenship from foreign-born citizens with dual nationality. His loyal minister Brice Hortefeux explained in remarks about Arab people that "when there's just one, it's okay. It's when there're a lot of them that there're problems."[2]

During the Sarkozy years, there was an extraordinary explosion of racist speech at the highest levels of the French government. I felt bullied and abused. More than ever, I had the feeling I was a second-class citizen. Under these circumstances, the Guerlain Affair was the straw that broke the camel's back.

On October 15, 2010, Jean-Paul Guerlain, heir to the perfume company of the same name and the former "nose" of the Maison Guerlain, was interviewed on France 2's nightly newscast by Élise Lucet. As part of a promotional tour for his autobiography, Guerlain described the process that had led him to create one of his best-selling perfumes. In a light-hearted tone, he explained, "For once, I set to work like a *nègre*. I don't know if *nègres* have always worked that much, but anyway . . ."

With the first words the perfumer spoke, Élise Lucet began to laugh, surely never imagining what would come next. But when he mentioned the work of "*nègres*," she merely nodded and moved on. The interview ended as if nothing had happened, in the same light-hearted vein, and without any request for clarification from the journalist.

The clip immediately made the rounds on Twitter and Facebook. That evening, on the eight o'clock news on France 2, Laurent Delahousse read the press release Jean-Paul Guerlain had sent to AFP. "My words in no way reflect the way I actually think. It was an inappropriate gaffe that I deeply regret."

I'm always surprised by how quickly people who make racist remarks in public call them "gaffes." Or claim their words were misinterpreted. Because, of course, those same people are ready to swear right here and right now, hand to god and doe-eyed, that they aren't racist. What surprises me even more is that the media goes along with the spin. The "racist gaffe" has become its own trope and regularly appears in newspaper headlines. Regarding Guerlain, the headline in the center-left newspaper *Libération* read, "Racist Gaffe on France 2 News."

A gaffe: a *dérapage*, from the verb *déraper*. The dictionary tells us that *déraper* is originally a nautical term referring to an anchor that becomes detached from the seabed, setting a boat adrift. A *dérapage* is what happens when control mechanisms break down, when the superego nods off and the id reveals itself in all its splendor. The so-called racist gaffes authentically express what their speakers think deep down.

Jean-Paul Guerlain quite obviously thought what he said. Less than two years later, he did it again, this time going after three railway workers—Black and Asian—who tried to help move his wheelchair after he had been denied access to a train because he had arrived late. "France," he said, "is a shit country, this is a shit train company, and to top it all off, we're only served by immigrants."[3] His "we're served" says it all—a turn of phrase that it would never occur to me to use with regard to French railway workers. It betrayed an upper-class white man's vision of the world, a caste-bound world where people of color are not only foreigners but inferiors in the master's service.

In 1995, Jean-Paul Guerlain bought extensive ylang-ylang plantations on the island of Mayotte. Highly prized by the perfume industry, the flowers were harvested by locals. After he was caught employing undocumented workers, he moved his operations out of French territory to the Comoro Islands. Had the world of his plantations birthed a colonial mentality in him? That was a friend of mine's argument when he rather awkwardly tried to convince me that Guerlain wasn't racist, and that he had only said what he had about *nègres* not working because of his environment.

The image of *nègre* laziness was indeed recurrent among white plantation masters, whether during slavery or colonialism. The *nègre* wasn't productive enough. He couldn't keep up the necessary pace. Yet this *nègre* wasn't a machine. And regardless of what those who made him work his fingers to the bone thought, he was endowed with a brain. He knew what it would cost him if he tried to escape the plantation or get out of forced labor. He protested as best he could with the extremely limited freedom he had. He used passive resistance. Not too much, though: he wanted to avoid the master's reprisals.

When forced labor was abolished in French African colonies in 1946, Ivorians previously subject to the practice on the country's large European plantations simply stood up and walked away. Who was going to work themselves to death for their former masters? The illusion of omnipotence must have been incredibly widespread for Europeans to believe that the very people whose bodies they had already taken would now be willing to give up their souls.

But let's return to October 15, 2010. On Facebook, my friends were in an uproar. It was all anyone was talking about. Spoofs of Guerlain's perfume ads were making the rounds. Already seething from three years of Sarkozysm, I too was pretty upset. It wasn't just that Jean-Paul Guerlain was racist; he had touched a nerve—the memory of slavery. Despite that, Élise Lucet said nothing, did nothing, refuted nothing. She apologized on France 2. But she claimed in the press that she hadn't heard the perfumer's remarks, a hearing loss belied by the skeptical "erm" she uttered following the second part of Guerlain's remark. Guerlain the company didn't react, nor did its multinational parent LVMH. The general impression from all this was that there would be no consequences to publicly insulting the country's Black population. I spoke to friends about it on the phone. We all agreed that something had to be done. But what?

Without putting much thought into it, I created a Facebook group that I mockingly named "I don't wanna work like a *nègre*, either!" and called for an "action" in front of the Guerlain store on the Champs-Élysées for a week later, Saturday, October 23. Fearing that a protest might be prohibited on the Champs-Élysées because of heightened anti-terrorist measures, I made sure not to mention the word "protest" in my post and spoke instead of a "silent action," during which those of us with Guerlain products would return them to the store. I imagined it as a kind of happening. The only problem was, whatever it was called—a gathering, an action, or a protest—I had no idea how to organize this kind of event. I wasn't an activist. I wasn't a member of any association. I had attended a protest just once, against Jean-Marie Le Pen, the hard-right politician who made it to the second round of the 2002 French presidential elections. I called Rokhaya Diallo, the founder of Les Indivisibles, an antiracist association which became known for its "Y'a bon" Awards ceremony, at which banana peels were given to French public figures who had made racist remarks. She thought it was an excellent idea—which, strangely, no one had come up with yet—told me that other associations were planning to act, and that a call to boycott Guerlain had just been launched on Facebook. She suggested that we combine the various initiatives. The idea of forming a collective emerged over the weekend. It all still seemed quite abstract to me. But on Monday morning, the online edition of the magazine *L'Express*, whose journalists were clearly tracking what was happening on social media, announced that people were gathering on Saturday, October 23. It was too late to turn back, even if I hadn't yet resolved the legal side: did I or didn't I have to register the event with the prefecture?

The same day, the Maison Guerlain finally issued a press release. That is, three days after Jean-Paul Guerlain's racist sortie—at a time when Internet already existed—which was simply too late. Its message, which read like damage control or the corporate version of "white fragility" (whatever you do, don't make this sound racist, too), didn't change anyone's minds.

The Maison Guerlain expressed its disapproval. The company, the press release stated, "promotes talent diversity from all backgrounds throughout the world." It plainly feared that the "unacceptable" remarks by the company's eponymous heir would tarnish its image. But it didn't have a word to say to French Blacks outraged by the insults from a man who just a few days earlier was still doing PR for the Guerlain brand.

As for French politicians, all we got was radio silence. Only Finance Minister Christine Lagarde mentioned Guerlain's remarks. The CSA had yet to issue a warning to the state-owned broadcaster France Télévisions, which included France 2. The one forceful response came from journalist Audrey Pulvar, who voiced an unsparing rebuke that Monday morning on the public radio channel France Inter, entitled, "*Nègre* I am, *nègre* I'll remain." In magnificent terms, she expressed what we were feeling.

> The lying Arab, the thieving Arab, the hard-working (but dirty) Chinese, the greedy Jew, the promiscuous French woman, the sex-crazed Latino, the lascivious *nègresse*, the dancing *nègre*, the laughing *nègre*, the football-playing *nègre*, the lazy *nègre* . . . Bingo! We don't have to look too far to find other ideas to add to Jean-Paul Guerlain's little roundup of racist clichés. But it was the cliché of the loafing, good-for-nothing *nègre* he chose to serve up amid mind-boggling silence on the set of last Friday's news on France 2. "I set to work like a *nègre*. I don't know if *nègres* have always worked that much, but anyway." It's the second part of the sentence, thirteen words, that earned him . . . Uh . . . What exactly? We've looked hard, we've been patiently waiting all weekend for the hint of a condemnation, a little emotion or indignation, from the mouths of our political leaders. Only Christine Lagarde has spoken up. We're still waiting on the others. In France, you can make racist remarks in prime time on a national network without a single major politician, intellectual, or artist batting an eye. The associations are doing what they're supposed to do by threatening to file a complaint. But has anyone used the word thug? Is anyone talking about an outrage? A disgrace? An obscenity? How about a slap in the face? The very slap in the face that the very distinguished Monsieur Guerlain just delivered not only

to every living Black person, but above all, dear Monsieur Guerlain, to the millions of dead in the holds of slave ships, at the bottom of the oceans, shipped off from their native land to the New World. The millions of people enslaved, debased, and dehumanized for four centuries, the millions reduced to the status of mere hands and legs for the cotton fields, for the cane fields, for the bite of the whip and the watchdog, all the slaves sold for their potential for work. Not men, mind you, not fathers, not mothers, whose children were stolen from them and turned into still more beasts of burden; no, not human beings, but tools, equipment, and merchandise. Dear Monsieur Guerlain, when I was a child, my mother wore one of your perfumes and its scent alone was enough to comfort me when she was away; your name has been with us as far back as I can remember, passed down from mother to daughter and sister to sister, but I will never let another drop touch my skin again. To you, Monsieur Guerlain, I, a *nègresse*, dedicate these lines written by Aimé Césaire:

> vibrate
> vibrate you very essence of the dark
> in a wing in a throat from so much perishing
> the word *nègre*
> emerged fully armed from the howling
> of a venomous flower
>
> the word *nègre*
> all filthy with parasites
> the word *nègre*
> loaded with roaming bandits
> with screaming mothers
> with crying children
> the word *nègre*
> a sizzling of flesh and horny matter
> acrid
> burning
> the word *nègre*
> like the sun bleeding from its claw onto the
> sidewalk of clouds
> the word *nègre*

like the last laugh calved by innocence

between the tiger's fangs
and as the word sun is a banging of bullets
and as the word night a ripping of taffeta
the word *nègre*
            dense, right?
from the thunder of a summer
            appropriated by
                        incredulous liberties.[4]

> As Aimé Césaire once said in response to the same insult: Well, you know what this *nègre* says, Fuck you![5]

Césaire and Audrey Pulvar gave us our slogan. On October 23, there were several hundred, perhaps close to a thousand, of us gathered throughout the afternoon in front of the Guerlain store on the Champs-Élysées.

In the end, I decided not to check in with the prefecture. Plainclothes police walked in and out of our group without bothering to keep a low profile. Riot police vans were parked in a side street not far away. There were obviously a lot of Black people in attendance, but also people from every background, as well as a few celebrities, who were shocked by what had taken place. The radio and TV personality Cyril Hanouna was there. The rappers Mokobé and Disiz la Peste. The actress Aïssa Maïga. The former French women's high-jump record holder, Maryse Éwanjé-Épé. The mood was both festive and very engaged. My friend, the actress Mata Gabin, collected the bottles of Guerlain perfume the protesters had brought. With each bottle that landed in her tray, there was a burst of applause. The politician Benoît Hamon stopped by on behalf of the Socialist Party. The actor-comedian Dieudonné showed up after his henchmen had scoped things out. He quickly realized he wouldn't be able to co-opt the event—no one was interested in him—so he left. Tourists asked us what was going on. Some joined us for a bit. Friends came, too. I was calm, as often happens when I'm living through something important. Because the strident repetition of protest chants isn't really my thing, I took a step back and observed. All the TV channels were there filming us. But the best shot of the day wasn't of us.

Guerlain's management had closed the boutique before we arrived. They had locked the metal shutters and the company executives were now gathered on the store's second floor to watch us from the wide floor-to-ceiling window. The symbolism was unmistakable. Entrenched in their fortress, the upper management of the largest luxury brand in the world, all of them white, observed the little Black folks amassed at their feet. I thought of the famous anecdote of Marie-Antoinette looking out from her Versailles window onto the starving people below. After someone explained the situation to her, she quipped, "They have no bread? Let them eat cake!"

Instead of engaging in dialogue, the lords of luxury treated us as if we were rabble. Our demands were nonetheless extremely modest. They came down to two things: that the Maison Guerlain and the conglomerate LVMH break off all contractual relationships with Jean-Paul Guerlain, who occasionally worked as a consultant for them, and that they announce the break publicly.

We thought that this way they would demonstrate that they had understood the gravity of the outcry he'd caused and send a public message of zero tolerance for racism. That was exactly what they'd end up doing after the Dior creative director John Galliano's anti-Semitic diatribe was caught on camera. But by then, the Guerlain protests had taught them a lesson. For the moment, when it wouldn't have cost Guerlain's CEO much—Jean-Paul Guerlain hadn't been employed by the company for many years—he refused even the small gesture we were asking for. He clearly figured that the company's press release was sufficient. The Maison Guerlain wasn't to blame. He certainly didn't want to look like he was giving in. And it should be said that, unlike the major antiracist associations SOS Racisme and LICRA, or even CRAN (the Representative Council of Black Associations), our group was absolutely unknown. We were no one. But we were stubborn.

Energized by the turnout, I ended my brief speech on October 23 by promising that if Guerlain refused to meet our demands, we would be back.

We returned to the store six Saturdays in a row. In the end, there was no more than a handful of us, but we stood firm. I continued to adhere to the same principle I had starting with our first protest and that seemed to me consistent with the idea of a grassroots movement: no leader, no loyalty tests; we would welcome whatever came and whoever wanted to join. I had learned this lesson at the age of thirteen in Abidjan, when I had gotten on a horse that was much too powerful for me. The best way for me to stay in the saddle was to go with the flow, without trying to control what I had no power to control.

I didn't know many of the people who stuck with our collective over those seven months. I didn't really know them afterward. But I took it as a given that anyone who chose to invest their time and energy in the movement did so whole-heartedly. And that held true: although some of those present at the very beginning slipped away as soon as the media faded away, those who stayed showed incredible resolve.

When the Maison Guerlain refused our demands, we called for a boycott, which was taken up in the West Indies by the LKP, the collective trade union group in Guadeloupe headed by Élie Domota, who had led the country's general strike in 2009. In Paris, Guerlain reopened its shop on the Champs-Élysées.

Saturday was the day of security guards—all Black men—hired just for us, even though we never caused even the slightest incident. They thought it was funny: "They think you're thugs, right?" They told us privately, "We're doing our jobs, but we're with you."

In early December, the Paris prefecture called me. They had already spoken with some of us to better understand our demands and had allowed us to protest peacefully on the Champs-Élysées. They told me that with the holidays approaching, anti-terrorist measures would be more stringent.

At the same time, the Reverend Al Sharpton, who had been outraged by Jean-Paul Guerlain's remarks but who the luxury conglomerate's CEO had refused to speak with, sent two representatives, Charles Steele, a civil rights activist and former Alabama state senator, and George Curry, now deceased, a journalist-activist close to Jesse Jackson. Both made common cause with us, floating the possibility of an international boycott if negotiations broke down. French executives at LVMH knew the devastating effect a boycott by the African American community would have. The conglomerate depended on the US market. I received a letter from Guerlain's CEO very dryly stating that "Monsieur Jean-Paul Guerlain is not and will not at any time in the future be an employee, shareholder, or beneficiary of the Guerlain Group."

A month and a half had passed since our first protest. A month and a half of tense negotiations during which we returned every Saturday to the Champs-Élysées. We felt that our efforts were worth more than a letter. Although we wouldn't have thought of it had our demands been met straightaway, we unanimously agreed that the company's lack of good faith now meant that the Maison Guerlain and LVMH would have to show an unmistakable commitment to ethnoracial diversity.

We figured that, given how poorly they had handled the situation, the company must simply have been clueless. Its executive class was almost exclusively made up of upper-middle-class white men all from the same Grandes Écoles, HEC or ENA, so I was convinced that, had there been people educated on the issues or from ethnoracial minorities themselves, they would have gone about things differently. Guerlain's CEO wasn't racist. But as often happens, people are so unused to thinking of racism in structural terms, he seemed to assume that it was enough that he and his employees weren't personally racist for the company itself to be in the clear.

We had no reason to back down. We decided, in all modesty, to inject a little more diversity into the LVMH conglomerate. That led to six long months of negotiations with the company's chief administrative officer, who was determined, out of sheer principle, to give nothing up. Six months of intense debates on our side at the local McDonald's (we had no other place to meet). And six months of email exchanges deep into the night and an incredible amount of self-sacrifice.

Several of my friends and family members couldn't understand why I would spend so much time and energy on this fight. They thought it was too much. They were right; it was. And that was why I threw myself into it. When you are as self-involved as writers so often are, the selflessness of collective action, the brief forgetfulness of oneself for the good of others, the discovery of a cause more worthy of defending than something you have created alone, can be extremely gratifying. Not to mention the adrenaline. And the moments—however brief—of such wonderful camaraderie.

Thanks to our unrelenting pressure, LVMH and Guerlain implemented sensibility training for their employees, including their upper management. For the next five years, the company paid the university tuition of three students from high schools in Martinique, Guadeloupe, and Saint Martin admitted to the Grande École Sciences Po as part of France's program of promoting students from Education Priority Areas. It invested in a sickle cell anemia program, led by the incredible young woman Fatiha, who joined us, she explained, because her brother, like her Moroccan mother, was Black, and for that reason was a victim of racism, which she was determined to fight.

I hadn't known that sickle cell anemia, a genetically transmitted disease, mainly affected people from the Southern Hemisphere—from India, North Africa, the Caribbean, and, especially, sub-Saharan Africa. Until conclusive clinical tests were carried out at the Necker Hospital in Paris in 2017, there was no cure, only methods for alleviating the acute pain caused by the disease and for preventing complications. It's the most widespread genetic disease in the Paris region. Throughout France, it affects 25,000 people, mostly of African and Caribbean descent,[6] which ranks it among the country's major rare diseases. But both sickle cell anemia research and the care for those with the disease—many are children—were underfunded by the French government.

We contacted Robert-Debré Hospital, whose pediatric services included a sickle cell anemia center. Within our broad focus on helping underprivileged groups, we thought that children had to be a priority. The hospital served the Seine-Saint-Denis department, an underprivileged area, as well as Paris's eighteenth, nineteenth, and twentieth arrondissements. The medical teams with which our collective met all described a lack of funding. Working in tandem with them, we presented a plan that would cover their research needs, ensure improvements in the care of young people afflicted with the disease, and created an awareness campaign about the disease—all of it paid by LVMH.

We also managed to get Guerlain to include a "diversity criterion" in its guidelines governing outside contractors such that, in the event of equivalent service offers, the new policy against racial discrimination would allow management to decide in favor of the more diverse choice. This clause was supposed to be extended to the company's other French subsidiaries, and it would have been, had we stuck to our guns. It was my view that although our talks with LVMH and Guerlain had initially been very strained, we had now established a decent working relationship. Guerlain's CEO had showed genuine goodwill. After that first period of conflict, we could work together to make change. But the central purpose of many associations is direct confrontation.

Our movement was unfortunately no exception to that rule and, as the composition of our collective shifted, some members escalated their calls for ethnoracial transformation, which represented a hardening of our position that I found unproductive. I had gotten involved in the antiracist struggle in order to try, in my own modest way, to restore a little justice to the world, not to reproduce against white people the exclusionary structures I myself suffered from as a Black woman. I therefore decided I no longer had a place within the collective.

I had done my part. It was time for me to go. I hoped that those who remained would continue what we had started. I was disappointed when that didn't happen. The urgency had passed. The group disbanded on its own.

I have thought a lot about my experience within a collective movement. I came to the conclusion that the most authentic way for me to be politically engaged was by being who I was, in other words, through my creative work. That was why I decided to make a documentary about being Black in France, a documentary based on my personal experiences and those of my family: *Trop Noire pour être française?*

Because of the Guerlain Affair, people often took me for an activist. I wasn't an activist. I was simply uncompromising. As much as I could, I tried to have the courage of my convictions. Even if, like everyone else, I didn't always succeed.

I was still very proud of what we had accomplished—with no money, no resources, no reputation, simply as French citizens. Several months after our agreement with LVMH, the company hired a Corporate Social Responsibility Officer, who is now responsible for training the group's new managers in non-discrimination practices and for promoting more diversity in recruitment. Our assessment of the company's shortcomings in these areas had been spot-on.

Many years later, LVMH continues to support one of the world's leading sites for sickle cell research at Robert-Debré Hospital. It holds an annual "Committed Companies Dinner," at which it asks its partners for donations, which have substantially increased the hospital's funding. I attended the dinner's first iteration. Naturally, our group was never mentioned, nor was there any mention of our role in creating the initiative. On the other hand, in its film describing the disease and the speech given by its director of social affairs, the company explicitly linked the lack of resources the government allocated to the fight against sickle cell anemia with the fact that the disease predominantly affects Black people, one of the most underprivileged groups in French society.

People have told me more than once that our protests established a precedent. Our protests supposedly heralded the arrival of Web 2.0 in antiracist mobilization in France and proved to French Black people that they could, even as mere citizens, fight and win. One thing is certain, since the Guerlain Affair, no one now turns a blind eye to even the slightest racist incident at French corporations. From time to time, I myself have reentered the fray. But like weeds, incidents like this proliferate; you root out one and another shoots up elsewhere. And they always follow the same pattern. It starts with a blend of ignorance, stupidity, and carelessness. Then the associations and social media go to work. They protest, petition, file complaints, and let nothing slide. Without fail, the companies or institutions quickly move to control the damage. Having a racist image is simply too costly. From this perspective, civil society has real power. On the other hand, when it comes to racism, some people in French society have remained impervious to any and every form of public pressure: politicians.

# 26 The Three Fears

French politicians on the left and the right—to say nothing of the extreme right—have established exceptionally well-honed arguments to stifle any and all demands from ethnoracial minorities. Their discourse is founded on three irresistible fears: victimization, communitarianism, and repentance.

Nowadays, the accusation of communitarianism essentially targets Muslims, whose religious and cultural practices allegedly endanger the nation's indivisibility and its special form of secularism, or *laïcité*, by introducing distinctive identities, which undermines the grand principles of the Republic. Even when those practices are perfectly legal and in no way violate the laws of French secularism. It makes one wonder if, in order for national unity to exist, every historical period needs a foil, a scapegoat that binds the majority population together in a common act of rejection. The Jews and communists were given that role; today, it's the Muslims, who, furthermore, are regularly confused with Arab-Berbers.

Yet the most prevalent form of communitarianism in France is whiteness. It seems such a normal thing that you don't notice it except when it comes from the French upper and middle classes, who really are past masters, with their clubs, society balls, elite private institutions, resorts, and, of course, territorial boundaries that guarantee their perpetual self-segregation. There are neighborhoods of the French capital where I can't rent an apartment no matter how much I earn. The landlords, concerned about the neighborhood's reputation and property values, would refuse to rent to me for the same reason they would refuse the presence of public housing or homeless shelters. They don't want poor people. They also don't want Black people, including middle-class Black people. They want to stay among their own, among other rich whites. They have no qualms about this. On the contrary, they consider their prejudice completely legitimate.

In an earlier chapter, I told the story of my being turned away from a very well-known hair-salon chain, which certainly didn't describe itself as communitarian, but where I was brusquely told that they didn't do Afro hair. At the time, my hair was straight and could have been done using the same techniques used for European hair. What the hair stylist was actually telling me was that the chain where she worked was only for a white clientele. But the communitarianism of whites who want to stay among whites is rarely questioned, even though it breeds and reinforces prejudice.

I have often found it difficult to make people with a moral view of racism understand that, although being Black is a reality of skin color, it is precisely that racial reality that produces social inequality. Whatever your standard of living may be, when you're a Black French person, you're in a more precarious position than a white French person, even if you belong to the same social class. Precarity—unemployment, disability, a single-family household, poverty, etc.—is exacerbated by the racism, discrimination, and denial of Frenchness encountered by Black people.

In a country that promises equality, I believe it's completely legitimate to protest against social inequalities engendered by racism and discrimination. Doing so as a personally affected minority is legitimate as well. The feminist struggle was started by women, the fight against homophobia by homosexuals, labor struggles by workers. Who's going to fight with you if you aren't already fighting for yourself? Yet as soon as an ethnic group speaks up for itself, it's disqualified with the label "communitarian." That's how a whole series of demands immediately get discredited.

The right to work, to housing, to truly equal opportunities, and to the respect of our bodily integrity shouldn't be a favor that the French Republic deigns to grant us at its pleasure or because of our skin color. These rights lie at the very core of the republican social contract. Reminding people of this isn't some thinly veiled defense of communitarian interests; it reflects the desire to be fully integrated into the life of French society. We have been so thoroughly conditioned to believe that it's wrong to express ourselves as Black people that we have come to forget that obvious fact. Or, like many Black personalities in France, we prefer to remain silent on these issues for fear of being reduced to only that one aspect of ourselves—a Black person. But if we don't speak on our own behalf, no one will do it for us.

Black people, Arab people, and Asian people are constantly told to integrate into French society, even when we're already French. When politicians demand integration, what they really have in mind is the disappearance of the *visible* differences, however slight, that break with the majority's cultural norms. They also want to forestall political organizing on an ethnic or racial basis. France, we are told, isn't the United States. It isn't a hodgepodge of ethnoracial communities partitioned off from one another. France is an indivisible whole. The trouble is that this "whole" doesn't wholly include me. To fully belong, I would have to get rid of everything that isn't "Gallic" in me, that is, a significant part of who I most deeply am. That's exactly what they demanded of my grandfather during the colonial period a century ago. Although the words have changed, at bottom the obligation remains the same: if you want to belong, assimilate.

But if France has managed to remain intact despite the separatism of Basques, Corsicans, and Bretons, and if it has accepted deeply rooted regionalisms within its own territory, how does my speaking Creole or Bambara, listening to African music, eating *allocos*, or enjoying time with people of African or West Indian descent threaten the integrity of the Republic? Is there really only one way to be French—with a baguette under one's arm and a beret on one's head?

Personally, I feel very French in how I think. But without the space to express the Ivorian part of myself, without the space to be fully myself and accepted as such, it's always somewhat hard for me to claim France as my own.

In 2006, as French Interior Minister, Nicolas Sarkozy made the following remarks in a speech to his party in Paris: "We've had more than enough of always feeling like we have to apologize for being French. And for that matter, if people are upset about being in France—I say this with a smile but with firm conviction—they should go ahead and leave a country they don't love."[1]

Make no mistake, the Black, Arab, and Asian people who criticize France do it out of love, because they feel attached to France and to being French. They would like to be able to live in France without being French only "under certain terms and conditions," for they too have had more than enough of always having to apologize for their non-European origins. They don't want to be the victim of an abusive relationship, where to be accepted they either have to suppress everything their partner doesn't appreciate or disguise themselves as their partner's exotic Other.

One day, during an interview for my documentary, the historian and anthropologist Sylvie Chalaye made the astute point that her mixed-race French-Ivorian daughter wasn't fifty percent Ivorian and fifty percent French, she was 100 percent both. Despite my mixed race, my double nationality, and my hybrid culture, whether I'm in France or in Ivory Coast, I always position myself as a native. That's how I feel. In both countries, I'm not from somewhere else, I'm from here. In Ivory Coast, it's totally accepted. In France, it's a whole different story.

In 2017, a very dear friend of African descent had an exhibition coming up at one of the most prestigious foundations in France. The curator was a major figure in contemporary art. The exhibition was in honor of Africa, the setting was sublime. But my friend was unhappy. Despite his twenty-year career and international reputation, he had been told in no uncertain terms that he would have zero control over anything; they had already done him the honor of exhibiting. "Am I in a zoo?" he asked me over the phone.

I came to see him the night of the opening. The curator was there as well as collectors and other art world people I didn't know. They didn't know me, either. And that was essential. As a complete unknown in their social circle, I was nothing. They could nonetheless see that I was very close with the same artist they were lavishing compliments on. They could have shown some tact. The first thing the curator said to me, eyeing me approvingly and speaking about me as if I wasn't there, was: "They're all so magnificent!"

Appallingly, she was referring to the Black women at the event. A guy with upper-crust airs one-upped her: "A true gazelle!" he observed, then stepped over to pose with my friend for the evening's official photographer. My friend asked me to stand next to him for another picture with the same photographer. Upon which, the same guy playfully blurted out, "That picture is *un*official!" In other words, I was nobody and he was somebody. Once again, I didn't know this person and he didn't know me, I didn't know what he did and he didn't know what I did. But his sense of superiority gave him the right to talk to me like this. I was an unidentified Black woman.

These people would have spoken with the same sugar-coated contempt to a working-class white woman. They would have made sure that she felt her inferiority, that she was under no illusion that her mere presence in the gallery put her on an equal footing with them. But they wouldn't have done so with the particular violence of treating her, as they had treated me, like an exotic novelty. They saved that violence for ethnoracial minorities and thus communicated an additional form of social superiority, their superiority as whites. I agreed with my friend: we were definitely in a zoo.

I spent the rest of the evening with the other Black people at the opening. They spoke to me like a human being. Did that make me a communitarian?

Besides communitarianism, French Black people are regularly accused of victimization. Blacks, we are told, have the unfortunate habit of constantly whining about their lot, ascribing their present misfortunes to the whites who enslaved or colonized them in the past. But "no one can ask the sons to repent for the mistakes of their fathers," as Nicolas Sarkozy reminded us, obviously very much on top of these matters when he was in power.[2] Some of my white family tell me the same thing, and I assume that that's what many French people think.

Of course, it isn't modern-day French people's fault if their great-grandfathers were colonizers or their great-great-great-great-grandfathers slave traders. It is, however, the responsibility of the French state and its leaders to assume the present consequences of France's past policies.

Perhaps the demands of French Blacks have focused too much on issues of memory, causing a certain fatigue among those who don't feel that this history, which is also part of their own history, has anything to do with them. But memory is where the wound is most acute, so it was only logical that our demands started there. Without the tenacious campaigns of West Indian associations, there would never have been the Taubira Law (May 21, 2001), which recognized the slave trade and slavery as crimes against humanity. Guadeloupe's Mémorial ACTe, a cultural center dedicated to the memory of the slave trade and slavery in the Caribbean, would never have seen the light of day. The city of Nantes, which was the largest slave port in European France, would never have built the Memorial to the Abolition of Slavery in 2012.

But France has a very hard time coming to terms with the dark periods of its past. It prefers sweeping them under the rug. It was only in 1995 that Jacques Chirac recognized France's responsibility in the Vel' d'Hiv Roundup, the mass arrest of foreign Jews in 1942. And not until 2012 that François Hollande officially recognized the Sétif massacre of Algerian civilians by the French army in 1945. But who would know that from 1955 to 1965, France violently suppressed Cameroonians' struggle for independence, authorizing the assassination of numerous independence leaders and waging a veritable war that according to estimates left between 100,000 and 300,000 Cameroonians dead? That episode doesn't appear in history books. Revisited in a damning 2008 documentary by Valérie Osouf and Gaëlle Le Roy,[3] the events were also recently the focus of several books published in France[4] in addition to being regularly evoked by the Cameroonian intelligentsia for decades. That didn't stop French Prime Minister François Fillon, during an official visit to Cameroon in 2009, from responding to journalists' questions by declaring, "I absolutely deny that French forces participated in any way in assassinations in Cameroon. It's all pure fiction."

As long as French leaders continue to deny the country's history, French citizens will continue banging on the walls of those leaders' consciences until the facts and consequences of its history are recognized—not only from the victors' perspective, but from the perspective of the vanquished as well. The more they resist, the harder we'll push to make ourselves heard. We aren't victims, we're guardians; we're the voice of France's repressed memories.

Because politicians are well aware of this, they have tried to keep public opinion bottled up by exploiting a third and still more formidable fear, the fear of repentance.

December 2012. François Hollande was on a state visit to Algeria. He intended to officially acknowledge the Sétif massacre. The day before his speech, he told journalists, "I didn't come here to repent or apologize."[5]

May 2007. On the evening of his presidential victory, Nicolas Sarkozy declared, "I want to put an end to repentance, which is a form of self-hatred, I want to put an end to the 'competition of memories,' which feeds hatred of others."[6]

2017. In its presidential program, in a chapter titled "A Proud France," the National Front advocated for reinforcing "national unity by promoting a single national narrative and refusing the divisiveness of French repentance."[7]

I could cite other examples. What struck me each time was the use of a religious term in a political context, a term that evokes such powerful notions as sin and atonement. I didn't recall it being part of the vocabulary of Black or Arab activist associations, nor had I heard any of them calling on France to repent. Ethnoracial minorities aren't God or the pope, after all, so they're in no position to grant absolution. Nonetheless, from the extreme left to the extreme right, with the possible exception of the Greens, the country's politicians keep hammering home the message that they won't repent.[8]

In reality, France's former colonies aren't calling for France to repent. They, like French minorities, whose ancestors endured slavery and colonialism, are calling for it to recognize what took place (and even then, many sub-Saharan countries aren't particularly vehement on the issue). In other words, instead of the three fears, three forms of recognition are demanded: recognition of the facts, recognition of French responsibility, and recognition of the harm done. This is a far cry from forcing the country to its knees to beg for forgiveness from the people it exploited. Yet that is precisely what these politicians are trying to convince the French public of when they use such an outrageous term. Why do they do it? Is it to prevent people from hearing demands that are in reality eminently more reasonable but that politicians themselves simply refuse to entertain?

The mere recognition of France's mistakes is intolerable for the right, the extreme right, and for nationalists on the right and the left, who see it as degrading—as if a nation couldn't be great if it recognized its mistakes. As for the socialists, they're no dummies: they understand that after recognition the next logical step is reparations. To avoid that expense, they wrap themselves in moral arguments, pretending to believe that no reparation could possibly make up for the wrongs committed.

In 2015, in a speech inaugurating Mémorial ACTe, François Hollande announced that during his trip to Haiti two days later, he would settle France's debt to the country. Haitians believed that the French president had finally accepted the idea of financial reparations. Indeed, despite Haiti's hard-fought independence in 1804, France officially recognized the Republic of Haiti only in 1825, in exchange for 150 million gold francs to compensate for the loss of its colony. To pay back the exorbitant sum, the young republic secured a loan at usurious rates from—how convenient!—French banks. The loan would hamstring its economy and take 150 years to pay back. Many people in Haiti, the United States, and even France argued that France should repay that debt. But Hollande soon clarified his remarks: what France would be paying off in Haiti was its moral debt. To justify his position, he quoted Aimé Césaire, who once said in an interview, "There is no possible reparation for something irreparable and unquantifiable." Césaire did in fact fear that European countries would absolve themselves of their responsibility by writing a check. However, he thought it was the duty of those responsible for the slave trade to help the countries they had driven into poverty. How should they help? Césaire didn't say.[9]

To escape their own sense of guilt and keep the image of France intact, there are others who claim, with still greater bad faith, that there is no reason to "repent" for a crime—slavery—that Europeans only committed in part. The argument used to relativize their country's responsibility? By providing slaves, African despots had also participated in transatlantic slavery.

Let's be serious. Does the active collaboration of the Vichy regime in the deportation of Jews from France erase Nazi crimes? That African kings raided neighboring African peoples is a terrible thing. Even so, they didn't institute slavery as it was practiced in European colonies. They played a fool's game. They thought they had won but they had lost. Europeans incited conflicts between neighboring peoples in order to ensure their supply of slaves. They waged war against kings who refused trading posts on their coasts. Once the Europeans had taken the people, they returned for the land.

The same denialism prevails when it comes to colonialism. Certain politicians insist on its benefits. Jacques Chirac, we should remember, wanted a law enshrining the positive role French colonialism had played in the country's overseas, and especially North African, colonies. At the time—this was in 2005—sixty-four percent of French people were in favor of the new legislation, which was ultimately retracted after an uproar by its opponents.[10]

The argument is every time the same. France built roads, railroads, and ports. It brought development to people deprived of modern Western civilization. To paraphrase Sarkozy, France allowed these people to finally enter history. What the disciples of positive colonialism forget to say is that all that infrastructure wasn't designed to improve local living conditions but to facilitate the delivery of raw materials to France. Built by the colonized peoples, that infrastructure came at a staggering cost in human lives. To take a single example, during construction of the Congo-Ocean railway between 1921 and 1934, no fewer than 20,000 African workers died under exceptionally harsh and cruel conditions.

As for colonial schools, their primary role was to provide the personnel that the colonial administration needed to serve French colonists. There were, of course, hospitals and clinics. Was that enough to justify depriving African people of their freedom, separating communities according to the colonizers' maps, or destroying the structures that had supported the newly colonized peoples until then?

> They talk to me about progress, about "achievements," diseases cured, improved standards of living. *I* am talking about societies drained of their essence, cultures trampled underfoot, institutions undermined, lands confiscated, religions smashed, magnificent artistic creations destroyed, extraordinary *possibilities* wiped out.[11]

Already in 1950, Césaire was forcefully reminding us that a people that dehumanizes others dehumanizes itself. His words remain relevant for anyone indulging in colonial nostalgia.

The three fears—communitarianism, victimization, and repentance—have nonetheless been embraced by France's entire political class—or just about, since, as I write this book, I don't know the official positions of Emmanuel Macron's party La République en Marche.[12] For now, it seems that on these issues Macron may be looking to do something different. When he wasn't yet a presidential candidate, he was straightforward in calling colonialism a "crime against humanity," thus breaking with his predecessors. Now that he is president, and after the right-wing uproar over his remarks, will he stick to his position and work, as he has claimed he will, toward a "reconciliation of memories"?[13] Or will he backpedal once he has to face the inevitable outcry?[14]

Well before Macron made the politics of "both right and left" the centerpiece of his presidential campaign, the French political class had found a common language. It was revealing that they united around the issue of race, that it was on this specific topic that they identified a convergence of interests sufficient to suspend their usual divisions. What were French politicians trying so zealously to defend?

Rectifying the inequalities caused by slavery and colonialism doesn't necessarily come down to cold hard cash. On the other hand, since these inequalities have created a dividing line that unites race and class, addressing them means threatening white privilege. Is that what traditional politicians are so adamantly against? The challenge to their own and their voters' privilege?

# 27 On the Advantage of Being White

Whites have a huge advantage they're not even aware of. Most of the time, they don't realize they're white. Furthermore, they don't like it when you remind them that they too belong to a racial group, the only one that has managed to make its skin color synonymous with power. White people aren't white; they're people, individuals, human beings. They're neutral, the standard against which French universalism is measured. They're the norm and we're the exotic. They're inherently legitimate, inherently competent, inherently innocent.[1] We, on the other hand, get stuck with all the negative expressions of the French language: *travailler au noir*, *colère noire*, *marché noir*, *magie noire*, *broyer du noir*, *voir tout en noir*, *regarder d'un œil noir*, *manger son pain noir*, *c'est ma bête noire*, etc.[2] And of course, *travailler comme un nègre*, *être un nègre (littéraire)*, *parler petit-nègre*, etc.[3]

White people have forgotten that they were once merely one ethnicity among others and that what they consider "normal" merely expresses particularities they have managed to impose on the rest of the world. Similarly, because white people are privileged, in France in any case, and because we don't name their skin color, they have now forgotten that their color gives them privileges. And these privileges are real. Easier access to scarce resources. Positive validation of their existence in history, school, the media, and society in general. Confidence in being represented at all levels of society. More rarely subject to discrimination.[4]

I'm not claiming that the mere fact of being perceived as white allows one to escape every form of inequality. Currently, the absolute jackpot, as we know, is the wealthy heterosexual white male.

He sits atop the social pyramid; he controls the levers of our fate. He also generally denies the non-negligeable advantages that his gender and class afford him, preferring the delusion that what he has he owes solely to his personal merit.

Simply put, white people who are discriminated against because of their age, gender, sexual orientation, or disability, to mention only these criteria, don't also confront discrimination based on their origins or race, as is the case for Black people in France. They don't suffer the added delegitimization of who they are.

Even so, white people today fear and feel threatened by minorities who often have plenty of reason to envy them. That fear takes different names: "Anti-white racism" (which, as we know, is generally reactive and not systemic), the "great replacement," and "cultural insecurity." The root cause is the same: whites feel that the supremacy that until very recently was theirs is threatened.

It goes without saying that before, things were a lot simpler. Whites held sway over the entire world. They persuaded themselves that they were biologically superior to anyone who, unlike them, didn't come from old Europe. They enslaved, they colonized, and did it all with a clear conscience. They took from the land what they considered their due, preferably land that didn't belong to them but that they were benevolent enough to "discover." Occasionally, when the people they were oppressing became too restless or threatening, they made public concessions then took back what they had conceded. That's what is so perversely beautiful about Françafrique.

Nowadays, it's more difficult to make the world obey. Former colonized people, the territories once under European domination, like India, China, and Brazil, are gnawing away at parts of a market once firmly controlled by the West, which has an acute fear of the conquering power of the Asian "monster." Within European countries themselves, formerly subjugated peoples, easily recognizable by their non-white skin color, which once allowed Europeans to know whom they were dealing with and how to treat them, now have the bad taste of demanding not only social equality but European nationality, which confuses things even more.

Politicians are up in arms. If there are no "wretched of the earth" to bear the brunt of capitalism's failures, what are they going to do with the most precarious of their citizenry, with the victims of a system that has made the West so rich for so long? Ship them off to America, to Africa, to Guiana, to the Caribbean, as they did in the past? There are no El Dorados left to conquer, nowhere left to dump their surplus poor. And as if all that weren't troubling enough, suddenly their very person is threatened by the random acts of religious fanatics who have declared war on the West and use Europe's own children to carry out their plots.

Given the context, what good would it do for our leaders to rob the majority—in the name of equality for all and reparations for crimes past—of one of the last significant privileges remaining to it?

Let's not kid ourselves. If certain people are ruled out for employment and housing because of their skin color, it means that other people have easier access to employment and housing. In 2007, a newly graduated French person of Moroccan descent had to send fifty-four résumés before landing a single interview for an accountant position. Her fellow citizen with a typically French-sounding first and last name only needed to send nineteen résumés before being called in for an interview.[5] If suddenly we really started to fight discrimination, if we decided, using affirmative action, to give the same opportunities to everyone who was equally qualified, what would happen? The typically French-sounding Pierre Dubois, who until now didn't realize he only needed to send nineteen résumés, would suddenly face much stiffer competition. Based on his idea of identity, if deep down he felt more legitimately French than his Moroccan-French counterpart, he may not understand why he now has to fight just as hard as she did to find a job. His resentment would express itself at the ballot box. What politician would risk turning a potential voter away?

Even the most disadvantaged of the majority population, the "petits Blancs," as it is now fashionable to call them in France, know that even if they lose everything, at least they still have the advantage of being "pure" French, which nothing and no one can take away from them. And they intend to hold onto it. After being neglected for so long, their expectations are justified by a political class that, to counter the National Front and capture its right-wing voters, obligingly caters to their fears.

It's more comfortable for everyone, at least for the majority of the population, to maintain a social hierarchy that continues to favor French white people. That doesn't prevent politicians, who, despite everything, still want ethnic-minority votes, from naming a few carefully selected Black, Arab, or Asian people to highly visible government positions. It's a low-risk, high-reward way to make people happy, ease the majority's conscience, and validate French universalism without fundamentally changing it at all. At which point we can all marvel at how well "integration" is working out.

In my own life, I have occasionally been considered a prime example of French integration. Better to stay clear-headed. I'm a perfect counterexample to French meritocracy. From preschool on I benefited from excellent private schools, foreign language programs abroad, and many family trips. I grew up in houses where I had the space and time to study, and where there was always a room specifically for books. I was taken to museums, concerts, and movies. Even though, from the age of ten on, I always worked in order to have pocket money—because I loved nothing more than my freedom—I was under no obligation to do so. When working as a receptionist or telemarketer no longer suited me, I could quit. My parents took care of my needs so I could study. And as long as my father was alive I knew that if I had an overdraft or an urge for something I didn't have enough money for, all I had to do was call him. It was the money and cultural capital of my parents, as well as their perfect understanding of strategies for success, that allowed me—broadly speaking—to avoid the obstacles that my country put in the way of people of my skin color. My parents also provided me with a way of thinking about life that allowed me to do it, because money is nothing without the thinking to go with it.

When I was at the Sorbonne, a friend just as intelligent as I failed her teaching-certificate exam. A mixed-race French-Ivorian woman like me, she had come from a very humble background, with a mother who worked as a ticket clerk for the metro and a father who, broken by his immigration experience, alternated between stays in a psychiatric hospital and long-term unemployment. She had managed to overcome the precarity of her family life, except for one thing: the essay test, the *dissertation* in French, a rhetorical and stylistic exercise that seemed to her impossible. Whatever her approach, and despite the advice I gave her, she systematically failed. The essay had come to symbolize her inferiority complex; succeeding had become something so wonderful in her mind that she didn't deserve it. After failing the exam twice because of anxiety, she gave up.

Other people from similar backgrounds, from a more stable family environment or endowed with greater resiliency, with more self-confidence, with a great deal of talent and, no doubt, a certain amount of luck, manage to escape the stigma of race and its consequences by working two, three, or even ten times harder than their peers. I admire the personal successes of these self-made women and men. But I fear superhumans. For me, these success stories don't tell us much about the French Republic. The stories are too few and far between. The republican values I would like to see are those that give the same opportunities for success to everyone, everyone according to their aspirations, by addressing structural inequalities, by giving real opportunities to people from underprivileged backgrounds, by lifting up the non-white twenty-five percent of the French population so that they are included in the same way as white French people. To me, that's precisely the equality promised in our country's motto, "liberté, égalité, fraternité."

We have a very long way to go.

And yet . . .

# 28 In It Together

In 2005, the French government ceded to grassroots pressure and decided to support ethnoracial minorities. Jacques Chirac gave a very inspiring speech and made a series of promises. During the years that followed, the word "diversity" was on everyone's lips. Ethnic minorities were much more visible. And then what? The pressure let up. French politicians went back to normal and moved on to other things. They only respond to force, someone told me. Politically unorganized, French Black people didn't represent a sufficiently influential or sufficiently damaging bloc for traditional political parties to bother trying to pander to it. These days, "diversity" isn't such a hot issue.

The riots of that year nonetheless led to the emergence of new community associations, of a new generation of activists freed from the dogma of assimilation, who had no problem calling themselves afrodescendant and made their voices heard through a wide variety of media.

If you're a French Black person today, even if you don't live in a city, there are all sorts of welcoming spaces online where you can learn new things, share with others, and take part in a community of common interests and experiences. When I was twenty, I felt completely alone with all the questions I had. Nowadays, even if mainstream media still offers next to nothing, you can find the resources and support necessary to construct your own identity.

In 2016, I was at Columbia University for a screening of my film. It took place against the backdrop of the rising Black Lives Matter movement. An African American student was my chaperon. As she showed me pictures from a cultural association that her boyfriend, also African American, had created, she told me, "They kill so many of us, we have to do all we can to stay alive."

In France, we still don't fully exist in the public sphere, but we can now find places to stay alive and feel alive, deeply sustained by who we are as complete (or nearly complete) human beings. To me, that's essential if we want to avoid giving in to bitterness or anger.

Among the new associations, French Afrofeminists speak with a unique voice. Started in the United States in the seventies, with intellectuals like Angela Davis and bell hooks, the Afrofeminist movement decried the patriarchal structure of the civil rights movement led by the major Black leaders of the fifties and sixties but didn't see themselves reflected in contemporary feminist movements, by and large composed of middle-class white women, who ignored the issue of racism. Why would the descendants of slaves fight for the same right to work as men when they had already been working their fingers to the bone for white women, many of whom continued to look down on them because of their skin color?

Like their older sisters in the United States, French Afrofeminists have positioned themselves at the intersection of gender, race, and class inequalities. They have also caused controversy. In June 2017, the Mwasi Collective announced a "non-mixed" festival with certain workshops reserved for Black women only. Falling into the trap of the National Front, which immediately accused the festival of anti-white racism (but, curiously, not of anti-Arab or anti-Asian racism), Paris's mayor briefly threatened to prohibit the festival. When Mwasi also faced criticism from LICRA and SOS Racisme, two forms of antiracist activism collided, as they often do, one claiming to be universalist, the other claiming to be guided by French minorities themselves.

Construct your identity. Call out. Condemn. The associations already do all that. But what about the fight for inclusion?

We Black people are a minority in France. A minority continually kept in check by being led to believe that our place in France isn't completely legitimate, that we still need to make more of an effort, integrate, and be patient for the day when we'll finally be recognized as fully French—and not "just on paper," as I often hear from disillusioned young Black people. Obviously, we're not fooled. We know that the people instructing us to integrate into French society are running twenty years behind. They haven't grasped the fact that we're already French, and that it's not up to us to integrate, it's up to them. We protest, usually in our own neighborhoods and among one another; sometimes our shouts reach people who aren't part of the Black community. But it seems that we're still too timid. It's time we take our proper place, the same place that every French citizen is entitled to, no more and no less.

There are plenty of contexts where our views are recognized as legitimate. As consumers. In labor unions and professional organizations. Within political parties. As parents of students. Or even as television viewers.

In May 2017, the TV news magazine *Enquête exclusive* broadcast an "exclusive investigation" titled "Black, chics et festifs: secrets et succès des Africains de Paris," that is, Black, Chic, and Festive: Secrets and Successes of Africans in Paris. "*Black*," in English: that was already a bad start. Universally panned by Black viewers on social media for the clichés of the African diaspora it peddled in, the episode inspired a young Black woman entrepreneur to write an open letter to the show's producer and host Bernard de La Villardière. The letter was published on a website devoted to the French Black community.[1] I suspect that it was mostly read by Black people, but perhaps it was read by its addressee, too. It was a courageous gesture. It was also an isolated gesture. With the support of an association, the episode would undoubtedly have been referred to France's TV regulatory authority, there would have been a letter to the network's board of directors and an "educational" meeting with *Enquête exclusive*'s team, which had already drawn attention to itself with an earlier episode in the same vein, called "Clothes Kings, Black Beauties, Street Vendors: the Amazing Life of Africans in Paris." Rather than a few tweets and an open letter, there would have been an organized political action.

In my own life, I have absolutely no desire to meet with my children's teacher to explain to her that, given the presence of students of African descent in her class, it would be prudent for her to foreground positive representations of Africa rather than teaching them simply that African children are very poor and walk a very long way to school. Like everyone else, I avoid conflict. In the end, however, even if it was a burden to act alone, I ended up speaking with her because I thought it was necessary for my children. But since I was acting alone, I had to rack my brains to put things in a way that wouldn't upset her so much that she would later take it out on my kids.

A young woman I know told me that her daughter's teacher had adopted a no-grades policy and instead handed out colored stars, among which a yellow star for average work. She explained to the teacher that, in view of world history, it really wasn't an appropriate choice. Although this young woman wasn't Jewish herself, the Holocaust was an integral part of French history, so she felt personally concerned. On the other hand, it hadn't occurred to her to mention the black star, which was the equivalent of an "F" in a class where the majority of the students were Black. She didn't think of it because the negative associations linked to skin color weren't part of her frame of reference; they weren't part of shared French history. The history of Black people in France is still not considered something that concerns all French people, even though that history is also the history of whites.

There are, however, several large parent associations represented on France's High Council for Education. When I looked over the associations' programs, which said little or nothing about diversity, I wondered whether and how much they considered issues specific to children from ethnoracial minority backgrounds: inequalities in grading and academic guidance, the significant obstacles to obtaining internships, the stereotypes propagated by learning materials and certain teachers. As for the parents of these children, I wondered if they were sufficiently present in the parent associations apparently representing them.

Many years after the 2005 riots, underprivileged neighborhoods still suffer from the same marginalized status. The unemployment rate is two and a half times the country's average.[2] Incidents of ethnic and racial discrimination remain widespread. France's Arab minority has become the country's number one bogeyman.

Weary of seeing so little progress, someone I consider to be very serious-minded recently told me, "Nothing will change for Black people in this country without an insurrection. It's the only way to create a more equitable balance of power."

Yet in the United States, Black people fought. Through their struggle for civil rights, they upset the balance of power and reclaimed their inalienable right to vote, forced the end of segregation, and brought the beginning of affirmative action, among many other achievements. They were heroes. Some of them lost their lives in the struggle. Thanks to these activists, the lives of American Black people were considerably transformed. But the country's underlying structure, its mental structure, didn't change. As James Baldwin explained in the sixties,[3] American white people's wealth and complacency—their immaturity, Baldwin calls it—are founded on two original sins: the extermination of Native Americans and the enslavement of Black people. To this day, America remains afflicted by the same deadly impulse. It has confined Native Americans to reservations where it lets them waste away, and it incarcerates massive numbers of Black people. As if driven by the unconscious desire to erase their presence in the country.

To be sure, Obama was elected and reelected. The first Black president. What did white America do? It made up for it by electing Trump, most of whose political "project" was aimed at undermining what Obama had accomplished.

In 2008, my biological mother and I watched Obama's inauguration on television. I couldn't stop thinking about Stanley Kramer's 1967 film *Guess Who's Coming to Dinner*, in which the protagonist, played by Sidney Poitier, calls his future white wife optimistic when she says she's convinced that one day their mixed-race children will become US presidents. And then the unthinkable happened, and sooner than anyone had imagined possible. It was an incredibly moving moment for me. But in the years that followed, I also thought that Obama ultimately wasn't a manifestation of America's resilience but an exception—and in more ways than one. His mother was a white American, his father a Black Kenyan. He grew up with his mother and her family. Slavery and segregation weren't part of his family DNA. He didn't have Black Americans' visceral distrust of whites. In the words of Ta-Nehisi Coates, Obama was able to offer white America what very few African Americans could: trust.[4]

My sense is that America won't really overcome the issue of race until it elects a descendant of slaves.

So, no, I don't think that a few riots or even an insurrection are going to force French people to address their own trauma, that part of French history that contradicts all of France's proclaimed Enlightenment ideals about human rights—the enslavement of Black people and the colonization of Africans and Asians. We're going to have to take different risks, no doubt slower to see through but more political in nature. And we're going to have to rely on a fair amount of willingness to change things. Or, if there is none, to generate it ourselves.

In big cities, we're accustomed to seeing people from all different backgrounds. That doesn't mean we spend time with them, but at least they're there, we rub elbows them, we interact, however superficially. On the other hand, as soon as you get out of France's urban centers, as soon as you plunge into the world of its villages and small towns, there are very few if any Black people. You suddenly find yourself in white France.

Jean, my grandmother's nephew, lived in the house in Gaillac where my grandmother was born until the day he died. As a little boy, he carried the train of her wedding dress when she was married at the local church. He was, I've been told, the apple of Rose-Marie's eye. The sincere affection he had for my grandparents, Alphonse's impressive presence—Jean called him uncle—and my grandparents' incredible love story, which long captivated the family's imagination, gave him a positive image of Black people. The only Black people he ever met were my grandfather and me and my kids, but thanks to that experience he was positively predisposed.

When I visit Georges's family, who have always lived in the Béarn region in southwestern France, I don't see a single Black person. The family doesn't keep company with Black people, as far as I know. This is an educated, well-traveled, multilingual family, but for the most part they inhabit a limited geographical and cultural area. They know their region in such minute detail that it seems like an entire country to them and Paris another world. One can only imagine where Africa and the West Indies fit in.

As French Senator Esther Benbassa put it, France is still "a country of the soil, of roots, attached to the notions of homeland and the nation."[5] And these are the people suddenly being asked to think globally enough to connect their history with the history of Africa and the Caribbean, let alone Asia?

One of Georges's cousins would go on and on about her research into Béarn poets who gloried in a regionalism that thrilled her but left me cold. This was in the early nineties. I had sent her an article about Alpha Blondy that I had written for *Afrique Magazine*. I was very proud of it. Alpha Blondy meant a great deal to me. Georges's cousin confessed that she didn't know what to make of the article. She didn't know who Alpha was. My piece sparked zero interest in her. It was then that I realized the enormous cultural gulf between us. We lived in parallel worlds that superficially came into contact during family dinners in the southwest. How could I make her understand who I was when her reality was hundreds of light-years away from mine?

How do you ask French people to have empathy for the injustices endured by their fellow citizens of non-European descent when they simply don't know any, don't meet any, and don't have any opportunities to develop positive feelings about them?

It's up to France's news and culture media, especially television, to do the narrative work necessary to produce both greater understanding and empathy among French people. The now-defunct TV network France Ô did a tremendous job with its cultural programming from throughout overseas France. But who watched it? Its viewership was tiny and less than one percent from mainland France. As for non-cable channels, they fall well short of the effort they need to make, not necessarily in terms of diversity but in terms of inclusion. Since they generally remain stuck in the mindset of assimilation, they don't allow those who depend on TV for their information to get to know French ethnoracial minorities from their own perspectives.

For these reasons, I'm not surprised—or, more accurately, I can understand—that in the countryside, where France is almost uniformly white and where local routines prevail, when you meet a Black, Arab, or Asian person, your first instinct is to take them for a foreigner, and your second instinct is to sense that you're more French than they are. It's nonetheless infuriating.

Every time I go to a small provincial town, I get so tired of people trying to explain France to me. "You know, here in France . . ." Thank you, I know, I'm French. I know the country's culture and customs. But I can see that in those places where it's even more necessary to instill in people that being French is a question of nationality and not of skin color, that educational work simply isn't being done.

It may also be partly our responsibility as Black people. Despite the attitude of victimization ethnoracial minorities are accused of, it is in fact rare for us to speak openly about what we have to deal with. Or we talk about it with people who share the same experiences in order to spare ourselves the burden of preliminary explanations and to protect ourselves from reactions that might diminish our experiences and hurt us a second time.

At my children's school, Arab mothers tell me about the discrimination they believe their children face because of their ethnic origin. They rightly assume that I understand what they're talking about. They don't say the same things to white mothers, with whom they stick to polite small talk. On the other hand, they tell me nothing about the discrimination their families are subject to due to their religion. They know or assume that I'm not Muslim. They don't know what I think about Islam. They don't want to run the risk of being rejected yet again by opening themselves up to me about it. An entire part of their lives remains unknown to me.

One evening on the train home, I fainted. A French Maghrebi couple very kindly offered to walk me to my apartment. I told them the street name. They lived in the neighborhood and knew more or less where it was. Still, they wanted to be sure they were leading me in the right direction. I lived next to a recently built mosque. I sensed all too well that they were dying to say the word, that the mosque was a reference point for them, but they didn't dare say it, no doubt fearing a negative reaction from me. I took the initiative and immediately saw their relief: I wasn't anti-Muslim. They could tell me they went there to pray, that they found it a lovely place. We continued to talk about this and that. I kept quiet about the acerbic remarks I heard about the "cultural center," as the city hall advertised it on the road sign in order to avoid writing "mosque."

The remarks came from some of my neighbors, who, because they're of African origin and from a Christian upbringing like me, take for given that I share their opinions.

Several months later, taking a detour from an errand I was running, I stopped in at a neighborhood block party. Under the benevolent eyes of the hijab-wearing North African ladies, and as the youngest kids scurried about, a few Black teenage girls put on a show of African pop music. Several blocks away, white bobos filled their carts at the organic minimart, never in the least suspecting that other forms of social life existed just nearby.

Without realizing it, we live in parallel universes, which, unless we deliberately go out of our way, don't ever come into contact with one another. Most white people I meet in Paris, especially those on the political left, tell me that racism is in the past, that today things have changed. According to a report from the National Commission on Human Rights, forty-five percent of French people admit to being "somewhat," "fairly," or "not too" racist.[6] In other words, nearly one in two.

Although statistically more numerous in calling themselves racist, upper-middle-class people on the right, true to their traditional class principles, tell me that racism is an attitude of the poor and poorly educated.

Idealists, always ready to let it rip, shake their little fists: "That's so disgusting! How could anyone be racist! We're all human beings!" So much earnestness and naiveté in indignation, it's almost touching. But once you've said that we're all humans, what have you said?

Before the first round of the presidential elections in April 2017, SOS Racisme launched an antiracist campaign called "We're the Same, My Buddies and I" in order to counter far-right candidate Marine Le Pen and mobilize voters. What did we see on its posters?

A young white woman or a young white man with their arm around their Black or North African "buddy." Because the young whites are foregrounded in the poster, and because they're the ones who have sanctified their colored friends with their embrace and not the other way around, we get the picture that the white people's voice is speaking the poster's slogan. And that they're the main target of the campaign. Personally, however nice he or she might be, I have no need of a white friend validating my existence. And although in theory we may all be the same, I know that in the world we live in, that just isn't the case. Wherever I go in France or in the world, except for sub-Saharan Africa, I'm likely to experience a racism that my white "buddy" will never know.

The SOS Racisme poster didn't help me at all. Nor did it help my "buddy" understand the roots of the country's rampant racism, how it is expressed, or how it can be fought. Because in reality, instead of looking after me, my white friends should be looking at themselves.

We sometimes get pleasant surprises. One afternoon, on the first day of a vacation, my car broke down in a tiny town in Normandy. When the mechanic showed up, white, blond, and pale, with blue eyes and straight hair—a Norman, at least as people usually imagine them—he gave me his card. His first name was Karim. His last name couldn't have been more Gallic—let's say, to keep things simple, Dupont. I asked him if he was mixed. He laughed. Not at all. His father, he told me, traveled a lot—I assumed to Arab countries—and had chosen his name out of personal preference. To the great displeasure of the local city hall, which had at first refused to enter "Karim" in the birth registry. But his father held firm and didn't change his son's name. Throughout school, Karim Dupont's teachers took attendance scanning the classroom for a little curly-haired brown boy, only to discover to their surprise a fair-haired kid, the color of a Norman poster child. He admitted that when he called prospective customers to advertise his garage, he introduced himself as Monsieur Dupont. When he added his first name, people hung up on him or the customers never came.

Karim Dupont doesn't need anyone to explain discrimination and racism to him. He doesn't even need to spend time with Arab people. Thanks to his father's humanistic impulse, he knows. He knows from the inside what it is to be excluded because of one's background, a background that, as it happens, he doesn't even have. We should all be Karim Duponts. We would then understand that affirmative action and quotas don't mean rewarding someone for their background, as we too often hear. Affirmative action and quotas don't shackle the beneficiaries to their race or ethnicity; they don't eliminate meritocracy. They simply balance the scales that aren't balanced from the start, so that everyone with the same skills has the same opportunities.

The problem, someone once quipped to me, is that in France, it's a small pie. Instead of baking a bigger one, we prefer fighting to keep our slice.

In that case, let's set the table and spread out the feast. Let's make a much bigger pie! In a country in crisis, tormented by its past grandeur and the fear of future decline, is it wise to deprive it of an entire young, dynamic, and resourceful population? Why not bet on the present instead of taking refuge in the glorification of the past? It's time we accept reality. French people from former colonies, who are now an integral part of the workforce, aren't going anywhere. They aren't immigrant workers. They aren't going back "home" when they retire. You can try to marginalize them, to contain them, to make them feel insecure, but it won't change a thing. "Home" is France, and given their numbers, "home" is necessarily changing. France has become multiethnic. But it now balks at becoming multicultural, too. It's going to happen, even if a portion of the French public seems deeply frightened by the change. I wonder why, honestly. After all, traditional French culture is going strong, and it's not going away. It's being enriched in new ways.

Instead of viewing our pluriculturalism, our double or triple nationality—if we choose to have it—as a threat, why not capitalize on our cosmopolitanism? French people with roots elsewhere are more likely than other French citizens to create economic and cultural links between France and abroad—when and if that's something they're looking to do (again, it's not a question of hemming people into strictly defined roles). Today, almost half of all French speakers live in Africa; in 2050, it will be eighty-five percent, with only twelve percent living in Europe.[7]

Our politicians tell us that France is a great country that must make its voice heard in the world. They promise us a return to grandeur. Personally, I'd prefer that they focus on our well-being. Scandinavian countries aren't "great nations" on the geopolitical scene, but they provide a good quality of life to those who live there. The French aren't as modest as the Scandinavians. France's grandeur is important to them. So be it. But in that case, they ought to be consistent. How can a country hope to have influence beyond its borders by casting aside the talented people who make up its present and future? Isn't it time for France to mobilize all of its potential instead of letting a portion of it go to waste for the sake an ethnocentric identity?

Remember: we're not the problem. We're part of the solution.

# 29 That's a Wrap

I would have been curious to know where my grandfather stood on these issues, but we never discussed politics. I was too young. All I know is that, even if he wouldn't have agreed with me, he would have heard me out and we would have talked about it, as we did about religion.

I didn't share his faith, which was a crucial part of his life. He would listen attentively to my arguments, without trying to dismantle them with his. Then he would tell me that, for his part, he preferred to believe in an afterlife. As if he were afraid that that was already a form of proselytism, he would always end by emphasizing that it was up to me alone to decide.

My grandfather, a reserved man with an awe-inspiring presence, was one of my rare role models in childhood. I appreciated his calm, his simplicity, his great kindness toward me, and the moral rectitude he embodied. In a country where the exercise of power often encouraged personal enrichment, he was content with living on his salary. When my mother urged him to change his government car, because he had been driving around in the same Mercedes for ten years and she found it beneath him, he looked at her in surprise: "But it's still running very well," he replied.

I often found a haven in his house, where, as he and my grandmother got old, everything seemed gently frozen in time, like in a palace in Snow White. Strong-willed and resolute, almost stern, when she was young, Rose-Marie had become a sweet, fragile, little woman with failing health. Too weak to go out, she spent her long days at home alone while my grandfather worked at his office. She could no longer remember my name or age. She'd ask me the same question ten times. But she couldn't be beat when it came to the past. To keep her busy, I spent whole afternoons with her unpacking souvenirs and old evening gowns. I loved my grandmother.

Unlike other mixed-race couples, I don't think she and my grandfather had much difficulty adapting to one other's culture. In his character, tastes, and manners, Alphonse was very French. I imagine that spending middle-school vacations with his friends and their families refined his mastery of French habits and customs. As for Rose-Maire, she had accepted from the outset that going with him to Africa was a precondition of their marriage; it was perhaps also one of the things that appealed to her, a woman who dreamed of leaving small-town Gaillac far behind.

My grandmother spent most of her life in Africa. She did it on her own terms, by remaining steadfastly French. Her daughters told me that she didn't like those of her compatriots who, because they lived in Africa or had married an African man, dressed and spoke like African women. Rose-Marie never lost her southwestern accent, whereas Alphonse spoke French without an accent. I don't think my grandmother was judging African culture. The pages of her manuscript where she describes her first impressions of Africa are very moving. She was full of enthusiasm. She wanted to understand everything. The colonial system disgusted her. She was outraged by the condescension with which the colonizers treated their houseboys and by the sight of poor Guineans transporting whites in sedan chairs in Conakry. She went so far as to compare this kind of exploitation to slavery. Even the use of the word "native" she couldn't stand, a term my grandfather didn't seem to mind. Her utter lack of prejudice was striking.

She simply refused to assimilate—the much-vaunted assimilation, rebaptized as integration today, that French society demands of Black people. That didn't stop her from obtaining Ivorian nationality when Ivory Coast became independent. Nor from assuming a certain number of official duties for what had become her country. She embraced the role expected of her. She did it while staying true to her original culture.

My grandparents, like my parents, lived in the French style, except for a few minor adjustments that revealed the limits of my grandfather's acculturation. During the week in their house in Abidjan, it was cheese soufflé, veal roast, pommes dauphine, green beans, and crêpes Suzette. French bourgeoise cuisine. When I expressed my surprise one day that my grandfather systematically refused to eat salad, he smiled at me and said he wasn't some cow to go around eating grass.

On weekends, my grandparents went to Tiassalé, Alphonse's hometown. For two days, the women of the family entourage made only Ivorian dishes. The employees, among them family members, addressed my grandfather as "Monsieur le Président." They called my grandmother "Maman," as they did with any Ivorian woman of a certain age to whom they wanted to show respect and affection.

After the end-of-year holidays, Rose-Marie would begin packing for her annual winter trip to France. The preparations lasted several weeks. The bags and suitcases piled up. I wondered what she was bringing in such great quantities—perhaps a holdover from the seasonal migrations she made by boat during her time in the colonies. Although she had spent fifty years in Africa, she couldn't tolerate the heat. She left for two months to breathe cold air and go skiing in her precious Pyrenees. My grandfather briefly joined her then returned home. During their engagement, Rose-Marie brought him to the mountains once. He couldn't understand what he was doing at the top of a snow-covered trail with skis strapped to his feet. From then on, they settled on playing tennis.

As I've mentioned, my grandfather was the big man of the family. As for Rose-Marie, she did her best to pursue her university degree but in the end never finished it. Nor did she complete her manuscript. Alphonse's ambitions became her own. In the pages I discovered, she tells her father as much shortly before her marriage: Only one thing matters now, Alphonse's career. Yet I'm certain she dreamed of becoming a writer.

She passed on her dream to her daughters, especially to her youngest daughter, whom she hoped, even before her youngest had written a line, would one day be Bernard Pivot's guest on the literary talk show *Apostrophes*, which for Rose-Marie was the ultimate achievement. When they didn't become writers, her daughters all become avid readers like her.

I think it was my mother who first spoke to me about Rose-Marie's unfinished manuscript, although she assured me that no one knew where it was. I was a child. I was still playing with my cousins, drawing fake treasure maps that we held over a lighter flame to give them a parchment look. The existence of a lost manuscript fascinated me. When my grandmother died, I set about finding it. It had simply been forgotten in a compartment of her little glass bookcase. I was fifteen years old. For twenty-five years, on each of my many moves, everywhere I went, I carefully brought with me a prized black leather satchel with a broken zipper. It contained the notebooks and typed pages where my grandmother, using pseudonyms, had recorded parts of her life story. But I never read them. I couldn't say why. I only began to look over them when I started working on my documentary and had to get a better grasp of her and Alphonse's story.

When I became the caretaker of Rose-Marie's manuscript, did I also become the keeper of her dreams? I'm the only one in the family who made writing a profession. But would discovering her manuscript have been as important for me if I didn't already have a passion for writing? On Thursday afternoons in Abidjan, at barely eight years old, I would go to my grandfather's secretary's office at the Supreme Court to type up the poems I had written that day. When I left, I stopped in on Alphonse and gave him a kiss on the top of the head.

The last time I saw him alive was in Paris in September 1989. He was eighty years old.

The weather was still mild. I took him for a drink on the terrace of Les Deux Magots. We had lunch across the street afterward at Brasserie Lipp. He was delighted to be back in the Saint-Germain-des-Prés neighborhood, which, he said, reminded him of his student days. Perhaps he was alluding to the time he spent in Paris to take the magistrate's exam, staying nearby with Father Duhil, the priest who had baptized him as a boy.

We continued talking in the lobby of his hotel. I walked him back to his room to help him undress for his nap. He sat down in a chair. Suddenly, he looked tired. A weariness I had never seen before swept over his face. His shoulders slumped. "I miss your grandmother so much," he sighed.

Rose-Marie had died two years earlier, on July 19, 1987, of a ruptured aneurysm. They had married on July 17, 1937. She had passed precisely two days after their fiftieth wedding anniversary. She held on until that date, so important for the both of them, then she let go.

To say that it affected my grandfather is an understatement. Overnight, one of his legs gave out. Without Rose-Marie, he literally couldn't go on. He needed several months to regain the use of his leg, but until his death he had a limp. He stopped taking the evening walks that had punctuated their fifty years of life together. It was a ritual they never missed.

When people who are old enough recall Alphonse and Rose-Marie, they tell me about a mixed couple, the first in Ivory Coast, walking for an hour every evening at dusk along the streets of Abidjan or the paths of Tiassalé, escorted, a good distance behind them, by a police officer. In a country where only poor people walked, it was quite a symbol.

When Rose-Marie died, I was in Abidjan. In an attempt to ease my grandfather's heartache a bit, I started having lunch with him once a week. I asked him questions about her. Talking about his wife brought a smile back to his face. It was at these moments, just the two of us, that he spoke to me about their youth. He agreed to do tape-recorded interviews with me to tell me about his life. I was a teenager, interested in the past, of course, but more concerned about the present and the possibilities then opening up to me. I postponed our interviews. Then I left for Bordeaux to take my baccalaureate exam.

Shortly after his trip to Paris, during a vacation in Toulouse, Alphonse had dinner in Gaillac with my grandmother's family, in the same house where he stayed every weekend during their engagement, where they lived for a year as he awaited his first assignment in Africa, and where my biological father was born.

Then he returned home to his apartment in Toulouse. That night I had a dream about him. I woke up in the morning with a bad feeling. My mother called. He had died peacefully in his sleep, in the same city where he had met Rose-Marie.

I thought back to what my grandfather—a man normally so reserved—had shared with me a few weeks earlier in his hotel room. "You know," he murmured, "I'd like to join your grandmother up there in heaven, but I can't. I haven't fulfilled my duty to my family yet."

His duty. Isn't that what he had tried to do all his life? From the day his family sent the fifteen-year-old to France to study law so that he could return afterward to protect them from the arbitrary laws of the colonizer.

My grandfather believed that Ivory Coast's independence had come too soon, before the country had the means to truly be free. But he had done his duty. He had followed the course set by Houphouët-Boigny. He had carried out the policies the president sought. By bending his moral principles to the president's wishes in 1964, he failed to live up to them. Whether or not he had a choice, this original sin prevented him from founding the reliably independent legal system for his country that his vast expertise and devotion had allowed its people to hope for. Nevertheless, he belongs to that generation of Africans who put a continent's hopes of freedom and dignity on their shoulders. As well as an ideal of justice, the ideal of former colonized peoples seeking equality. My grandfather was no revolutionary, but he taught me to be proud of who I am. He and those of his generation only partially succeeded in the mission that history had confided to them. They did what they could, given who they were and the value system of the time, especially as it related to France. But they tried. They had the courage, the courage of pioneers. Can we find a similar courage today?

# Notes

2. A BLACK PRINCESS AND WHITE NANNIES

1. On this topic, see Caroline Ibos, *Qui gardera nos enfants? Les nounous et les mères* [Who Will Look After Our Children? Nannies and Mothers] (Paris: Flammarion, 2012).

2. Kathryn Stockett, *The Help* (New York: Penguin, 2009).

3. Stockett, *The Help*, 251.

3. YOU WILL PLAY BALTHAZAR, MY DEAR

1. Catherine Nay, *The Black and the Red: François Mitterrand, the Story of an Ambition*, trans. Alan Sheridan (San Diego: Harcourt Brace Jovanovich, 1987).

2. Delivered on June 6, 1958, in Mostaganem, Algeria.

3. Translator's note: Colombey-les-Deux-Églises translates literally as Colombey-the-Two-Churches, Colombey-les-Deux-Mosquées as Colombey-the-Two-Mosques. Alain Peyrefitte, *C'était de Gaulle* [That Was De Gaulle], vol. 1 (Paris: Gallimard, 2002).

4. "We need to keep a balance in our country, which also means a cultural majority. We are a Judeo-Christian country, General de Gaulle said, of the white race, one that welcomes foreigners." Nadine Morano on the television program *On n'est pas couchés*, September 26, 2015.

5. Alain Peyrefitte, *C'était de Gaulle*, vol. 2 (Paris: Gallimard, 2002).

4. DOES CLASS ERASE RACE?

1. Aníbal Quijano, "'Race' et colonialité du pouvoir," trans. Jim Cohen, *Mouvements* 180 (2007), which is the French translation of "¿Qué tal raza?" *Río Abierto* 11 (2004). In English, see Aníbal Quijano, "Coloniality of Power, Eurocentrism, and Latin America," trans. Michael Ennis, *Nepantla: Views from South* 1:3 (2000).

2. Chloé Maurel, "La question des races," *Gradhiva* 5 (2007). See UNESCO, *Four Statements on the Race Question* (Paris: UNESCO, 1969).

3. Edgar Schneider, *Jours de France* 1121, June 7–13, 1976.

4. 50 Cent, "Candy Shop," featuring Olivia.

5. A "LITTLE FRENCH GIRL" IN IVORY COAST

1. *Les Enfants du Blanc* [The White Man's Children], directed by Sarah Bouyain (Athénaïse, Pyramide Films, Stalker Films, 2000).

2. Translator's note: Throughout the book, the word *nègre* has not been translated. Although broadly speaking it may be translated by "Negro" or the N-word, depending on the context, both are fraught with a particular social, cultural, and political history in the United States such that neither term seems appropriate or adequate to convey the specificity of its usage in French. However, as the author makes plain in the pages ahead, the term is often no less derogatory, no less degrading and traumatizing, in the French contexts she describes, despite the variability in meaning and connotation between the two languages.

The N-word appears in certain English-language texts quoted in the book, and as such has been retained.

## 6. MY GRANDFATHER, ALPHONSE BONI

1. Translator's note: The French term *magistrat*, here and elsewhere translated as "magistrate," encompasses both judges (*juges*) and prosecutors (*procureurs*); both are part of the judiciary in the French legal system. Over the course of Alphonse's long career as *magistrat*/magistrate, he holds positions of judge and prosecutor.

2. Jean-Noël Loucou and Françoise Ligier, *La Reine Pokou: Fondatrice du royaume baoulé* [Queen Pokou: Founder of the Baoulé Kingdom] (Paris: Nouvelles Éditions Africaines, 1977).

3. Delafosse was a French colonial administrator, ethnologist, and Africanist stationed for several years in Ivory Coast. He was also the father of one of the country's most influential mixed-race families.

4. Maurice Delafosse, *Essai de manuel de la langue agni, parlée dans la moitié orientale de la Côte d'Ivoire. Ouvrage accompagné d'un recueil de légendes, contes et chansons en langue agni, d'une étude des origines et des migrations des tribus agni-achanti, de vocabulaires comparatifs des différentes langues agni-achanti, d'une bibliographie et d'une carte* [Practical Guide to the Agni Language, Spoken in the Eastern Half of Ivory Coast. With a Collection of Legends, Tales, and Songs in the Agni Language, a Study of the Origins and Migrations of Agni-Ashanti Tribes, Comparative Vocabularies of the Various Agni-Ashanti Languages, a Bibliography, and a Map] (Paris: J. André, 1901).

5. Here and elsewhere in the book, I quote form Rose-Marie's unpublished manuscript, which I discovered after her death. I describe the circumstances of that discovery in Chapter 29.

6. Bruno Gnaoulé-Oupoh, *La littérature ivoirienne* (Paris: Karthala, 2000).

7. AOF (Afrique occidentale française) and AEF (Afrique équitoriale française) were federations of French colonial territories in Africa.

8. Janet G. Vaillant, *Black, French, and African: A Life of Léopold Sédar Senghor* (Cambridge, Mass.: Harvard University Press, 1990).

9. Pascal Blancard, Sylvie Chalaye, Éric Deroo, eds., *La France Noire: Trois siècles de présences des Afriques, des Caraïbes, de l'océan Indien et d'Océanie* [Black France: Three Centuries of Presence from Africa, the Caribbean, the Indian Ocean, and Oceania] (Paris: La Découverte, 2011).

## 7. SLAVERY AND THE HOLOCAUST: WHY I AM A HUMANIST

1. Popular open-air bar-restaurants in Ivory Coast.

2. Joël Kotek, "Afrique: le génocide oublié des Hereros" [Africa: The Forgotten Genocide of the Herero People] *L'Histoire*, no. 261, vol. 2, 2002.

3. *Namibie. Le génocide du IIe Reich* [Namibia: The Second Reich's Genocide], directed by Anne Poiret (Les Films d'ici, 2012).

4. Kotek, "Afrique: le génocide oublié des Hereros."

5. *Namibie. Le génocide du IIe Reich.*

6. Serge Bilé, *Noirs dans les camps nazis* [Blacks in the Nazi Camps] (Paris: Le Serpent à Plumes, 2005).

## 8. WHEN MY GRANDMOTHER MARRIED A BLACK MAN

1. Birago Diop, *À rebrousse-temps. Mémoires II* [Against the Flow of Time] (Paris: Présence africaine, 1982).

2. From the announcement published in the *Journal official*, the French Republic's official gazette, on May 6, 1934.

3. Passing the magistrate's exam would qualify Alphonse for positions of judge and prosecutor, both part of the judiciary in the French legal system.

## 9. AN "AFRICAN GIRL" IN BORDEAUX

1. A contemporary art museum was created in Cocody, a suburb of Abidjan, in 1993.

2. Renamed the Musée des Civilisations de Côte d'Ivoire in 1994.

## 10. WHAT COLOR IS THE FRENCH LANGUAGE?

1. *La Dépêche du Midi*, April 1, 1990.

2. *La Dépêche du Midi*, May 18, 1990.

3. *La Dépêche du Midi*, May 22, 1990.

4. Dominique Vieu, *La Dépêche du Midi*, March 30, 1990.

## 11. WHY RACE TRUMPS CLASS

1. The opening verse of "Four Women," written, composed, and performed by Nina Simone. First released on the album *Wild Is the Wind* (1966).

2. *Dictionnaire de l'Académie française*, 9th edition.

## 12. ALPHONSE AND ROSE-MARIE : A MIXED-RACE COUPLE IN THE COLONIES

1. "Dix choses que vous ne saviez pas sur OBO" [Ten Things You Didn't Know about OBO], *Journal de l'Afrique en expansion*, January-February 2006, based on *Blanc comme nègre* [White as in *Nègre*], interviews with Omar Bongo by Airy Routier (Paris: Gasset, 2001).

## 13. A LITTLE STORY ABOUT DISCRIMINATION

1. "Les stéréotypes sur les origines: comprendre et agir dans l'entreprise" [Stereotypes and Origins: Understanding and Taking Action in the Workplace], study led by Patrick Scharnitzky and IMS-Entreprendre pour la cité, 2014.

2. Marcel Dorigny, "Introduction," in *La France noire* (Paris: La Découverte, 2011).

3. Dorigny, "Introduction."

4. The Parisian zoological garden where plants and animals from the colonies could "acclimate" to France's climate. Today called the Jardin d'Acclimatation.

5. "Rempilé" is an informal term referring to a non-commissioned officer or draftee who has re-enlisted in the army after prior military service.

6. Bureau pour le développement des migrations dans les départements d'outre-mer [Office for Migration Development in Overseas Departments]. It was closed in 1992 by François Mitterrand.

7. *Le Matin*, September 21, 1898, quoted by Gérard Noiriel, "L'humiliant apprentissage du premier député 'nègre,' Hégésippe Légitimus" [The Humiliating Apprenticeship of the First "*Nègre*" Deputy, Hégésippe Légitimus], *Le Monde*, February 23, 2021.

## 14. MY FIRST BLACK ROLE MODELS

1. Jacques Chirac, speech delivered in Orléans, June 19, 1991. Source: *Nouvel Obs*, INA.

2. Interview between Basquiat and Marc Miller and Paul Tschinkel as part of the program on "Young Expressionists" by the video magazine *ART/new york* in 1982.

3. Andy Warhol, *The Andy Warhol Diaries*, ed. Pat Hackett (New York: Grand Central Publishing, 2009), 629.

4. Anthony Haden-Guest, "Burning Out," *Vanity Fair*, April 2, 2014.

## 15. THE ADVENTURE OF 'REVUE NOIRE'

1. *Afrique sur Seine* was made in Paris in 1955 by Paulin Soumanou Vieyra, Mamadou Sarr, and Jacques Mélo Kane. Mamadou Touré's 1953 *Mouramani* is believed to be the first African short film, but all copies have been lost.

2. Sophie Hofflet, "L'Émergence d'un axe Sud/Sud dans la coopération cinématographique africaine" [The Emergence of a South/South Axis in African Cinema Cooperation], *Clap Noir*, March 17, 2003: http://www.clapnoir.org/spip.php?article415. By way of comparison, according to France's National Center of Cinema and the Moving Image (CNC), 2,684 French films were produced in the same period.

## 16. FRENCH "INTEGRATION"

1. National School for the Image and Sound Professions.

## 17. WHERE ARE YOU FROM?

1. Derald Wing Sue, *Microaggressions in Everyday Life: Race, Gender, and Sexual Orientation* (Hoboken, New Jersey: John Wiley & Sons, 2020).

2. LICRA, Ligue internationale contre le racisme et l'antisémitisme (International League Against Racism and Anti-Semitism). SOS Racisme is an antiracist organization founded in France in 1984.

3. The party was renamed National Rally, le Rassemblement national, in 2018.

4. Manuel Valls, on the political talk show "Politiquement parlant" (*Direct 8*, June 10, 2009), referred to white people as "les whites" instead of the usual French term *les blancs*.

## 18. COMING OUT OF THE RACE CLOSET

1. Pap Ndiaye, *La Condition noire. Essai sur une minorité française* [The Black Condition: Essay on a French Minority] (Paris: Calmann-Lévy, 2008).

2. Isabelle Boni-Claverie, interview with Claire Denis, *Revue Noire* 15 (December 1994–January/February 1995).

3. *I Am Not Your Negro*, directed by Raoul Peck (Velvet Film, 2016).

## 19. GOOD HAIR

1. This and the following paragraph are based on the work of Juliette Sméralda, *Peau Noire, Cheveu Crépu. L'Histoire d'une aliénation* [Black Skin, Kinky Hair: A History of Alienation] (Pointe-à-Pitre: Jasor, 2004), which draws on Willie L. Morrow, *400 Years Without a Comb: The Untold Story* (San Diego: California Curl, 1990) and *Cosmetology: The Art and Science of Curly Hair* (San Diego: Morrow's Unlimited, 1993).

2. Juliette Sméralda, *Peau Noire, Cheveu Crépu.*

3. Relaxing paste made from a mix of lye, potatoes, and eggs.

4. Malcom X and Alex Haley, *The Autobiography of Malcolm X* (New York: Ballantine Books, 1992).

5. Malcom X and Alex Haley, *The Autobiography.*

6. *Good Hair*, directed by Jeff Stilson. Produced by Chris Rock (Lionsgate, 2010).

7. *Coming to America*, directed by John Landis, with Eddie Murphy (Paramount Pictures, 1988).

8. Chimamanda Ngozi Adichie, *Americanah* (New York: Knopf, 2013).

9. The first professional degree with a specialization in curly and kinky hair was finally created in September 2023.

10. Juliette Sméralda, *Du cheveu défrisé au cheveu crépu* [From Straightened Hair to Kinky Hair] (Paris: Publibook, 2012).

11. Juliette Sméralda, *Du cheveu défrisé au cheveu crépu.*

12. Rokhaya Diallo and Brigitte Sombié, *Afro!* (Paris: Les Arènes, 2015).

## 20. ALPHONSE'S DILEMMAS

1. "Hommage à Alphonse Boni," *Notre école*, November 15, 1989.

2. Frédéric Grah Mel, *Félix Houphouët-Boigny*, vol. 1 (Paris: Maisonneuve et Larose, 2003).

3. Jean-Noël Loucou, "La Seconde Guerre mondiale et ses effets en Côte d'Ivoire" [The Second World War and Its Effects in Ivory Coast], *Annales de l'université d'Abidjan*, issue 1, vol. VII, Histoire, 1980.

4. Frédéric Grah Mel, *Félix Houphouët-Boigny*, vol. 1

5. Grah Mel, *Félix Houphouët-Boigny,* vol. 1.

6. Monthly political report from September 1945, Centre d'acceuil et de recherche des Archives nationales, cited in Grah Mel, *Félix Houphouët-Boigny*, vol. 1

7. "Journées du dialogue," October 1969, in Frédéric Grah Mel, *Félix Houphouët-Boigny*, vol. 2 (Paris: Cerap/Karthala, 2010).

8. François Mitterrand, *Ma part de vérité. De la rupture à l'unité* [The Truth as I See It: From Rupture to Unity] (Paris: Fayard, 1969).

9. Aristide R. Zolberg, *One-Party Government in the Ivory Coast* (Princeton: Princeton University Press, 1964).

10. Grah Mel, *Félix Houphouët-Boigny*, vol. 2

11. Chris Beauchemin, Christelle Hammelle, and Patrick Simon, *Trajectories and Origins: Survey on Population Diversity in France* (Paris: INED, 2015).

21. FAULT LINES

1. Maxime Cervulle, *Dans le blanc des yeux. Diversité, racisme et médias* [In the Whites of the Eyes: Diversity, Racism, and Media] (Paris: Éditions Amsterdam, 2013).

2. Chris Beauchemin, Christelle Hammelle, and Patrick Simon, Trajectories and Origins*: Survey on population diversity in France.* No. 168.1. 2010.

3. "Dixième baromètre de la perception des discriminations dans l'emploi" [10th Survey of Perceptions of Discrimination in the Workplace], Défenseur des droits/OIT, 2017.

22. FRENCH TV: KEEPING OUT THE COLOR

1. Centre National du Cinéma, "La place des femmes dans l'industrie cinématographique et audiovisuelle" [The Place of Women in the Film and TV Industry] (Paris: CNC, 2017).

2. Camille Haddouf and Isabelle Wolgust, "La place des femmes parmi les auteurs écrivant dans le cinéma français sur 10 ans (2003–2012)" [The Place of Women among Authors Writing for French Film over a 10-Year Period)] *Guide française des scénaristes*, May 2014.

3. In 2023, Alice Diop won the César for Best First Film for *Saint-Omer.*

4. Gérard Noiriel, "Chocolat, tu t'es battu, tu as été l'acteur de ta vie" [Chocolat, You Fought, You Were the Actor of Your Own Life], interview with Natalie Levisalles, *Libération*, January 6, 2016.

5. Jay Weissberg, "Untouchable," *Variety*, September 29, 2011.

6. Régis Dubois, *Les Noirs dans le cinéma français. De Joséphine Baker à Omar Sy* [Blacks in French Cinema: From Joséphine Baker to Omar Sy] (La Madeleine, France: LettMotif, 2016).

7. Conseil Supérieur de l'Audiovisuel [High Council for Television and Radio]. After a merger with the internet regulatory authority in 2022, the CSA became the Autorité de régulation de la communication audiovisuelle et numérique (ARCOM), the Regulatory Authority for Audiovisual and Digital Communication.

8. Marie-France Malonga, "Présence et representation des 'minorités visibles' à la télévision française" [Presence and Representation of "Visible Minorities" on French Television], CSA Report, June 2000.

9. CSA, "Les résultats de la vague 2016 du baromètre de la diversité" [Results of the 2016 Diversity Survey], January 13, 2017.

10. Robin DiAngelo, "White Fragility: Why It's So Hard to Talk to White People about Racism," *The Huffington Post*, June 30, 2015. Also see her book *White Fragility* (Boston: Beacon Press, 2018).

11. Éric Macé, "Des 'minorités visibles' aux néostéréotypes. Les enjeux des régimes de monstration télévisuelle des différences ethnoraciales" [From "Visible Minorities" to Neo-Stereotypes: The Stakes of Systems of Televisual Monstration of Ethnoracial Differences], *Journal des anthropologues* 5 (2007).

12. Hélène Ferrarini, "Plus de soixante-dix ans après, les résistants antillais sortent de l'ombre" [More than Seventy Years Later, West Indian Resisters Come Out of the Shadows], *Slate*, August 20, 2015. See also: Eric T. Jennings, *Vichy in the Tropics: Pétain's National Revolution in Madagascar, Guadeloupe, and Indochina, 1940–1944* (Stanford: Stanford University Press, 2002).

13. In recent years, with the arrival of streaming services like Netflix and Amazon in France, the situation has changed: a number of shows invite French viewers into the lives of characters from ethnoracial minority backgrounds.

## 23. THE WHITE NORM

1. Chris Beauchemin, Christelle Hammelle, and Patrick Simon, *Trajectories and Origins: Survey on population diversity in France*, No. 168.1. 2010

2. Fortunately, in the last few years, the name for the color is no longer "gazelle."

3. The appearance of Rihanna's Fenty Beauty products in France was also a game-changer.

4. In 2023, the Malian-born French pop singer Aya Nakamura became Lancôme's brand ambassador.

5. From a study by the consulting agency Ak-A, cited in Marianne Bailly, "Peaux ethniques, un marché en pleine extension" [Ethnic Skin, an Expanding Market], *Cosmétiquemag*, April 2012.

6. Since I first wrote these lines, things have changed. Nowadays, in 2024, French women's magazines try to be more inclusive. They've dropped the word "ethnic" and feature more models of every race and ethnicity. On the other hand, when they discuss French society, they still have some trouble including the experiences of non-whites.

7. See "Back to the Fro'," *Black Beauty Bag*, October 12, 2013: http://www.blackbeautybag.com/2013/12/back-to-fro.html.

8. Marie-Félicité Ebokea, *À l'eau Mariétou!* [Get In the Water, Mariétou!] (Paris: Éditions du Sorbier, 2010).

9. Thankfully, since I wrote these lines, *Black Panther* arrived in French move theaters and radically changed the lives of millions of children of African descent in France. They finally have Black superheroes whom everyone knows and can identify with.

## 24. RUN, BLACK MAN, RUN!

1. Frantz Fanon, *Black Skin, White Masks*, trans. Charles Lam Markmann (London: Pluto Press, 2008).

## 25. THE GUERLAIN AFFAIR

1. "Le discours de Chirac, le 14 novembre 2005," *Le Nouvel Obs*, October 26, 2006. The speech can be viewed in English translation on C-Span: https://www.c-span.org/video/?189944-1/french-president-address.

2. "Ce que Brice Hortefeux a vraiment dit" [What Brice Hortefeux Really Said], *Le Monde*, September 11, 2009.

3. "Racisme: Jean-Paul Guerlain, un parfum de récidive?" [Racism: Jean-Paul Guerlain, the Whiff of a Repeat Offender?] *Slate Afrique*, March 9, 2012.

4. Aimé Césaire, "Word," *The Complete Poetry of Aimé Césaire*, trans. A. James Arnold and Clayton Eshleman (Middletown, CT: Wesleyan University Press, 2017). Translation modified.

5. Audrey Pulvar, "Nègre je suis, nègre je resterai," France Inter, October 18, 2010. Available online: https://www.dailymotion.com/video/xf9yue. See also, Aimé Césaire and Françoise Vergès, *Nègre je suis, nègre je resterai: Entretiens avec Françoise Vergès* (Paris: Albin Michel, 2003), in English, *Resolutely Black*, trans. Matthew B. Smith (Cambridge: Polity Press, 2020).

6. Source: Association pour l'information et la prévention de la drépanocytose [Association for Sickle Cell Anemia Awareness and Prevention].

## 26. THE THREE FEARS

1. Delivered on April 23, 2006: https://www.vie-publique.fr/discours/161443-declaration-de-m-nicolas-sarkozy-ministre-de-linterieur-et-de-lamena.

2. Speech delivered at the University of Dakar, Senegal, July 26, 2007: https://www.vie-publique.fr/discours/167388-declaration-de-m-nicolas-sarkozy-president-de-la-republique-sur-sa-co.

3. *Cameroun. Autopsie d'une indépendance* [Cameroon: An Autopsy of Independence], directed by Valérie Osouf and Gaëlle Le Roy (Paris: Program 33/France 5, 2008).

4. Thomas Deltombe, Manuel Domergue, and Jacob Tatsita, *Kamerun! Une guerre cachée aux origines de la Françafrique* [Kamerun! A Hidden War at the Heart of the Françafrique] (Paris: La Découverte, 2011) and by the same authors: *La Guerre du Cameroun* [The War of Cameroon] (Paris: La Découverte, 2016).

5. "Hollande à Alger: 'Je ne viens pas ici faire repentance ou excuses,'" [Hollande in Algiers: I Didn't Come Here to Repent or Apologize], *Le Monde*, December 19, 2012.

6. Speech delivered in Paris, May 6, 2007: https://www.vie-publique.fr/discours/166610-declaration-de-m-nicolas-sarkozy-president-de-lump-lannonce-de-so.

7. French presidential candidate Marine Le Pen's program from 2017 is available at: https://www.politique-animaux.fr/fichiers/prises-de-positions/pieces-jointes/projet-presidentiel-marine-le-pen-2017.pdf.

8. Since Emmanuel Macron was elected president in 2017, he, too, has consistently rejected any form of repentance in his speeches.

9. Alain Louyot and Pierre Ganz, "Aimé Césaire: 'Je ne suis pas pour la repentance ou les réparations'" [Aimé Césaire: I Am Not For Repentance or Réparations] *L'Express*, September 13, 2001.

10. A CSA-*Le Figaro* poll from December 2, 2005, regarding Article 4 of the law of February 23, 2005. Respondents were asked: "Are you or are you not in favor of the law requiring school programs to recognize the positive role of French colonialism?"

11. Aimé Césaire, *Discourse on Colonialism*, trans. Joan Pinkham (New York: Monthly Review Press, 2000).

12. The party was renamed Renaissance in 2022.

13. Patrick Roger, "Colonisation: les propos inédits de Macon font polémique" [Colonization: Macron's Remarks Cause Controversy], *Le Monde*, February 16, 2017.

14. My remarks here were written in the early days of Macron's presidency. Since then, during his two terms as president, Macron has veered hard to the right, pushing an extremely repressive law through the French legislature in January 2024 designed to "curb immigration." France's Constitutional Council found certain parts of that law so draconian that it ruled that they violated the French constitution.

## 27. ON THE ADVANTAGE OF BEING WHITE

1. Ségolène Roy, "L'autre versant du racisme: le privilège blanc" [The Other Side of Racism: White Privilege], *Mediapart*, March 5, 2014, drawing on Horia Kebabza, "'L'universel lave-t-il plus blanc?': 'Race', racisme et système de privilèges" ["Is the Universal a Whitewash?": "Race," Racism, and the Privilege System], *Les Cahiers de CEDREF* 14 (2006).

2. *Travailler au noir* (literally, work in the black/idiomatically, work under the table), *colère noire* (black anger/blind rage), *marché noir* (black market), *magie noire* (black magic), *broyer du noir* (be in a black/dark mood), *voir tout en noir* (see everything in black/see only doom and gloom), *regarder d'un œil noir* (look with a black eye/give a dirty look), *manger son pain noir* (eat one's black bread/go through a rough patch), *c'est ma bête noire* (it's my bête noire/pet peeve).

3. *Travailler comme un nègre* (literally, work like a *nègre*/idiomatically, to slave away), *être un nègre (littéraire)* (a (literary) *nègre*/a ghostwriter), *parler petit-nègre* (speak little-*nègre*/speak pidgin).

4. For a more detailed list, see Peggy McIntosh, "White Privilege: Unpacking the Invisible Knapsack," Wellesley College Center for Research on Women, 1989.

5. Observatoire des Inégalités, "Discriminations à l'embauche des jeunes d'origine immigrée" [Discrimination in Hiring among Young People from Immigrant Backgrounds], June 13, 2007.

## 28. IN IT TOGETHER

1. "Enquête exclusive spécial 'Blacks': la lettre ouverte d'une entrepreneure noire" [*Exclusive Investigation*'s "Blacks" Special: Open Letter from a Black Woman Entrepreneur], *Nofi*, May 15, 2017.

2. Observatoire des Inégalités. In 2012, the unemployment rate was 24.2 percent in disadvantaged urban areas compared to 9.9 percent in the rest of France.

3. *I Am Not Your Negro*, directed by Raoul Peck (Velvet Film, 2016).

4. Ta-Nehisi Coates, "My President Was Black: A History of the First African American White House—and of What Came Next," *The Atlantic*, January/February 2017.

5. Esther Benbassa, "La libération de la parole politique favorise l'intolérance" [The Loosening of Political Speech Promotes Intolerance], *Public Sénat*, March 22, 2013.

6. Commission nationale consultative des droits de l'homme, "Rapport 2016 sur la lutte contre le racisme, l'antisémitisme et la xénophobie" [2016 Report on the Fight against Racism, Antisemitism, and Xenophobia] (Paris: La Documentation Française, 2017).

7. Organisation internationale de la francophonie, "Estimations des populations francophones dans le monde en 2017" [2017 Estimates of the Worldwide French-speaking Population], 2018.

**Isabelle Boni-Claverie** is a French filmmaker, screenwriter, and author. At eighteen, she won second prize for the Young Francophone Writer Award for her first novel, *La Grande Dévoreuse*. In 2005, Danny Glover asked her to adapt Valérie Tong Cuong's novel, *Où je suis*, into the screenplay *Heart of Blackness*. She has since written numerous television dramas and series, including the comedy *Sex, Okra and Salted Butter* (ARTE), *Seconde Chance* (TF1), *Coeur Océan* (France 2), and *Plus Belle La Vie* (France 3), the most watched TV series in France. Two of her first short films, *Pour la nuit* and *Le Génie d'Abou* won international awards. Broadcast for the first time on the Franco-German television channel ARTE in 2015, her documentary *Too Black to Be French?* was a hit both with audiences and the media and screened internationally. She has produced and cowritten a documentary about diversity at the Paris Opera that will air on ARTE this year.

**Joshua David Jordan** is Senior Lecturer in French at Fordham University. He has translated works by Etienne Balibar, Jean Hatzfeld, and David Lapoujade and is a two-time winner of the French Voices Award.

**Kaiama L. Glover** is Ann Whitney Olin Professor of French and Africana Studies at Barnard College. She is the author of *A Regarded Self: Caribbean Womanhood and the Ethics of Disorderly Being* (2020) and *Haiti Unbound: A Spiralist Challenge to the Postcolonial Canon* (2010).